Gay Life Stories

Jón Ingvar Kjaran

Gay Life Stories

Same-Sex Desires in Post-Revolutionary Iran

Jón Ingvar Kjaran
University of Iceland
Reykjavik, Iceland

ISBN 978-3-030-12833-3 ISBN 978-3-030-12831-9 (eBook)
https://doi.org/10.1007/978-3-030-12831-9

Library of Congress Control Number: 2019933128

© The Editor(s) (if applicable) and The Author(s) 2019
This work is subject to copyright. All rights are solely and exclusively licensed by the Publisher, whether the whole or part of the material is concerned, specifically the rights of translation, reprinting, reuse of illustrations, recitation, broadcasting, reproduction on microfilms or in any other physical way, and transmission or information storage and retrieval, electronic adaptation, computer software, or by similar or dissimilar methodology now known or hereafter developed.
The use of general descriptive names, registered names, trademarks, service marks, etc. in this publication does not imply, even in the absence of a specific statement, that such names are exempt from the relevant protective laws and regulations and therefore free for general use.
The publisher, the authors and the editors are safe to assume that the advice and information in this book are believed to be true and accurate at the date of publication. Neither the publisher nor the authors or the editors give a warranty, express or implied, with respect to the material contained herein or for any errors or omissions that may have been made. The publisher remains neutral with regard to jurisdictional claims in published maps and institutional affiliations.

Cover credit: © gevende / iStock / gettyimages

This Palgrave Macmillan imprint is published by the registered company Springer Nature Switzerland AG.
The registered company address is: Gewerbestrasse 11, 6330 Cham, Switzerland

For my parents, Ingunn Jónsdóttir and Snorri Páll Kjaran

PREFACE

Writing a book has often been compared to a journey, from the initial idea to the publication of the book. For me, this book started with an actual journey to Iran in 2014—a journey that, back then, I did not know where it would take me in the end. I became fascinated with Iranian culture and the hospitality of its people, and met, for the first time, gay Iranians, who then became my friends and main informants during my subsequent fieldtrips. Until then, I had never met any gay- or lesbian-identifying Iranians and had only read about their situation in the Western media, which usually depicted them as sexually oppressed victims of the "Islamic-fascist" state, who were in need of being saved by the liberal democracies of the West. Hence, during my first trip there, I encountered a different world of gay life than the one depicted in the Western "gay" media: It was neither a world full of fear and oppression nor optimal in terms of gay livability. It was somehow a world or a place "in between," being constantly made and remade by its occupants—some kind of heterotopia in a Foucauldian sense. It was a place/space that was somehow "other," a world within a world, hidden and underneath mainstream society. It was a world with many more layers than immediately met the eye.

That was exactly my experience. To begin with, there were many aspects of gay life in Iran that did not straight away meet the eye of the researcher—the gay outsider coming from the West. I therefore had to "dig" deep into this world and meet different people, in different places/spaces, to get a glimpse of the many layers of the Iranian gay community, and to try to understand what it means to live as a gay subject in the Islamic Republic of Iran. I was guided from the beginning with the following question:

How are Iranian gay males constituted as subjects in the Islamic Republic of Iran and how do they negotiate and navigate their lives within the limits of their cultural and social context? I gradually found out that there is no one answer to that question and therefore I present in this book different stories and versions of gay life in Iran; stories told by my friends and informants, who all identify as gay or non-heterosexual. Their stories and embodied experiences form the basis of the book and through them we gain insight into the livability of gay-identifying/non-heterosexual men in Iran. That being said, I do not claim to be giving a representative account of being gay or non-heterosexual in Iran. Rather, the book should be seen as presenting different aspects among many, in terms of gay livability in contemporary Iran. The main focus is predominantly on gay-identifying men living in Tehran, the capital of Iran.

Four years later, and after several fieldtrips to Tehran, I come to an end of my journey and present in a book the stories I was trusted with, told by my informants and friends. In Chap. 1, I give an overview of the main arguments of the book and its objectives. I also introduce the field and context of the research, as well as discuss my positionality and the ethical issues of conducting ethnographic research "underground." Chapter 2 lays out the theoretical foundations, where I particularly draw on, and discuss the work of, Foucault and other post-structural theorists. Chapter 3 is co-written with my colleague and friend Wayne Martino. In Chap. 3, we engage with important historical sources and accounts that speak to the historical contingencies of the emergence of same-sex desire and the category of "the homosexual" in Iran. We incorporate into this account the political and social history of Iran from the latter part of the twentieth century until the present. Chapter 4 addresses the power of the pink press and how the Iranian gay subject is constructed through different discourses outside of Iran. Here I raise important political questions of misrepresentation in the reporting of the current situation of sexual minorities in Iran. In Chap. 5, I turn to ethical relationality and draw on the embodied experience of gay-identifying Iranian men. I take up a particular Foucauldian analysis and work mainly with Foucault's ideas on the technologies or practices of the self. Throughout the chapter, I present empirical examples of how gay Iranian men constitute themselves, and how they are constituted by dominant discourses of gender and sexuality. By providing different accounts of gay existence in Iran, the aim of the chapter is to juxtapose the one-dimensional liberationist discourse presented in the West of the victimized Iranian gay male, discussed in

Chap. 4. Chapter 6 focuses on gay/queer activism among Iranian gay men, living inside of the Islamic Republic of Iran. It discusses what it means to be a gay activist, drawing attention to the socio-cultural context and particular historicity. It draws on interviews with gay-identifying Iranian males that could be seen/defined as activists, not only fighting for sexual rights but also political rights in general. Chapter 7 draws on Foucauldian analytical frameworks, as well as on Judith Butler's writings on abjection, and addresses the intersection of sexuality, gender, and bodies in terms of HIV/AIDS. It explores how the discourse on HIV/AIDS has evolved within Iran and how those bodies, who live outside of what can be considered culturally intelligible in terms of seropositivity, sexuality, and gender, are constructed. Chapter 8 provides empirical insights into how gay/queer Iranian men navigate their lives between different spaces—social, virtual, and physical—in order to accommodate their gay identity and sexual desires within the legal-social and Islamic frame of modern Iran. By employing Foucauldian analytic frameworks that attend to questions of heterotopic spatiality, and in conjunction with Massey's notion of power geometries and how space is produced, I illuminate the complexity of queer Iranian men's spatio-temporal modes of sociality in relation to sexual practices and being gay/queer. The final chapter, Chap. 9, synthesizes my main arguments and discusses how we can go beyond the binary thought of utopia/dystopia, when addressing interpretive questions of quality of life and livability for gay-identifying men in a transnational context such as Iran.

In terms of language, the interviews were conducted either in English or in Farsi (Persian) with the help of a translator, often one of my main informants. Together we transcribed the interviews in Farsi, which were then translated into English. For Persian words and names, I have adopted a modified version of the transliteration system of *Encyclopedia Iranica* (e.g., I use the vowels o and e in addition to a, i, and u). I have omitted all diacritical marks except hamzeh or ain. For the spelling of commonly known words in Arabic or Persian, I have reverted to the *International Journal of Middle East Studies* (*IJMES*) word list.

Reykjavik, Iceland   Jón Ingvar Kjaran

Acknowledgments

I would like to express my gratitude to the many people who saw me through this book; to all those who provided support, talked things over, read, wrote, offered comments, allowed me to quote their remarks, and assisted in the editing, proofreading, and design. I would especially like to thank professor Wayne Martino for encouraging me to write this book and giving me constructive comments and feedback through the whole writing/production process. I give my special thanks to Arash, my main informant and friend in Tehran. Without him I would not have been able to establish so many contacts in Tehran and gain access to the underground gay community under the city surface. I would also like to thank Martin, my informant and friend, who read the whole manuscript and gave me valuable information about Iranian culture and life. Arash and Martin, and all the participants and informers who shared their experiences and trusted me with their stories, made this book a reality. I dedicate this book to them—it is their stories I try to tell. Also, I wish to personally thank the following people for their contributions to my inspiration and knowledge and other help in creating this book: Sólveig Friðriksdóttir for preparing the index and reading through the bibliography and other references; Karen Jordan for proofreading the book at different stages; the University of Iceland for giving me leave from teaching responsibilities when I was working on the book; and Paul Magnusson and the Ott family at LAS (Leysin American College) for giving me the opportunity to stay with them in the Alps as a guest for two weeks, during which I worked on a chapter of the book. I would also like to express my thanks to everyone who gave me their kind permission to use or quote their material in this book. And last but not least, I express my gratitude to the field, Iran, and its people who embraced me with open arms, especially the gay community and my gay friends there, and who made me feel at home during the time I conducted the fieldwork there.

CONTENTS

LIST OF FIGURES

LIST OF TABLES

CHAPTER 1

Introduction

When the controversial Iranian president Mahmoud Ahmadinejad
addressed New York's Colombia University in 2007, he was asked about
the situation of gays in Iran. He replied that "In Iran, we don't have homosexuals. In Iran we don't have this phenomenon. I don't know who has
told you we have it" (Whitaker 2007, September 25).[1] These remarks
caught the headlines in the Western media and drew widespread criticism,
as well as cries of disbelief. Once again the Islamic Republic of Iran was in
the spotlight regarding its treatment of sexual minorities, particularly due
to the fact that same-sex sexual acts are punishable by death in Iran. Well-
established discursive themes about the "barbaric" and "evil" nature of the
Islamic Republic re-emerged in the Western media: Iran, because of its
inhuman treatment of sexual minorities, is depicted as "uncivilized" and
"primitive" in comparison to the progressive and civilized global north,
where gays and lesbians enjoy freedom and full civil rights. In fact, this
discourse about the "civilized" global north depicted against the "uncivilized" global south, particularly the Middle East, in terms of the sexual/
civil rights of gays and lesbians, is part of a wider neoliberal political discourse, which has in the aftermath of 9/11 changed the political discourse
in the West and the concept of "good" citizenry (Puar 2007). For instance,
in many Western liberal democracies, certain "respectable" LGBTQ subjectivities have now been included as part of the "national imaginary,"
which then presents those societies as tolerant and open, in contrast to
allegedly homophobic and barbaric Islamic countries. This kind of rhetoric,

© The Author(s) 2019   1
J. I. Kjaran, *Gay Life Stories*,
https://doi.org/10.1007/978-3-030-12831-9_1

which Puar has defined as homonationalism, has in the first decade of the twenty-first century, contributed to inciting racist, anti-Arab, and Islamophobic discourses in many Western countries—both with regard to foreign and domestic policy/politics.

The question thus remains as why President Ahmadinejad renounced that "this phenomenon," referring to homosexuality, existed in Iran, knowing that it would raise anti-Iranian sentiments based in part on homonationalistic rhetoric? Was he unaware of the reaction his comments would cause or was he evading this sensitive topic altogether by declaring that homosexuality did not exist within Iranian culture/society? Of course Ahmadinejad knows that there are gays, lesbians, and other members of the LGBTQ community living in Iran today. It is an "open secret, everybody knows about it," as one of my informants told me. Moreover, Iranian cultural history gives plenty of examples of same-sex desire and homoerotic love, which can be found in classical Persian poetry and literature (Homosexuality iii. In Persian Literature 2012, March 23). However, this kind of love or desire has always been expressed figuratively, and throughout Iranian history homosexuality/same-sex desire has been an open secret, something neither talked about nor expressed in public. It is to be kept within the private sphere, where one can express one's true feelings and remove the "social mask." In fact, when Ahmadinejad was publically denying the existence of gays and lesbians, he was indirectly referring to that kind of cultural division between the private and the public, which many Iranians still embody today. Moreover, gays and lesbians are not officially recognized in Iran and in that sense they do not exist, and therefore in that sense Ahmadinejad was referring to the official rhetoric and erasure of sexual minority subjects. In fact, gays and lesbians in Iranian society are a hidden minority, as one of my informants told me:

> They don't actively try to kill [gay] people they just want to hide it. They don't want these activities to become public. ... [Thus] you have to put up a mask and you have to do everything in order to hide yourself. You have to lie to survive. So Iranian gays are perfect liars and perfect actors.

The book is therefore about masking/unmasking, the construction, and enactment of gay identity and same-sex desire in contemporary Iran. In that respect it addresses the livability of self-identified Iranian gay males, who are not actively being killed by the state, although executions of gays and men who have sex with men have been reported by various NGOs, but are forced to live in hiding and without any official recognition or social support. The book tells the story of a masked existence. It explores the strategies, which Iranian gays use to survive and pursue their lives within the limits set by the legal-religious discourse of the Islamic Republic of Iran. Thus, the following research question, which has guided my work on this topic, and has previously been formalized in a paper with my co-author Wayne Martino, emphasizes the nuances which need to be taken into consideration when studying sexuality in a cultural context such as Iran: "How are the terms of recognizability, enactment and livability of same-sex desire […] understood and negotiated by gay Iranian men under historically specific social and Islamic jurisprudential conditions of disavowal and criminalization of homosexuality?" (Martino and Kjaran 2019).

The book draws on ethnographic data and it engages with self-identified gay Iranian men's lived experiences. Keeping in mind that studies on men and the intersection of masculinity and sexuality in (and from) Middle Eastern contexts remain few and insufficient, the focus of the book on gay Iranian men is important, as it contributes to research on queer issues in the Middle East and extends the knowledge of the experiences and livability of this group within that region. The ethnographic data was collected during several fieldtrips to Iran, mostly in the capital city of Tehran. It consists of interviews with gay-identifying men, field notes, research diary, as well as historical and online sources. In analyzing and interpreting the data the focus is on different theories on space in connection to Foucault's analytic perspectives on power, self-knowledge, confessionary practices, and ethical relations of subjectification, which have the capacity to draw attention to sexual embodiment and identificatory possibilities. Through these analytical lenses, different spaces will be examined in order to draw attention to how they are constructed in terms of gender and sexuality. Furthermore, the focus will be on how the gay Iranian subject has been constituted through discourses, both in the past and the present, both within and outside of Iran. Although being positioned by different discourses, the book emphasizes how the gay Iranian male positions himself as an active agent in taking care of the self and in terms of queering/resisting dominant norms in their social environment through their embodiment and actions.

"Tintin" in Tehran—Entering the Field

It is February 10, 2015, and I am waiting for my flight to Tehran at the departure gate at Sabiha Gokcen airport in Istanbul. After going through security and immigration I sit down close to the boarding gate, making the final preparations for my second trip to Iran and my actual fieldtrip over there. Right in front of me is a screen, which indicates the boarding time and the destination: Tehran, this large, modern and multilayered city that captured all of my senses when I first arrived there in April 2014. Looking at the screen and seeing my destination, where I will be in a couple of hours, all kinds of feelings start to flow through my mind, feelings of fear about the unknown, but also curiosity and enthusiasm to start my fieldwork there. I start to recollect how I first became introduced to Iran, and how my perception and understanding of its history, society, and culture has evolved and changed over time. I remember that I first heard about Iran when I watched with my father the mini series called *On the Wings of Eagle*, based on a non-fiction thriller by Ken Follet. It is set against the Iranian Revolution and tells the true story of the rescue of two executive managers of the company Electronic Data System. At that time, the American billionaire Ross Perot owned the company. He is said to have paid Follett to write the book, which he based on conversations with people that directly took part in the rescue operation. It is estimated that at least 25 million Americans watched the mini series (Posner 1996). For those millions of Americans who saw the series, it influenced their perception of revolutionary Iran, and in many ways established the current stereotypical image of Iran and Iranians in the West: an uncivilized fanatic mob, demonstrating on the streets, burning the American flag, and hating everything coming from the West (Beeman 2005; McAlister 2005). At the time, I also internalized this image of Iran, being a young teenager living in the final era of the cold war during the presidency of Ronald Reagan, on a small island in the North Atlantic, between the two superpowers. However, at the same time I wanted to learn more about this mystical country, which raised feelings of both fear and curiosity. Consequently, I started to read and follow news about Iran, which during this time was mostly related to assumed terrorism, and the war between Iran and Iraq. The news coverage about Iran in the West mostly depicted the country in a negative light. In fact, as William O. Beeman (2005) has pointed out in his book *The Great Satan vs. the Mad Mullahs*, since the Islamic revolution, the discourse of demonization, particularly regarding the relationship between Iran and the US, has been part of the official political rhetoric and discourse of both countries. This discourse has then been cited by the media in both countries, and contributed to the stereotypical image of Iran, which most people have in the West.

Coming back to the wait for boarding the plane to Tehran, a friendly old man in his late 80s woke me up from my contemplation and asked me if he could take the empty seat next to me. I smiled to him in approval and he sat down. He started to talk to me in German, assuming that I was from Germany. I speak fluent German, so we were able to converse easily. He told me that he was on his way to Tehran to visit his family there. He was actually from Afghanistan and lived in Munich. He had studied epidemiology at the University of Tehran in the 1950s, and after that he worked in Iran and in different Persian Gulf countries, before returning to Afghanistan. When the war in Afghanistan culminated with the intervention of the Soviet Union in December 1979 he moved back to Iran. In fact, many Afghans immigrated to Iran during that time and today there is still a continuous flow of Afghan migrants and workers over the border to Iran. I met some of them in Tehran, where they work in low-paid jobs, such as in restaurants or on building sites. Many Afghans speak Farsi quite well, and in fact Dari, one of the two official languages in Afghanistan, is related to Farsi and is often referred to as the Afghan Persian. They can therefore quickly adapt to Iranian society. However, they face some prejudices in Iran and until recently, children of migrant workers were not allowed to attend public schools (Moinipour 2017; Undocumented Afghan refugees get a chance at school in Iran, 2017, October 26).

The old man continued to talk to me: "I lived as a young university student during the time of the Shah [the last emperor of Iran, Mohammad Reza Shah Pahlavi] and then I experienced the [Islamic] Revolution—and I am still alive." He talked rather positively about the Islamic Revolution and Ayatollah Khomeini, of whom he referred to as the "full moon." In Iranian culture, "full moon" (*mahe shabe chahardah*) is normally used to describe the beauty or perfection of a young woman. In the context of our conversation, the old man was not using *mah* or moon in that sense, but rather citing the rhetoric (metaphoric language) of the revolution, which portrays the image of Ayatollah Khomeini in the moon (Najarian-Najafi 2017, July 13). One of my informants mentioned that many Iranians refer sarcastically to the story of "seeing" Khomeini in the moon. Hence, it was not fully clear for me during our conversation whether the old man was being sarcastic or an ardent supporter of the regime/the Islamic revolution. Boarding has started and I say goodbye to the old man and walk to the plane.

Finally, I arrive early in the morning in Tehran, after three hours flight from Istanbul. Everything goes smoothly through immigration and other formalities. My prearranged taxi driver greets me in the crowded arrival hall of the Iman Khomeini airport. It is February 11, a public holiday in Iran, the Islamic Revolution Day (*Rooze Pirozie Enghelabe Eslami*), commemorating the Islamic Revolution in 1979. I therefore wonder if the airport is so crowded because of that day, people coming to the capital from other cities to visit family and friends. We walk to his taxi parked some meters away from the terminal building. On our way he asks me if I am from Belgium. I am bit taken by surprise by his question and then I tell him that I have come from Germany, and live in the capital, Berlin. He then says: "I thought you were from Belgium because you look a bit like Tintin, your hair and blue eyes. Welcome to Iran." I smile to him, and we enter his unofficial taxi, making our way toward the city. The taxi driver is in his 30s, wearing an old leather jacket and blue jeans. He does not have a beard, which is often the rule for men his age in Iran. He is friendly, talkative and smiles a lot. He tells me that he is married and that his wife is a music teacher. They do not have any children he tells me, which is in many ways a bit uncommon in this child-centered society, but perhaps a sign of changing times.

The taxi driver had now put on some Iranian pop music, which today is mostly produced outside of Iran, by Iranian diasporic musicians living in Los Angeles. Iranians often refer to LA as Tehrangeles, because of the high number of diasporic Iranians living there.[2] While we drove into the city and passed the enormous mausoleum of Imam Khomeini, this modern Iranian music coming all the way from Tehrangeles, from the land of the "Great Satan," blasted through the air. Hearing the music while driving through the almost empty highway this early in morning, I thought about how much Iran had changed since Khomeini passed away in 1989. The children of the revolution, now in their late 30s, especially those living in big cities like Tehran, have in many ways turned their back on the revolution and the theocratic ideology of the Iranian state. Perhaps even their parents and grandparents have by now distanced themselves from the Islamic Revolution, if they were ever sympathetic to it in the first place. Instead, the young generation wants to embrace Western lifestyle and personal freedom, as I will discuss later in the book. Moreover, the children of the revolution have in many ways started their own "revolution," which entails, for example, different attitudes toward sex and sexual behavior, appearances, and use of social media, such as Instagram and Facebook (Varzi 2006; Khosravi 2008; Mahdavi 2008). This was one of the many paradoxes of Iranian society that I encountered and experienced during my time in Iran. In fact, Iran is the land of many layers, and as one of my main informants, Arash, said about his country: "Iran is like an onion, there are many layers, you open one and another appears." Finally I reached my guesthouse close to Imam Khomeini Square and said farewell to the taxi driver. I entered the room and shortly afterwards I was in bed, in order to rest for couple hours before I started the fieldwork by meeting Arash, my main informant (see Box 1.2). However, I was not able to sleep immediately as my mind was spinning, going through and reflecting on my experiences so far.

The "Naive" Researcher: Some Thoughts About My Positionality

The conversation with the taxi driver and him comparing me to Tintin was somehow stuck in my mind when I finally woke up later that morning. I began thinking about Hergé's books about the adventures of Tintin and why the taxi driver identified me with his main protagonist. Having read all the Tintin books in my youth, I had never identified with the cartoon figure of Tintin. However, I find the comparison interesting and even helpful for me now, after returning from the field, to reflect upon my own positionality within the field: The adventurous journalist Tintin, who is, figuratively speaking, embodied in me, the ethnographer. In fact, the ethnographer is sometimes compared to an adventurer who enters unknown territories or cultures. This can involve risk and danger, not only for the ethnographer but also his informants, as I will discuss in the next section (Lee 1995). Moreover, like Tintin, I have blue eyes, white skin and ginger hair. In that sense I was clearly an outsider and a source of curiosity among Iranians, especially those that identified as gay, that I met during my time in Iran. In that sense my appearances signified something exotic and different in the eyes of some of my informants and those that I encountered. This was confirmed during my first days in Tehran, when Arash, my main informant, referred to the color of my eyes by saying: "In Iran blue eyes have power, they are magical, and can open doors."[3] These words had some grain of truth as I will explain later on, but they also got me thinking about my own privileged position, being a white, middle-class, male researcher from Western Europe, a continent with a colonizing past and a history of unjust political meddling in this part of the world. Although coming from Iceland, a small island in the North Atlantic, which did not participate in the nineteenth-century colonial project, simply being from the West made me part of the colonial discourse of the past. Today, it has taken some new forms, interwoven into racial, gendered, and nationalistic ideologies, where the racial/ethnic other is more than often constructed as a threat in the public discourse and the media. Furthermore, whiteness continues to be invisible as a position of power to many contemporary Europeans. Thus, for me, an ethnographer working in a non-Western cultural context, it was important to be aware of my position and the underlying power imbalances when conducting my fieldwork in Iran—a country that since the middle of the nineteenth century up until the overthrow of the Shah in 1979 experienced foreign meddling in its internal affairs.

Coming back to being blue-eyed, in Iceland, it can also mean to be naive, which in my case meant being innocent or inexperienced in terms of doing fieldwork abroad and in a culture/society that was quite different from my own (Gokah 2006). Amanda Coffey (1999) has argued that the ethnographer has often been depicted as a "naive explorer" who during the fieldwork progresses into an "informed knower." However, this representation of the ethnographer is itself a naive construction. According to Coffey "the self and the field are seen as symbiotic, and the writing seen as establishing the interconnectedness of the two" (Coffey 1999, p. 125). In other words, representing the ethnographer as a naive explorer can be misleading, as it does not fully take into account the symbiotic nature of the fieldwork. Keeping in mind how the field interacted with my ethnographic self and vice versa, and how I was able to make "interconnections" through my field notes, diary and reflections, I still found it useful during my fieldwork to be "blue-eyed," asking "silly" questions about something that was perceived by Iranians as an obvious truth or fact. By this I was trying to make the familiar strange and the strange familiar: in other words, peeling through the many layers of Iranian society with regard to my research topic.

Thus, having blue eyes and being blue-eyed "opened doors" during my fieldwork but so did the disclosure of my sexuality toward my informants and those I interviewed. It somehow reduced hidden power imbalances and increased the rapport during the interview. Thus, in terms of sexual orientation and sexual identity, I shared some common experiences with my informants. In that sense I was to a certain extent an insider, and could relate as a gay man myself when I was talking to them as, Sharyar, who identifies as gay told me:

Sharyar: Can I ask you one question?
Jón: Yes, ask me anything.
Sharyar: Are you gay?
Jón: Yes, I am gay.
Sharyar: Good. Then you can understand these things. Some straight
            people cannot.

Coming from the West and being non-Iranian earned me a "stranger-value" and positioned me outside the cultural grid and customs of Iranian society. In that sense I was an outsider. However, being an outsider also had an advantage. I felt, for example, that some of my informants were often eager to tell me their story, without having to worry about being judged by their fellow gay Iranians. As I understood from some of my informants, the Iranian gay community thrives on gossip and talking behind each other's back is rather common. As one of my informants told me: "They want to show [you] that they are successful or a good person." Thus, the eagerness of some of my informants to talk and tell me their story might have been to impress the Western stranger:

> For example when you ask them [gay informants or interviewees] questions they have [a] totally different response than when I ask them questions[,] because in front of you, [a] white, non-Iranian, European foreigner, they want to impress you, but when they talk to me they don't want to impress me, they want to have my support.

The quote above is taken from an interview with a gay Iranian activist who has been working outside of Iran, helping Iranian queer refugees living in Turkey to resettle in the West. He draws attention to the different responses that those gay Iranians might give in terms of whether the person asking is an insider, meaning gay Iranian like himself, or an outsider like me, a foreigner from the West. However, during my fieldwork, I mostly interviewed or talked to Iranian gays inside of Iran. I was of course aware of this insider/outsider dilemma (bias) and sometimes I noticed in the narratives that some of my informants/interviewees were trying to impress me with their stories. However, as my research focus was also on how they constructed themselves or positioned themselves as gay-identifying subjects living in contemporary Iran, I was not solely interested in seeking the "truth" in their narrative. But generally speaking, my informants were most often sincere in their narrative and trusted me with their story. For that I am grateful and dedicate my book to all my informants and interviewees who I met and talked to. In the next section I will introduce and describe the field of my research.

Welcome to Iran: The Field of My Research

Iran, officially called the Islamic Republic of Iran, has a long and rich cultural history, which spans more than 2500 years. Today, Iran is a modern society with a rather young population. According to the latest statistics, in 2016, the mean age for both genders was 31.1 years, considerably higher in urban centers (31.5) than in rural areas (30.1) (Statistical Center of Iran). In 2016, Iranians, in the age range 15–34, were 36% of the total population (see Table 1.1).

In big urban centers such as Tehran, the percentage of the population in the age range 15–34 is slightly lower, or 35% (see Table 1.2). Thus, more than one-third of the population is in the age range 15–34, which marks Iran as one of the world's most youthful nations.

Table 1.1 Age distribution in 2016 for Iran as percentages of the total population

Age group	Males (%)	Females (%)	Total both genders (%)
15–19	7	7	7
20–24	8	8	8
25–29	10	10	10
30–34	11	11	11
15–34	36	36	36

Source: Statistical Center of Iran

Table 1.2 Age distribution in 2016 for Tehran as percentages of the total population

Age group	Males (%)	Females (%)	Total both genders (%)
15–19	6	6	6
20–24	7	7	7
25–29	10	10	10
30–34	11	12	12
15–34	35	36	35

Source: Statistical Center of Iran

Internationally, this age group is usually rather mobile and quite active, whether in terms of sexual activities, consumption or use of the latest technology. The Iranian post-revolutionary generation in the age range 15–34 is no different in that sense, and one could say that, in some ways, these children and grandchildren of the revolution are gradually changing Iranian post-revolutionary society. They are technologically savvy, which is, for example, manifested in their frequent use of social media, such as Instagram and Telegram. In fact, it is estimated that around 40 million Iranians use the social application Telegram on regular basis, with those in the age range 15–34 being the most frequent users (see Box 1.1) (Dehghan 2017, December 31). Additionally, individuals in this group are often more

---

Box 1.1   Telegram: Temporal and Spatial Extension of the Field

Telegram is today the most popular social media app in Iran. It is estimated that half of the population uses the app for daily communication, whereas the younger generation are the most active users. Tied to their phones, they can share videos and photos and subscribe to groups, both private and public, where everyone can broadcast their messages to their followers. Within the online gay community in Tehran, I was informed that there are different closed (private) groups on Telegram. It is often the main source of information for many gay-identifying individuals. Telegram, with its high performance at low bandwidth speed, is outside the official *filternet* and has so far not been censored by the authorities.[6] That also explains its popularity. Moreover, it is a rather secure media as it is highly encrypted, and its users can set their messages to be deleted after a certain period of time. This means that it can be rather difficult to follow or track messages on Telegram. Another feature, which explains the popularity of the app, is that it gives its users a certain feeling of privacy from the overarching state. Political activists have therefore used the app to organize meetings and protests. This has caused the Iranian authorities concern and during the latest protest at end of 2017 and beginning of 2018 the app was blocked temporarily (Dehghan 2017, December 31). In fact, before the protest, Iranian authorities pressured Telegram to install some automatic censoring devices (CDN—Content Delivery Networks) for its public channels (Alimardani 2018, January 1). These measures, as well as insufficient encryption

---

(*continued*)

Box 1.1   (continued)

protocol, have gradually made Telegram unsecure for its users, or at least not as secured as it used to be, according to the Internet researcher Alimardani (2018, January 1). Thus, with the government's official focus on how to control and censor Telegram, the Iranian public is in danger of losing the "save" social media for communication. All this depends on whether the owner of Telegram will collaborate with the Iranian authorities by extending further controls and censorship. That remains to be seen. However, before the December/January protest, Telegram was not under the scrutiny of the government. It was more or less a pretty secure platform to express your views and communicate with others.

That is why I chose to communicate with some of my informants via Telegram. I did so before, during, and after my fieldwork in Iran, mixing traditional fieldwork with virtual or online ethnography (Kozinets 2010; Sade-Beck 2004). In fact, during the writing of this book, I have contacted informants to get more information, hear their opinions, or ask them more about their experiences. In that sense, with the help of Telegram, my fieldwork has continued online long after I left the field, and in turn the field has been extended both spatially and temporally. This also raises the question of how and when to end fieldwork. In other words, when does fieldwork really end? Is it after you leave the field and start a new research project at another site/field? Or is it when you write up your fieldwork and publish it/disseminate it? There are no clear answers to these questions and as Miller has pointed out in her chapter about "Messy ethics" (Miller 2013), there is little discussion on this in the literature. Thus, the researcher needs to find the right moment when and how to end their research within the field. However, here it needs to be emphasized that the researcher/ethnographer has established connection and even made friends in the field during the time of the fieldwork. Thus, one can end research but not terminate relationships so easily. For me, the field, Tehran, and the friendships that developed there during my fieldwork, will somehow always be part of me. In that sense, the field and my fieldwork had a profound influence on me, and how I see things today.

educated than their parents and, as Shahram Khosravi (2008) has argued, are becoming more defiant toward the authorities, particularly in terms of dress, fashion, and lifestyle. In other words, they want to embrace Western culture and lifestyle, and as one informant told me: "We want [to] be Western. We don't want to be Middle Eastern or oriental. Say that in your book." This applies particularly to the big cities such as Tehran, which in recent years has seen the construction of public spaces that particularly cater to young people, such as coffee shops and shopping malls. Although the government tries to keep things under control, even closing some coffee shops that get too popular, this is now part of Iranian reality. I sensed and experienced these changes when I was conducting my fieldwork in Iran. Shopping malls were full of young people and I often met my informants in new and fancy coffee shops, full of young people. Even in small provincial cities like Yazd, in central Iran, I found a small and trendy coffee shop run by young Iranian couples. In fact, coffee shops, malls, and public parks are often the only venues for young people to meet or hang out as there are no bars or nightclubs allowed in Iran. I will come back to this topic later in the book when I discuss the intersection of space, gender, and sexuality, and how gay Iranians carve out their own space to meet and socialize with each other.

Tehran, the capital city of Iran with more than 13 million inhabitants, was the main site of my fieldwork. It is a modern city and the economic and administrative center of Iran (Fig. 1.1). The city began to grow rapidly

Fig. 1.1 Grey February day in Tehran with the Alborz mountains in the background

at the beginning of the twentieth century. Every year it attracted ever-larger numbers of people from the rural provinces who came to Tehran to seek work in the nascent industries and service sector. This "exodus" from the rural provinces to the capital was further accentuated after the last Shah, Mohammad Reza Pahlavi, initiated the so-called white revolution, land reforms in 1962. Thus, migration to Tehran from the countryside, which has continued up to this day, has changed the city considerably. Today, it is a multilayered city in every sense, with its diverse and mixed population in terms of economic status, social class, and ethnic/cultural background. The city can roughly be divided into two parts on the basis of economic well-being and social class: the northern part of Tehran, close to the Alborz mountain range, occupied by the highly affluent Iranians and the upper middle class; and the southern part, mostly occupied by the working class and those working in low-paid jobs. Travelling from the north to the south only takes about one hour if the traffic is not too heavy. However, during the journey everything gradually changes as one gets closer to the very southern part of Tehran. In the south the air is more polluted, the streets are narrower, and the houses are cheaper and older. The people dress more conservatively and one can see more religious people there. The north on the other hand is totally the opposite and it is like entering a different world, which in many ways resembles some neighborhoods in big cities in the West. It is also where the best cafés, restaurants and big malls are located, which attract young people from all parts of the city. During my fieldwork in 2015, I frequently visited both parts of the city and stayed in both parts with friends/informants. I went to Iran three times in 2015 and stayed each time between two weeks and one month. I mostly spent my time in Tehran but during my second trip I travelled to one of the holiest cities in Iran, Mashad, for two days and did some interviews/fieldwork there.

I conducted my fieldwork in Iran undercover, which meant that it was undertaken without any permits from the Iranian authorities. For example, when I applied for the visa I did not state the true purpose of my trip. Thus, I travelled to Iran on a tourist visa and the official purpose of my trip was to visit friends and the main tourist sights, as well as learn about Iranian culture and history. This was partly true, as I was exploring and learning about one aspect of Iranian culture: its sexual culture and the underground gay community of Tehran. In that sense my fieldwork not only involved me as a covert researcher regarding the authorities, but it was also conducted "underground," where I secretly and discreetly met

members of the hidden gay community of the capital city. In order to
gain access to the members of the gay community in Tehran I opened an
account on *Manjam* in 2014.[4] It used to be a popular dating site/app
among Iranians but recently other dating apps, such as *Hornet* and
Grindr, are taking over. All these apps are open in Iran and you don't
need a VPN (Virtual Proxy Network) app or program to use them.[5] Even
when other sites are blocked or censored by the government, these gay
dating sites/apps stay open. This raises some questions as to why the
Iranian authorities keep these sites/apps uncensored. Is it to trap its
users, in order to arrest and prosecute them? Or as one of my informants
told me, to gather more information about its users, as he expressed in
the following quote:

> [W]hen they [the government] leave these applications accessible, it means
> they are eager to get more information. [For example,] one of the website[s]
> that never became censored was Manjam. People use Manjam very actively.
> In 2007, an Iranian gay man was arrested in Isfahan and he was moved to
> the intelligence office. He told us that they put a thick picture album in
> front of him and said to him that he had to identify at least five people in
> [the] picture album if he wanted to leave [the] room. This was [a] cross-
> checking examination in order to make sure that all the information was
> accurate. He told me that all of those pictures in the album had [a] Manjam
> trademark on them.

Being aware of the panoptic nature of *Manjam*, I was quite careful
when conversing with men there, and did not reveal anything about my
future research or myself. Thus, for the first few weeks I was just exploring
this platform and chatting with random men. Most of them were looking
for sex and my most common questions were about sexual preferences,
which revolved around being "bottom" (penetratee in sex) or "top" (penetrator in sex), age, height, and other physical characteristics. Then the
most important question of all often came at the end of the conversation:
"Do you have a place," which meant a private space to have sex. In Tehran,
having a "place" increases one's success and popularity on dating apps
such as *Manjam*. As I was not situated in Tehran and I was not looking for
a hookup, all my conversations ended with me saying that I did not have
a "place." It therefore took me some time on *Manjam* until I got messages
from guys that I somehow felt that I could trust. Why I felt so is difficult
to explain, as it was a gut feeling, which in the field, in my case the virtual
field of *Manjam*, the ethnographer sometimes has to act on. I had some

criteria, which I followed indirectly, in evaluating the trustworthiness of the person I was conversing with. One of those criteria was to exclude those who only talked about sex and emphasized setting up a meeting for sexual encounters in our conversation. Another criterion was if a person asked me early in our conversation about some personal information or wanted to have my email address or my name on Facebook. After some weeks of doing informal fieldwork on *Manjam* and finding a way to gain access to the gay community in Tehran, finally, I got a message from Arash (see Box 1.2). He became my main informant and in fact acted as a "gate opener" into some parts of the gay community in Tehran. Shortly afterwards, other informants sent me messages and became both my friends and participants in my research. In Appendix I give an overview of my informants/participants.

Box 1.2   My Friend Arash—Main Informant and a Gateway into the Tehran Gay Community

I first met Arash during my initial trip to Iran in April 2014. This was not a formal fieldtrip but more a combination of an exploration of the field and a holiday. It gave me the opportunity to travel around Iran and get an impression of Iranian society and its people before starting my formal fieldwork there. I visited the countryside and other cities, such as Shiraz, Isfahan, and Yazd. Arash was 22 when we first met and before our meeting in Tehran, we had been chatting for a while on Telegram. I told him about my research project and he offered to help me find interviewees and informants. He told me that he knew the city and its gay community quite well, and that he had contact with gays in most layers of society—rich gays living in luxury in the north of Tehran, and poor gays, in the southern part of the city. Thus, from that day on our research relationship started and gradually during my fieldtrips it grew into a deep and lasting friendship. In fact, Arash got rather emotionally attached to me and in some ways regarded me as his older brother, whom he could tell everything, without having to worry about being judged or misunderstood. He mentioned this several times during our long conversations, through which I gradually got to know him quite well. Arash is an open, sensitive, resourceful, and caring person. He took good care of me when I was in Tehran—making sure that I was eating

(*continued*)

Box 1.2   (continued)

properly and getting enough sleep. He showed me the best of what Iranian hospitality can offer its foreign guests. He was also concerned about our safety during my fieldwork, and so was I. For example, before I came to Tehran in February 2015, he sent me a message on Telegram and told me to send him a short message (SMS) to his phone, where I should write that I had cancelled my trip to Iran. He informed me later on that this was just a precaution, for example, if authorities were monitoring his phone this information might somehow mislead them. However, as discussed previously, all went well during our research cooperation and we generally felt safe.

Arash came out to his parents and sister when he was 20 years old. His parents reacted badly to this news and did not show any support. The day after, his father took him to the official medical office, affiliated to the police authorities, because he regarded his son to be sick. He wanted to have confirmation of his son's "sickness," perhaps hoping for a possible treatment/cure for the "gay disease." Luckily they met a sympathetic doctor who advised his father to go back home and support his son, who was going through a difficult time in his life. Home they went, but Arash did not receive any support from his family. Instead, he got silence and emotional distancing from them. He was, in fact, alone, and his family did not trust or treat him well after he took off his mask. This experience deeply impacted Arash and when we met in Tehran for the first time, these events were still going on and fresh in his mind. I will come back to Arash's story later in the book and reflect on it in connection to other similar stories about gay life in Iran. But why did Arash agree to help me and participate in my research? In fact, he chose to become my main informant, and to provide a gateway into the gay community in Tehran. There were several reasons for his involvement, for example, personal reasons, which revolved around finding a purpose in life after having been renounced by his family. Another reason was to see the world differently and to try to help others and make a difference. At the end of my fieldtrip in August 2015, I asked Arash about our research cooperation and if the research had changed him. He replied with the following, where one can also read between the lines as to why he decided to participate in the first place:

(*continued*)

Box 1.2 (continued)

Yes, being with you and helping you with this research has really changed me ... I have for example stopped judging people, whether they are poor or rich does not matter anymore for me. In the past I never talked to guys on dating apps who were from the southern part of Tehran. But now, having met people from this part of the city through your research has changed my perspectives. This research has also opened my eyes regarding transsexuals/trans people. Before I thought they were all bitches standing near the street offering sex for money. But now I don't think like that anymore. I see the multilayers of society better and things are not only black and white. Your research and you changed my thoughts about all this and I thank you for that.

ETHICS UPSIDE DOWN: DOING ETHNOGRAPHY UNDERGROUND

In order to protect both my future informants and myself we did not talk about anything related to the research on *Manjam*. Instead we moved our chat to a more secure social app called Telegram (see Box 1.1). This was part of managing risk involved when conducting fieldwork underground and in a "hostile" environment (Gokah 2006; Lee 1995). Other measures I took in managing risk and protecting my informants and myself were the following: I wrote all my field notes in Icelandic, which would make it harder for someone to understand if my notebook got stolen or taken by the authorities. Moreover, interviews recorded were stored on a USB stick, which I kept hidden in my room. No data was stored on my phone, which I used to record interviews, nor in my computer. I always used a pseudonym for my informants/interviewees and we always met in public places, such as cafés, public parks, or tourist sites in order to avoid any suspicion. After all, my cover was that I was a tourist, and therefore if asked, my informants were showing me around and accompanying me to interesting places within the city. After talking further with Arash about possible risks and how we could manage them when I arrived in Tehran, we decided that I should not reveal too much about myself and change some minor details regarding the background I gave when I was conducting my research and doing interviews.

For example, we decided that my nationality should be German, that I was living in Berlin, and that I had come to Iran to learn about its culture and history. Therefore, if something were to happen, the authorities would be looking for a German. We chose Germany because I have in fact lived in Berlin and speak fluent German. Moreover, many Iranians know about Germany and Germans are highly respected in Iran. Finally, Arash emphasized that if he ever called me and told me to go to a certain place twice, I should go directly to the airport and take the first plane out of Iran. When he first told me this at our first meeting in Tehran, I got a bit scared. Although I knew the risk involved and had thought about it before I left home, sitting in a café in Tehran and discussing this with Arash made everything more real. However, Arash reassured me and said that we should not worry too much and this was more of a precaution for both of us, and it was highly unlikely that anything would happen. In fact, he emphasized that the authorities would not be able to trace anything and all the potential interviewees/informants were reliable and would not report anything to the authorities. The question then remains whether it was ethical of me to involve Arash in the research, and how did I minimize the risk involved?

Viewing ethics as static or fixed, manifested in disciplinary guidelines on ethical practices, researchers should neither cause harm to its research subjects nor put them at risk. Moreover, participation should be voluntary and a written informed consent should be acquired before formal participation (Miller 2013). As there was no formalized ethical approval required from my university at the time of my research, I followed these ethical guidelines, but adjusted them to the specific context and nature of my research. Thus, during my fieldwork in Iran, I approached ethics as a process in which the researcher addresses unforeseen ethical issues as the research unfolds. This, for example, meant that I sometimes did not follow the disciplinary guidelines literally, and had to adjust ethical practices to the specific nature of the field. Conducting fieldwork underground means that you never know beforehand exactly what will or can happen (Gokah 2006; Lee 1995). As a researcher, you have to be able to step in and make a decision on the spot, in order to avoid harm and not put your participants or yourself at risk. Thus, in order to reduce the risk involved for Arash, my participants, and myself, I made special arrangements regarding my data, as mentioned previously. Furthermore, before I met my informants, I carefully went through all the details with Arash in order to evaluate potential risk involved. If I felt something was too risky or not right—here again often relying on my gut feelings—I would decide to cancel an appointment or a meeting. This happened only once when I decided that we should not meet an informant late at night in a public park. It was both late in the evening and Arash could not fully disclose how he had come into contact with him. In all other instances, everything went well and generally we never felt unsafe during interviews or meetings with informants.

When I met my informants for the first time, I informed them about my research and also disclosed information about myself, for example, being gay and living in Germany, which, as already mentioned, was partly true. I then normally asked them if they were willing to participate and tell me about themselves and how they experienced being gay in Iran. However, diverting again from the official ethical guidelines, I did not require my participants to provide written consent. This would have put them at a potential risk, for example, if those papers or forms had gotten into the hands of the authorities. Thus, protecting my participants from a potential risk weighted more than obtaining written consent. My loyalties and care were toward my participants, and it was my duty to protect them, but at the same time tell their story from their perspective. Thus, most of the time I accepted my participants' stories at face value and did not question what they told me. I saw them as my collaborators and co-conspirators in generating knowledge about gay life in contemporary Iran. Scheper-Hughes (2004) has referred to this practice in her research as "hermeneutic generosity" which she juxtaposes with "hermeneutics of suspicions." The line between the two is not always clear, and sometimes the same informant can be taken at face value regarding particular issues/themes, whereas other aspects of his story should be viewed with suspicion. In my case, this did not happen often, as my participants were mostly from the gay, non-heterosexual population. I therefore trusted them to speak honestly about their experience of being gay in contemporary Iran. However, when I interviewed someone who belonged to or was affiliated with a governmental institution, such as a hospital, organization, or health clinic, my focus shifted from "hermeneutic generosity" to "hermeneutics of suspicions." In other words, I was more alert during the interview with those participants, and took a bit more critical stance toward their accounts.

NOTES

1. According to Ahmadinejad's media adviser Mohammad Kalhor he meant that "compared to American society, we don't have many homosexuals" (President misquoted over gays in Iran: Aide 2007, October 10).
2. In the past years this has been changing and today lot of pop or modern music is produced in Iran. These artists are often more popular than those coming from Los Angeles because their fans can buy their music in Iran, see their faces on the billboards, and go to their concerts (see e.g., Semati 2017; Robertson 2012).
3. To summarize, a person with blue eyes is for many Iranians a symbol of the West and something that can be considered to be foreign or even exotic. One of my informants said the following when I asked him what blue eyes meant for many Iranians: "Iranians who immigrate to EU or North America are obsessed by finding a spouse with blue eyes and blond hair! It is considered a big achievement!".
4. *Manjam* is a social/dating network website that enables gay and bisexual men to connect. The website has been translated into 28 languages, among other Persian (Farsi) and Arabic. Thus, the website has been and still is quite popular with users that speak these languages. *Manjam* enables its users to travel virtually from one location to another. This, for example, enabled me to be virtually located in Tehran when I was doing my fieldwork and finding access into the Tehran gay community.
5. VPN or Virtual Proxy Network allows you to connect your device to a secure connection to another network over the Internet. VPN enables you to access blocked websites from your home network and put your IP address in a land far away. You can also download the apps or open the sites blocked in your country.
6. Filternet is software that constantly filters one's Internet traffic.

REFERENCES

Alimardani, M. (2018, January 1). What Telegram Owes Iranians. Never in History Has a Protest Movement Depended so Much on One Technological Platform. Will the Company Uses Its Power Wisely? *Politico Magazine.* Retrieved from https://www.politico.com/magazine/story/2018/01/01/irans-telegram-revolution-216206.

Beeman, W. O. (2005). *The Great Satan vs. the Mad Mullahs. How the United States and Iran Demonize Each Other.* Chicago: University of Chicago Press.

Coffey, A. (1999). *The Ethnographic Self. Fieldwork and the Representation of Identity.* London: Sage Publications.

Dehghan, S. K. (2017, December 31). Iran Correspondent. Rouhani Acknowledges Iranian Discontent as Protests Continue. *The Guardian*. Retrieved from https://www.theguardian.com/world/2017/dec/31/protesters-who-spread-fear-and-violence-will-be-confronted-says-iran.

Gokah, T. (2006). The Naïve Researcher: Doing Social Research in Africa. *International Journal of Social Research Methodology, 9*(1), 61–73. https://doi.org/10.1080/13645570500436163.

Homosexuality iii. In Persian Literature. (2012, March 23). In *Encyclopædia Iranica*. Retrieved from http://www.iranicaonline.org/articles/homosexuality-iii.

Khosravi, S. (2008). *Young and Defiant in Tehran*. Philadelphia: University of Pennsylvania Press.

Kozinets, R. V. (2010). *Netnography: Doing Ethnographic Research Online*. London: Sage.

Lee, R. (1995). *Dangerous Fieldwork*. London: Sage Publications.

Mahdavi, P. (2008). *Passionate Uprisings. Iran's Sexual Revolution*. Stanford: Stanford University Press.

Martino, W., & Kjaran, J. I. (2019). The Politics of Recognizability: Giving an Account of Iranian Gay Men's Lives Under Repressive Conditions of Sexuality Governance. *International Journal of Middle East Studies, 51*(1), 21–41.

McAlister, M. (2005). *Epic Encounters. Culture, Media, and U.S. Interests in the Middle East Since 1945*. Berkeley: University of California Press.

Miller, T. (2013). Messy Ethics. Negotiating the Terrain Between Ethics Approval and Ethical Practice. In J. MacClancy & A. Fuentes (Eds.), *Ethics in the Field. Contemporary Challenges* (pp. 140–155). New York: Berghahn.

Moinipour, S. (2017). Refugees Against Refugees: The Iranian Migrants' Perception of the Human Rights of Afghans in Iran. *The International Journal of Human Rights, 21*(7), 823–837.

Najarian-Najafi, Z. G. (2017, July 13). The Ayatollah in the Moon: On Class Power and Dynamics in Islamist Iran. Retrieved from https://medium.com/@zacharygeorgenajariannajafi/the-ayatollah-in-the-moon-on-class-power-and-dynamics-in-islamist-iran-c248fc5cbe06.

Posner, G. (1996). *Citizen Perot: Escape from Iran*. New York: Random House.

President Misquoted Over Gays in Iran: Aide. (2007, October 10). *Reuters*. Retrieved from https://www.reuters.com/article/us-iran-gays/president-misquoted-over-gays-in-iran-aide-idUSBLA05294620071010.

Puar, J. K. (2007). *Terrorist Assemblages: Homonationalism in Queer Times*. Durham, NC: Duke University Press.

Robertson, B. (2012). *Reverberations of Dissent: Identity and Expression in Iran's Illegal Music Scene*. New York: Bloomsbury Academics.

Sade-Beck, L. (2004). Internet Ethnography: Online and Offline. *International Journal of Qualitative Research, 3*(2), 45–51.

Scheper-Hughes, N. (2004, March). Parts Unknown: Undercover Ethnography of the Organs-Trafficking Underworld. *Ethnography, 5*(1), 29–73. https://doi.org/10.1177/1466138104041588.

Semati, M. (2017). Sounds Like Iran: On Popular Music of Iran. Popular Communication. *The International Journal of Media and Culture, 15*(3), 155–162.

Varzi, R. (2006). *Warring Souls: Youth, Media, and Martyrdom in Post-Revolution Iran*. Durham and London: Duke University Press.

Whitaker, B. (2007, September 25). No Homosexuality Here. *The Guardian*. Retrieved from https://www.theguardian.com/commentisfree/2007/sep/25/nohomosexualityhere.

CHAPTER 2

Reading Foucault in Tehran

The French philosopher, Michel Foucault, visited Iran twice in 1978. He went there as a correspondent for the Italian newspaper *Corriere della sera*, in which he published several articles on Iran (Afary and Anderson 2005). During the time Foucault spent in Iran, mostly in Tehran, protests and demonstrations against the regime of the Shah were cumulating day by day. Less than a month after his final visit to Iran, the Shah had left the country, in January 1979. Soon afterwards, on February 1, 1979, Ayatollah Khomeini arrived in Tehran from his exile in Paris, an event that marks the height of the revolutionary fervor in Iran. The days of the regime were numbered and during the next months, Khomeini and his Islamic Republican Party consolidated their power (Amanat 2017).[1] As Afary and Anderson have pointed out in their book *Foucault and the Iranian Revolution*, the events in Iran during that time, especially the religious nature of the Iranian revolution, had a considerable impact on Foucault. In fact, he embraced the religious rhetoric and discourse of the revolution, and in his writings on Iran, he was rather sympathetic to the Islamic fraction of the revolution (Afary and Anderson 2005). As argued by Afary and Anderson, Foucault was, during that time, in search of "alternate forms of non-Western modernity that could rejoin spirituality and politics" (Afary and Anderson 2005, p. 10). In other words, he was on an intellectual or spiritual mission, in search of "political spirituality." This he saw in the Islamic rhetoric of the revolution, and particularly how the Shi'a notion of martyrdom was used as an instrument of propaganda and agitation, in

© The Author(s) 2019
J. I. Kjaran, *Gay Life Stories*,
https://doi.org/10.1007/978-3-030-12831-9_2

order to stimulate protests and actions against the Shah (Afary and Anderson 2005). For Foucault, the figure of Ayatollah Khomeini and his followers embodied "transgressive power" and "irrationalities" that had the potential of creating something new, break "new boundaries," like the artist who pushes the limits of rationality in his creative work (Afary and Anderson 2005, p. 2). Thus, the Iranian experience influenced Foucault's consequent works. His writings on the Iranian revolution were part of his reflections and theoretical writings on power and "hazards of modernity," as Afary and Anderson (2005) have argued. The Iranian chapter in Foucault's life, although short and controversial, can therefore be seen as an inspirational bridge between his previous works on power and resistance, for example, in *Discipline and Punish*, and his writings on the *Use of Pleasure* and the *Care of the Self* in the second and third volumes of the *History of Sexuality*.

But how does Foucault, his works and experience in Iran, relate to my fieldwork in Tehran 37 years later? Preparing for my trip to Iran in February 2015, I decided to pack four books by Foucault: *Discipline and Punish* and the three volumes of *History of Sexuality*. I had first read these books during my undergraduate studies, and ever since they had influenced my theoretical thinking. In fact, Foucault's works, particularly on power, subjectification, and resistance, have inspired me throughout my academic life and given me a useful heuristic framework to employ in my own research. Moreover, his writings on sexuality, knowledge production, and the marginalized "other" have influenced my ontological and epistemological self as a researcher. Thus, taking Foucault with me to Tehran was not only symbolic, due to the fact that he had visited Iran some 37 years prior to me, but also constructive: reading Foucault and reflecting on his work in the field, connecting it to my fieldwork and the data generated. In that sense, I was not only reading Foucault in Tehran but also reading the data, which I collected in Tehran through a Foucauldian analytical lens. Foucauldian concepts, such as *panopticon, docile bodies, biopower, heterotopia,* among others, as well as his notion of bodies as a site of power and resistance, often went through my mind when I was writing up my field notes and reflecting on my data. I was, however, aware of not letting my theoretical framework blind me during the data collection. I emphasized the use of my own hermeneutic gaze, when observing and reporting during the fieldwork, as well as involving my informants and interviewees in generating knowledge/data from their perspective. In that sense, I tried to minimize what Edward Said has referred to as the "exteriorly of representation" (Said 1978, p. 29), in which what is noted or represented about the "other" is observed and noted from the outside, rather than observed and noted from the inside—meaning from the perspective of those one is supposed to be representing in one's writings or research.[2]

Thus, during my fieldwork and writing this book, I have emphasized learning from my informants, from the "inside"—as far as that is generally possible—in order to reduce the difference between the actual subject and its representation according to an outsider. However, this also requires an awareness of the danger of producing a simplified or a singular image of gay life in Iran; an image that then carries with it the authoritative "signature" of the Western theoretical discourse. I have therefore constantly reminded myself that the analytic categories, which I employ in my work, take their primary point of reference in Western philosophical thought. These, in turn, cannot always be applicable to a non-Western cultural context, such as Iran. In his *Prison Notebooks*, Gramsci stated the following:

> The starting-point of critical elaboration is the consciousness of what one really is, and is "knowing thyself" as a product of the historical process to date, which has deposited in you an infinity of traces, without leaving an inventory. (Gramsci 1995, p. 324)

My task was therefore to be consciously aware of this and expose my hidden "inventory," both in terms of theories and concepts used, but also—as discussed in Chap. 1—my own background as a white middle-class researcher coming from the West. In this chapter, I bring into the open my theoretical inventory, mostly based on a Foucauldian theoretical framework and concepts, which helped me to analyze my data and write up my research.

A Foucauldian Lens on Power

In the first volume of *The History of Sexuality*, Foucault states the following: "Where there is power, there is resistance, and yet, or rather consequently, this resistance is never in a position of exteriority in relation to power" (Foucault 1978, p. 95). Power and resistance are thus interrelated and one needs to analyze them together. Thus, resistance is a perpetual component to the relations of power, even becoming an effect of these. Therefore, resistance always involves power, requires it, releases it, and generates the impact of power (Foucault 1978, 1980, 1991; Lynch 2011;

Mendieta 2011; Sharp et al. 2000). Furthermore, power is relational, omnipresent, and has various manifestations. It is not only repressive but also productive, in the sense that it both constrains and creates the individual subject, as argued by Foucault in the following quote:

> The individual is not to be conceived as a sort of elementary nucleus, a primitive atom, a multiple and inert material on which power comes to fasten or against which it happens to strike, and in so doing subdues or crushes individuals. In fact, it is already one of the prime effects of power that certain bodies, certain gestures, certain discourses, certain desires, come to be identified and constituted as individuals. The individual, that is, is not the vis-à-vis of power; it is [...] one of its prime effects. (Foucault 1980, p. 98)

Thus, as indicated in the quote above, modern regimes of power operate to produce subjects who become both objects and modes of power. Moreover, individual subjects, produced by power, exercise it in all social interactions and its effect can be either dominating or resisting. As an example of the former, Foucault mentioned disciplinary power, which creates docile and obeying bodies through operations of normalizations. This kind of power is not repressive but productive, as it incites individual subjects to obey it (Foucault 1978; Lynch 2011). Disciplinary power is directed at the individual, it functions at the micro-level, directed at the body and its subjugation to the dominant discourse (Foucault 1990, pp. 100–101). Its primary function is to regulate and produce subjectivities through subjectification (*assujettissement*)—that is, how the subject is constituted through the conditions under which they are made possible through relations of power.

In terms of resistance, Foucault takes a cautious stance and emphasizes that resistance can sometimes support or strengthen the power relations that are being resisted. He takes sexuality as an example, when he discusses the repressive hypothesis in the first volume of the *History of Sexuality*. By liberating ourselves from sexual repression, we are at the same time constructing ourselves as sexual subjects. In turn, having confessed to a sexual identity makes us subjects of study and control. For Foucault, there were different strategies in the workings of sexuality, in terms of regulation, normalization and disciplining of the (sexual) subject—that is, pathologization of sexuality, medicalization of those deemed sexually abnormal, and formation of sexuality as an object of public concern (Foucault 1978). As will be discussed in the next chapters, these strategies of sexuality are all in place in contemporary Iran, regarding the exclusion and othering of the "homosexual/gay" subject. In addition to those strategies, which have the overall aim of disciplining the general population in terms of sexual behavior, they also draw on religious arguments and the moral economy. Thus, as Foucault has argued, sexuality ties together multiple "technologies of power," both disciplinary power and "biopolitics." In *The Will to Knowledge* (first volume of the *History of Sexuality*), Foucault defined these combinations of "technologies of power" as "biopower" (Foucault 1978).

Foucault introduced the concept of *biopower* in the first volume of the *History of Sexuality* (Rabinow and Rose 2006). There he argues that from the seventeenth century onward, power within the modern state was increasingly being situated and exercised at the level of life. Thus, differing from what Foucault called "sovereign power," the "right to decide life and death," *biopower* is centered on the administration, management, and preservation of life. This new form of power over life coalesces around two poles: One pole focuses on the politics of the body, and how power is inscribed on it and exercised through it, in order to train, regulate, and discipline the human body; the second pole is concerned with the efficient government of the population as a whole, a *biopolitics* of the population. As such it focuses on the management of the life processes of the social body, such as regulation of birth, mortality, sickness, disease, health, and sexual relations (sexuality) (Foucault 1978). In fact, Foucault argues that the power of life—*biopower*—places great emphasis on the preservation of health, as well as the contamination of diseases, as can be seen in the following quote:

> It's the body of society which becomes the new principle [of biopolitics] in the nineteenth century. It is this social body which needs to be protected, in a quasi-medical sense. In place of the rituals that served to restore the corporeal integrity of the monarch, remedies and therapeutic devices are employed such as the segregation of the sick, the monitoring of contagions, the exclusion of delinquents. (Foucault 1980, p. 55)

Thus, the "social body" becomes the object of politics in the modern *biopolitical* state, with its aim to safeguard the welfare of the whole population. However, as Foucault indicates in the quote above, the *biopolitical* state creates a division or distinction between those lives or bodies that must be preserved—bodies that matter—and those bodies that do not, as they might be a threat to the well-being and health of the general population. In other words, the *biopolitical* logic of exclusion or "social death" of those "abjected bodies" serves two colliding aims: firstly, to make the life of the whole population better; and, secondly, to increase population's productive potential in order to secure the highest profit for the *biopolitical* nation-state. Therefore, in line with the *biopolitical* logic, those bodies that are not (re)productive are considered a threat to the population— whether for reasons of age, sanity, race, health, or sexuality—and must therefore be excluded, even eliminated (Ojakangas 2005). In that context, regulations and control regarding sex and sexual behavior have often been the focus of the *biopolitical* state, as it influences the reproduction of the population, and thus its future productive potential.

In the Islamic Republic of Iran, *biopolitical* logic is employed regarding reproductive and sexual controls, which will be discussed further in Chap. 7. The same logic has also been applied to sexual minorities, gays, and lesbian subjects. The official rhetoric pathologizes this group, and their sexuality is depicted as being morally reprehensible and alien to Islam and Iranian culture. They are thus excluded from the *biopolitical* nation-statehood through three discourses that intertwine and collide in creating abjected bodies: The medical discourse of pathologization; the religious discourse; and the cultural or nationalistic discourse, in which being gay or lesbian is seen as something foreign and alien, outside the Iranian cultural grid—I will elaborate further on this in Chap. 3. Thus, the only way for those abjected bodies to be included in the *biopolitical* nation-state is to submit to these discourses and seek a "cure" for their "disease," for their "abnormal" social and sexual behavior. Otherwise they risk repercussions from the state, their family, or society in general, not necessarily physical death, although that is still a reality for gay Iranians who have sex with men, but more a "social death," meaning living an unrecognized and masked life, as will be discussed in the following chapters. I argue here that the government of the Islamic Republic of Iran is in fact modern state, and as such follows *biopolitical* rationality, in which the main objective is to take care of its subjects, to foster life instead of taking life. Thus, the workings of exclusion and state homophobia against sexual minorities intersect and produce two types of power: *biopower* and juridical-sovereign power (the right to end life), which in the case of sexual minorities is still practiced in Iran, although *biopower* is more commonly exercised today.[3]

Space of Other: Disciplinary and Heterotopic Space(s)

Subjectivation not only takes place within particular spaces and contexts, subjects are also produced by spatialized power. In his work, Foucault engaged with the intersection of power and space and how (liminal) subjects were constructed within marginal institutional spaces of society, for example, in prisons, hospitals, or mental institutions (Foucault 1991, 1988a, 1994; Ingrey 2013). Foucault was less concerned with the effects of power within these particular spaces, but more so with how disciplinary power within these marginal spaces is translated or transposed upon other spaces and contexts. In other words, drawing attention to how liminal or "abjected" subjects are constructed and regulated within marginal spaces underscores how subjects in general are produced through institutional discourses and practices of disciplinary power.

A key aspect of disciplinary power is the concept of panopticism, or panoptic view. Foucault developed this concept from the *panopticon*, an architectural concept regarding the construction of prisons, introduced by the English philosopher Jeremy Bentham (1748–1832). It consists of a circular arrangement of prison cells. In the center of the circle is the guard's observation tower. However, the inmates are not able to see whether they are being watched from the guard's tower or not. Therefore, they always have to assume that they are being watched, which makes the watchful eye of the guard omnipresent. Thus, because of the invisibility of the sovereign, the inmate feels highly visible and internalizes the watchful eye of the prison guard. He in fact takes over the duty of his own control. In that sense the *panopticon* serves as a condensed form of disciplinary power, as it initiates a feeling of being constantly watched. Therefore, within disciplinary space(s) the subject internalizes the gaze of the environment through the implementation of a "coercive view" (Foucault 1991, p. 171), the panoptic view, influencing its behavior and actions. Among the most effective disciplinary space(s) for gays and lesbians in Iran is the institution of the family, discussed in the next chapters, which enforces heteronormativity and gendered norms upon its members, through the "marriage imperative" and other disciplinary processes. Other disciplinary spaces are schools, circles of friends, and the public society in general that, for example, impose strict rules and regulations in terms of dress code, appearances, and behavior, as well as gendered segregation in public spaces. Thus, for those individuals, as I will discuss later on, there are two strategies: either to internalize the dominant societal norms and censor their actions and behavior, or to challenge those same norms, but run the risk of being excluded from the society, of becoming an abject (Butler 1990).

However, as Foucault emphasized throughout his work, productive power not only creates and constrains the individual subject, it is also to be resisted and should not be viewed as external to modalities of power (Callis 2009). In my engagement with the interrelation of power and resistance, and how I view and understand various modalities of transgression my participants undertook, discussed in Chaps. 5–7, I draw both on Foucault and Butler. According to Foucault, resistance is not a choice or decision of an individual subject, as it is dependent on power relations and vice versa (Foucault 1990). In that sense, he rejects the liberatory/ individualizing discourse from modern humanism, further emphasizing that relations of power are "very complex," and indeed contradictory and ambiguous (Foucault 1982, p. 209). Butler agrees with Foucault that the individual is only able to resist relations of power from within those same relations. In terms of norms, Butler argues: "the subject who would resist such norms is itself enabled, if not produced, by such norms" (Butler 1993, p. 15). In that sense, subjects who resist are only partially agentic because they are always subsumed by their very subjection/subjugation to norms.[4] For Butler, resistance is therefore a possibility, but within the limits of discourse or what is indeed "culturally intelligible" (Butler 1990, p. 40). Accordingly, one way to imagine resistance is by expanding the norms of what is considered to be culturally intelligible. Resistive acts in that sense can include various forms of opposition and modalities of transgression that are more inconspicuous, subjective, subtle and, unorganized (see e.g., Ball 2005; Casey 1995; Fleming and Sewell 2002; Fleming and Spicer 2003; DePalma and Atkinson 2009; Knights and McCabe 2000; Kunda 1992; Mathiesen 1989). For example, resignification of identity labels, words, or bodily performances, or failing to repeat particular performances of gender, can be understood as a resistance. In Chaps. 6 and 8 I give examples of how some of my participants extended the limits of what was considered to be culturally intelligible in terms of gender and sexuality, and how these acts of transgression produced them as subjects, not in the sense of achieving full agency or liberation but by carving out a space, within the limits of the dominant juridical-religious discourse on gender and sexuality.

Parallel and in contrast to disciplinary space(s), Foucault put forward the concept of heterotopia, or the space of other. According to Foucault, heterotopia describes places and spaces that function in non-hegemonic conditions. These spaces are outside the traditionally normative or dominant institutional spaces of power (Foucault 1984a) and according to Johnson refer "to varied spatial and temporal disruptions that imaginatively interrogate and undermine certain formulations of utopia" (Johnson 2006, p. 75). In that sense, heterotopias are temporal spaces, which for the individual subject are constantly in the making and have the potential to transgress and disrupt the utopian ideal. Foucault depicted various types of heterotopias, for example, crisis heterotopia, heterotopia of deviation, or heterotopia in general. Heterotopias as power geometries and "counter sites" are applied in my work to spatial relationships and exchanges that come to define particular forms of gay relationality, sociality, and interaction, and come to define the possibility for gay Iranian men to carve out a "sexual" counter-space (Foucault 1984a, p. 3). Heterotopias are described as "an effectively enacted utopia in which the real sites, all the other real sites that can be found within the culture, are simultaneously represented, contested, and inverted" (Foucault 1984a, p. 3). Foucault argues that while these spaces are "outside of all places," they indicate "a location in reality" where one can live in the shadows and oneself "where I am not" (Foucault 1984a, p. 4). In that respect, "he uses the metaphor of the mirror to capture this sense of being re-constituted or of constituting one's relationality as a presence, which is simultaneously denied in other sites constrained by power geometries within the broader society" (Martino and Kjaran 2019, p. 14):

> I am over there, where I am not, in an unreal virtual space that opens up behind the surface; I am over there, there where I am not, a sort of shadow that gives my visibility to myself, that enables me to see myself where I am absent: such is the utopia of the mirror. But it is also a heterotopia … where it exerts a sort of counteraction on the position that I occupy. From the standpoint of the mirror I discover my absence from the place where I am since I see myself over there. Starting from this gaze that is, as it were, directed toward me, directed from the ground of this virtual space that is on the other side of the glass, I come back toward myself; I begin to direct my eye toward myself and to reconstitute myself there where I am. (Foucault 1984a, p. 4)

As previously argued by Martino and me, heterotopias can be seen as "spaces for enacting the livability of gay Iranian men, [and] are places of legitimacy and reclamation in response to geometries and geographies of power and subjection that render embodied queer sociality as abjected and outside of the norm" (Martino and Kjaran, 2019, p. 14). In fact, this is about creating a space for the queer gaze to be enacted in the form of material embodiments realized in spaces that afford a reconstitution of the self on the other side of the glass. In other words, within the heterotopic space(s), sexualities can be constructed, practiced, and performed: that is, sexualities that both transgress and contest the heterosexual discourse (Steyaert 2010). Heterotopia can also be seen as a space where individuals feel secure and experience a supportive environment, where they can explore different identities. I will come back to this topic and explore it in Chap. 8, where I discuss different spaces—physical, virtual, and imagined—for enacting gay livability in Tehran/Iran.

Foucault's writing on productive power in disciplinary and heterotopic spaces gives me the opportunity to draw attention to the various micro-politics of power found within different institutions of society. Understanding power as productive also increases the potential for resistance, which complies with one of the main objectives of my research. I, thus, view my participants both as active subjects who resist their social environment in the sense of expanding the limits of what is "culturally intelligible," and as individuals who are subjectified by the dominant discourse of sexuality and gender. Within the strict limits set by that discourse, there are some possibilities and strategies to "do sex," express their sexuality, and live as gay men. In that sense they are both resisting and engaging with their liminality in terms of sexuality, although they do it more subtly than overtly. In the next two sections, I will discuss Foucault's writing on the technologies of the self or the ethics of being, and confessions of the self. This theoretical framework can be used to cast light on the various practices individuals use to take care of the self, in the sense of reconstituting or transforming the self, but also in order to gain knowledge of the self.

Technologies of the Self: Caring and Knowing

In the last section I discussed the Foucauldian notion of agency and how Butler reframed it as "conditional agency." In that sense, subjects are never fully agentic because they are always subjected to the very norms they are trying to resist. In fact, construction of the subject (subjectivation) is

a compromise or an act of negotiation between resistance and confor-
mity. Moreover, subjects are not only constituted through the regimes of
truth, as much as they constitute themselves "through a certain numbers
of practices which were games of truth, applications of power" (Fornet-
Betancourt et al. 1987, p. 121). In this section and the next, I engage
with Foucault's later work on the technologies of the self and how we
become subjects through practices embedded in power relations and
normalizing practices. As mentioned in the beginning of this chapter,
Foucault started focusing on these issues shortly before and after his
trips to Iran in 1978. In fact, Afary and Anderson (2005) have argued
that his experience in Iran had considerable influences on his later works
on ethics. By reading between the lines, it is, according to them, possible
to see some connection between his thoughts about the ethics of being
in antiquity and the ethics practiced in Islamic/religious societies such as
Iran (Afary and Anderson 2005). In this section I will draw on Foucault's
later work, mainly the last two volumes of the *History of Sexuality*, and
focus on how subjects can transform themselves within the "grids of
intelligibility" through the ethics of being. In Chap. 5, I draw on this
theoretical framework, as well as Foucault's work on practices of the self
and Butler's understanding of conditional agency, to focus on how gay-
identifying Iranian men, within the limits of the *biopolitical* space of contemporary Iran, construct their understanding of themselves as sexual
and gendered subjects.

In a seminar about the technologies of the self, Foucault defined these
practices as the following:

> Specific techniques that human beings use to understand themselves ...
> [These consist of] a certain number of operations on their own bodies and
> souls, thoughts, conduct, and way of being, so as to transform themselves in
> order to attain a certain state of happiness, purity, wisdom, perfection, or
> immortality. (Foucault 1988b, p. 18)

In this seminar, as well as in the lecture *The Ethic of Care of the Self as
a Practice of Freedom*, Foucault traces the development (genealogy),
discontinuities and changes in respect to the construction and understanding of the self, from antiquity until modernity, focusing particularly on Greco-Roman and early Christian practices of the self
(Fornet-Betancourt et al. 1987). Foucault distinguishes between the
Greco-Roman notion of the care of the self, which was in a way more

transformative, and an ethical practice, a way to relate to and thus also care for others; and the Christian understanding of the self through knowledge and a preoccupation with truth through the mechanism of the confessional (see a further discussion of this in the next section). Thus, the Greco-Roman care of the self was more involved with the ethics of being, constructing a "subject of truth" without sacrifice of self (Foucault 1988b). Friedrich Nietzsche influenced Foucault's work on ethics of being considerably (Fleming and Sewell 2002). For Nietzsche, the self was linked to ethics or ethos, the conduct of the self. He understood ethics as a "space of agency and self-transmogrification."[5] Foucault took Nietzsche's thought even further, and for him subjectivity became "an ethico-political engagement," a way to "transform one's self and to attain a certain mode of being" (Fleming and Sewell 2002; Fornet-Betancourt et al. 1987, p. 113). Allan (2008) emphasizes the ethical aspects of transgression in Foucault's works in her writing about disability and agency. She argues that it is "a form of resistance involving the crossing of limits or boundaries" (Allan 2008, p. 92). Thus "crossing of limits or boundaries" informs my understanding of technologies of the self as an ethical task. Moreover, I agree with Jennifer Ingrey that the subject is "capable of transformation through resistances," which are then part of the technologies of the self, or ethics of being (Ingrey 2013, p. 21). In order to understand the ethical nature of transgression (transformation), I turn my attention to Foucault's four ethical dimensions. These are practices (activities), which have the purpose of repositioning the individual subject and moving them away from a disadvantaged state (see Allan 1999, 2008; Foucault 1984b, 1988a; Tobias 2005; Winch 2005). The dimensions are not separate entities. Instead, they overlap and work together in forming the practices of the self as it was understood in antiquity.

The first dimension refers to the determination of ethical substance, which means that the individual subject must identify an aspect of the self, which he needs to embrace through ethics (Foucault 1988a, 1988b). This depends on the subject position one takes each time. In the case of gay Iranian men, one could assume that their ethical substance would be to focus on their sexuality and livability. The second dimension is the mode of subjection, within which individuals position themselves in relation to certain rules, moral codes, or even norms (Foucault 1988a). How do individuals find different ways of obeying or conforming to rules and moral codes? The rules and moral codes, which regulate gay subjects in Iran, are, in this context, mainly the disciplinary space of the family, as it pertains to the regime of truth of heteronormativity, as well as the moral-religious-juridical norms and regulation within the *biopolitical* nation-state. Under these conditions, gay-identifying Iranian men try to find different ways of conforming at the same time as they resist through the ethics of being.

A third dimension, the self-practice or ethical work, entails asking: "What are the means by which we can change ourselves in order to become ethical subjects?" (Foucault 1988a, p. 265). How do individuals transform themselves, in order to achieve *telos* or the fourth dimension? One can take different paths in order to change oneself into an ethical subject. Foucault, for example, stressed *parrhesia* as ethical work, which refers to telling the truth about oneself and the environment, not in the confessional Christian way, but more in order to relate to others and become a "subject of truth" without sacrifice of the self. *Parrhesia* has, according to Foucault, five important characteristics: frankness, truth, danger, criticism, and duty, which intersect with each other. For example, when telling the truth, or being frank, one can be critical and even place oneself in danger, especially if the person who receives the message is more powerful than the one who is telling the truth. Thus, ethical work can refer to different modalities of transformation, for example: transgression, passive existence, positive thought, diminishing the effect of or excusing heterosexism, *parrhesia*, or bodily expressions. The fourth dimension is *telos*, the ultimate aim of the ethical work, which concerns the goal of practices of the self (Foucault 1988a, 1988b). What state of being do we aspire to through our ethical work? Thus, the fourth dimension is the goal that many may try to reach through their ethical work in order to come to terms with themselves and gain a sexual or a gendered state of being. However, gaining sexual and gendered being, or more precisely becoming a sexual and gendered subject, can also involve "truth telling" in the Christian notion of confession, particularly in the Western discourse, as I will turn to in the next section.

In Chap. 5, I will draw on the four ethical dimensions formulated by Foucault in order to describe and analyze the various modes some of the participants used when caring for the self, while claiming a space, both discursive and material. In order to do so, I interpreted the narrative of my participants with the aim of describing the practices of the self. I stress that the process of taking care of the self is an ethical task, as presented by Foucault in his later works.

CONFESSIONS OF THE SEX(UALITY)

[T]he confession became one of the West's most highly valued techniques for producing truth. We have since become a singularly confessing society [...]. When it is not spontaneous or dictated by some internal imperative, the confession is wrung from a person by violence or threat [...]. Western man has become a confessing animal. (Foucault 1998, p. 59)

The quote at the beginning of this section is from Foucault's first volume of the *History of Sexuality*. There, Foucault first discusses the genealogy of confessions in Western thought/societies, in which he draws attention to the importance of confessions in the constitution of the individual subject. Thus, confessions produce truth(s), not only about the individual self but also about others. Foucault traces the use of confessionary practices from the ancient Greeks to modernity, and how these self-exposing practices changed dramatically in terms of power and scope with Christianity, gradually institutionalizing confessional or pastoral power. These practices became productive because "speaking the truth about oneself also makes, constitutes or constructs forms of one's self [...] [and] through these technologies a human being turns him or herself into a subject" (Besley 2005, p. 85). Thus, confessions were about knowing oneself in order to improve the self and renounce any sins in the presence of the priest/pastor, or someone who requires it:

One does not confess without the presence (or virtual presence) of a partner who is not simply the interlocutor but the authority who requires the confession, prescribes and appreciates it, and intervenes in order to judge, punish, forgive, console and reconcile. (Foucault 1990, pp. 61–62)

Through confessional practices the subject created a new self who was pure and relieved from the previous sins (Foucault 1998).

Foucault draws attention to how Christian confessional practices have become normalizing practices in modern society and in fact multiplied outside the ecclesiastical institution: in psychology and counseling, in reality shows, and more recently on social media such as *Facebook* or *Instagram* (Foucault 1982). Today, it can be argued that confessionary practices play an important role in the construction of the modern subject by modifying the person making the confession through truth telling and exposure of inner self. This can take the form of experiencing a sense of liberation, of being unburdened or being forgiven for one's sins.

In that sense, confession works directly on the confessor, who in most cases "no longer perceive[s] it as the effect of a power that constrains us" (Foucault 1990, p. 60). This is particularly true with regard to sexuality and the confessional discourse connected to the "infamous" closet, which has in fact greatly influenced Western thought, as argued by Sedgwick in the book *Epistemology of the Closet* (Sedgwick 1993; Foucault 1990). The discourse of the "closet" and "coming out" draws on the Christian practices of taking care of the self, meaning declaration and knowledge of the self, and the idea of "pastoral power" (Ingrey 2013).[6] Thus, coming out, revealing or confessing one's sexual or gender identity has, at least in the Western discourse on sex and sexuality, the purpose of gaining "a condition of salvation, a fundamental principle in the subject's relationship to himself [*sic*], and a necessary element in the individual's membership of a community" (Foucault 2005, p. 364). In other words, by confessing a truth of the self, one also becomes recognized as an intelligible gendered or sexual subject, a part of a community of others, whether seen as "deviant" or "normal" (see e.g., Butler 1990).

The question remains whether the metaphor of the "closet" and the Western discourse of "coming out" can be applied in other cultural settings, such as in Iran. As will be discussed in the book, my participants were aware of the discourse of "coming out" in the West and sometimes referred to it indirectly in their narratives. However, they did not cite that discourse specifically, when they referred to their wish or action to make their sexual identity known to others. As a matter of fact, the practices in the West of "coming out," which are often combined metaphorically with the word "closet," are for most gay Iranian men not a possibility. Thus, instead of referring to the confessionary practices of the "closet" and "coming out" of it, they talk about masks, which for them means having both a public and private face. The distinction between the public and private sphere has a long cultural history in Iran and in the Middle East, particularly in relation to gender and sexuality. For example, traditional houses in Iran were divided into *andaruni*, the inner private part of the house, reserved for women and close family members, and *biruni*, the public space, mostly occupied by men (Arjmand 2017). This architectural division on the basis of gender symbolically represents the gender divide in society at large, as well as the division between private and public in terms of confessions of the self. For gay Iranian men, which in regard to their sexual identity have internalized this strict division, being "out" means negotiating your sexuality depending on the spatial relations, whether within the private space of friends and those you can trust, or out in the public. Thus, as opposed to the metaphor of the closet, which indicates a private, non-social and dark space, the Iranian mask entails being able to shift between and adapt to these two spaces, which rarely become one and the same. Thus, for my participants/informants, confessions of one's sexual identity belong to the private space. This, as will be discussed in Chaps. 5 and 7, influenced their willingness to enter "public" confessionary spaces such as offices of the official medical examiner to gain the military exemption card, or HIV-testing points/centers.

*   *   *

Six years after his visit to Iran, Foucault died of AIDS in June 1984. At that time the "political spirituality," which Foucault had seen in the Iranian revolution, had turned into well-established theocracy. Foucault's optimistic vision of the Iranian revolution and its "irrationalities," had in reality been transformed into a rational, "biopolitical" state, where today well-developed surveillance and disciplinary mechanisms are in place in order to control and regulate its population. Thus, for me, employing Foucault's theoretical framework and his concepts in my research and writing on gender and sexuality, and how these factors intersect, in contemporary Iran, is a useful heuristic tool. I have therefore laid out the theoretical framework of the book in this chapter, which is mostly inspired by Foucault's work which I will refer to and draw on in later chapters: In Chap. 8, I engage with spatial dimensions of same-sex desires and will particularly draw on Foucault's notion of spatial power when analyzing the intersection of space, gender, and sexuality. Chapter 3 is again framed around Foucault's work, especially the first volume of *The History of Sexuality*, where he emphasizes the discursive formation of sexualities. This perspective has guided me through my research. Moreover, Foucault's writing about the technologies of the self and the ethics of being will be referred to and connected to when discussing the empirical data in Chaps. 5 and 6. However, as discussed in this chapter, one needs to be conscious of the limitations of any theory, and whether it fits the cultural context under study. I have tried to take this into account and have attempted to address this by exposing my hidden "inventory" with regard to theoretical perspective and cultural background in both this, and the previous, chapter.

NOTES

1. The Islamic Republican party was established in mid-1979 to support Khomeini and the formation of theocracy in Iran. It was disbanded in 1987 (see Axworthy 2013).
2. Said drew on Foucault's (2002) *Archaeology of Knowledge* in his discussion/ arguments regarding the "exteriorly of representation." Foucault termed the boundaries between the "excavator" (the observer or the researcher) and subject "exteriority." This means that the knowledge about the subject or discourse is produced and made known by someone who is outside that discourse, someone who because of his or her position cannot wholly identify with those who are the subjects of that discourse.
3. According to Amnesty International, Iran is ranked as second, after China, in terms of number of executions in 2016. This indicates that the "sovereign power" in Foucauldian sense, take life instead of foster it, is still exercised quite aggressively in Iran (see Amnesty International 2017, April 11).
4. Butler refers to this as the conditional agency of the subject (see Butler 2005).
5. Transmogrify means to change or alter greatly, and often with grotesque or humorous effect. Nietzsche and Foucault use this verb to stress the transgressive aspect of change (Foucault 1984b). According to Butler (1990) this would mean to extend the limits of the norms or what is culturally intelligible, for example, through resignification or other means.
6. In fact the confession chambers in Catholicism resembles the closet and the effects of salvation coming out of those chambers after having confessed.

REFERENCES

Afary, J., & Anderson, K. (2005). *Foucault and the Iranian Revolution. Gender and the Seductions of Islamism*. Chicago: Chicago University Press.

Allan, J. (1999). *Actively Seeking Inclusion: Pupils with Special Needs in Mainstream Schools*. London: Falmer.

Allan, J. (2008). *Rethinking Inclusion: The Philosophers of Difference in Practice*. Dordrecht: Springer.

Amanat, A. (2017). *Iran. A Modern History*. New Haven: Yale University Press.

Amnesty International. (2017, April 11). The Death Penalty in 2016: Facts and Figures. Retrieved from https://www.amnesty.org/en/latest/-news/2017/04/death-penalty-2016-facts-and-figures/.

Arjmand, R. (2017). *Public Urban Space, Gender and Segregation. Women-only Urban Parks in Iran*. London and New York: Routledge.

Axworthy, M. (2013). *Revolutionary Iran. A History of the Islamic Republic*. London: Allen Lane/Penguin.

Ball, K. (2005). Organization, Surveillance and the Body: Towards a Politics of Resistance. *Organization, 12*(1), 89–108. https://doi.org/10.1177/135050840504857.

Besley, T. (2005). Foucault, Truth Telling and Technologies of the Self in Schools. *Journal of Educational Enquiry, 6*(1), 76–89.

Butler, J. (1990). *Gender Trouble. Feminism and the Subversion of Identity.* New York: Routledge.

Butler, J. (1993). *Bodies that Matter. On the Discursive Limits of Sex.* New York: Routledge.

Butler, J. (2005). *Giving an Account of Oneself.* New York: Fordham University Press.

Callis, A. S. (2009, November 25). Playing with Butler and Foucault: Bisexuality and Queer Theory. *Journal of Bisexuality, 9*(3–4), 213–233. https://doi.org/10.1080/15299710903316513.

Casey, C. (1995). *Work, Self and Society: After Industrialism.* London: Sage.

DePalma, R., & Atkinson, E. (2009). *Interrogating Heteronormativity in Primary-Schools: Project.* London: Trentham Books.

Fleming, P., & Sewell, G. (2002, November 1). Looking for the Good Soldier, Svejk: Alternative Modalities of Resistance in the Contemporary Workplace. *Sociology, 36*(4), 857–873. https://doi.org/10.1177/003803850203600404.

Fleming, P., & Spicer, A. (2003, February 1). Working at a Cynical Distance: Implications for Power, Subjectivity and Resistance. *Organization, 10*(1), 157–179. https://doi.org/10.1177/1350508403010001376.

Fornet-Betancourt, R., Becker, H., Gomez-Muller, A., & Gauthier, J. D. (1987). The Ethic of Care for the Self as a Practice of Freedom: An Interview with Michel Foucault on January 20, 1984. *Philosophy Social Criticism, 12*, 112–131.

Foucault, M. (1978). *History of Sexuality. Volume I: An Introduction.* New York: Random House.

Foucault, M. (1980). *Power/Knowledge: Selected Interviews and Other Writings, 1972–1977* (C. Gordon, Ed., and C. Gordon, L. Marshall, J. Mepham, & K. Soper, Trans.). New York, NY: Pantheon Books.

Foucault, M. (1982). Afterword: The Subject and Power. In H. L. Dreyfus & P. Rabinow (Eds.), *Michel Foucault: Beyond Structuralism and Hermeneutics* (pp. 208–226). Chicago, IL: University of Chicago Press.

Foucault, M. (1984a). Of Other Spaces, Heterotopias. *Architecture, Mouvement, Continuité, 5*, 1–9.

Foucault, M. (1984b). Nietzsche, Genealogy, History. In P. Rabinow (Ed.), *The Foucault Reader* (pp. 76–100). New York: Pantheon.

Foucault, M. (1988a). *The Care of the Self: The History of Sexuality.* New York: Vintage.

Foucault, M. (1988b). Technologies of the Self. In L. Martin, H. Gutman, & P. Hutton (Eds.), *Technologies of the Self: A Seminar with Michel Foucault* (pp. 16–49). Amherst: University of Massachusetts Press.

Foucault, M. (1990). *The History of Sexuality: Vol. 1. An Introduction* (R. Hurley, Trans.). New York, NY: Vintage Books.

Foucault, M. (1991). *Discipline and Punish. The Birth of the Prison.* London: Penguin.

Foucault, M. (1994). *The Birth of the Clinic: An Archaeology of Medical Perception.* New York: Vintage Books.

Foucault, M. (1998). *The History of Sexuality: The Will to Knowledge.* London: Penguin Books.

Foucault, M. (2002). The Archeology of Knowledge (A. Sheridan, Trans.). London: Routledge.

Foucault, M. (2005). *Hermeneutics of the Subject: Lectures at the College de France: 1981–1982* (F. Gros, Ed. and G. Burchell, Trans.). New York, NY: Palgrave Macmillan.

Gramsci, A. (1995). *Selections from the Prison Notebooks of Antonio Gramsci.* New York: International Publishers.

Ingrey, J. C. (2013). *The Public School Washroom as Heterotopia: Gendered Spatiality and Subjectification.* Electronic Thesis and Dissertation Repository. Paper 1768. Ontario: University of Western.

Johnson, P. (2006). Unravelling Foucault's Different Spaces. *History of Human Sciences, 19*(4), 75–90. https://doi.org/10.1177/0952695106069669.

Knights, D., & McCabe, D. (2000, August 1). 'Ain't Misbehavin'? Opportunities for Resistance under New Forms of 'Quality' Management. *Sociology, 34*(3), 421–436. https://doi.org/10.1177/S0038038500000274.

Kunda, G. (1992). *Engineering Culture: Control and Commitment in a High-tech Corporation.* Philadelphia: Temple University Press.

Lynch, R. (2011). Foucault's Theory of Power. In D. Taylor (Ed.), *Michel Foucault. Key Concepts* (pp. 13–27). Durham: Acumen.

Martino, W., & Kjaran, J. I. (2019). The Politics of Recognizability: Giving an Account of Iranian Gay Men's Lives Under Repressive Conditions of Sexuality Governance. *International Journal of Middle East Studies, 51*(1), 21–41.

Mathiesen, T. (1989). *Makt og medier. En innføring i mediasosiologi.* Oslo: Pax.

Mendieta, E. (2011). The Practice of Freedom. In D. Taylor (Ed.), *Michel Foucault. Key Concepts* (pp. 111–127). Durham: Acumen.

Ojakangas, M. (2005). Impossible Dialogue on Bio-Power. Agamben and Foucault. *Foucault Studies,* (2), 5–28. https://doi.org/10.22439/fs.v0i2.856.

Rabinow, P., & Rose, N. (2006). Biopower today. *BioSocieties, 1,* 195–217. https://doi.org/10.1017/S1745855206040014014.

Said, E. (1978). *Orientalism.* London: Routledge.

Sedgwick, E. K. (1993). Epistemology of the Closet. In H. Abelove, M. A. Barale, & D. M. Halperin (Eds.), *The Lesbian and Gay Studies Reader* (pp. 45–62). New York: Routledge.

Sharp, J. P., Routledge, P., Philo, C., & Paddison, R. (2000). Entanglements of Power. Geographies of Domination/Resistance. In J. P. Sharp, P. Routledge, C. Philo, & R. Paddison (Eds.), *Entanglements of Power. Geographies of Domination/Resistance* (pp. 1–43). London: Routledge.

Steyaert, C. (2010, December). Queering Space: Heterotopic Life in Derek Jarman's Garden. *Gender, Work & Organization, 17*(1), 45–68. https://doi.org/10.1111/j.1468-0432.2008.00404.x.

Tobias, S. (2005). Foucault on Freedom and Capabilities. *Theory, Culture and Society, 22*(4), 65–85. https://doi.org/10.1177/0263276405053721.

Winch, S. (2005, March). Ethics, Government and Sexual Health: Insights from Foucault. *Nursing Ethics, 12*(2), 176–186. https://doi.org/10.1191/0969733005ne774oa.

CHAPTER 3

The Historical Contingencies and the Politics of Same-Sex Desire in Iran

Jón Ingvar Kjaran and Wayne Martino

Jón was reminded of the importance of history and how it is kept alive through the historical or collective memory of a nation when he arrived in Tehran for his first fieldtrip on February 11, 2015. This important date is, according to the official rhetoric of the Islamic Republic of Iran, regarded as the day of the final victory of the Islamic revolution in 1979. In fact, the ten days leading up to February 11 are called *Daheh-ye Fajr*, ten days of dawn, framing the return of Ayatollah Khomeini on February 1, 1979, and the toppling of the monarchy ten days later (Axworthy 2013). It is a public holiday, observed all over Iran. In Tehran, during that day, the most ardent supporters of the government gather around the Azadi Square with flags, slogans, and pictures of fallen heroes and martyrs of the revolution. The state television broadcasts live from these events and throughout the day most national TV channels show programs devoted to the history of the revolution. However, for most Iranians, this day is just another holiday, though it is also a reminder of the past and how the past is interconnected to the present. Arman, one of Jón's main informants, made the following comment when asked about his feelings regarding this day:

> I just feel the pain and sadness in my heart when you ask me about this particular day. The day when a glorious civilization went backwards. The sun went down and the darkness took over.

© The Author(s) 2019
J. I. Kjaran, *Gay Life Stories*,
https://doi.org/10.1007/978-3-030-12831-9_3

For Arman, and many other young Iranians, the past is alive, and one is constantly reminded of the history of the Islamic revolution; it is a part of one's everyday existence. In fact, when walking or driving through the streets of Tehran, the past is ever present, kept alive through various images, particularly paintings of the martyrs and heroes of the revolution, which in many ways resemble photographs, located at visible spots or busy thoroughfares on billboards, houses, and public buildings (see Figs. 3.1 and 3.2).

Those images tell a story of the past and remind the present self of its place in history and how history is located in the present. It is also a reminder of the Islamic revolution and part of the Islamification of public spaces. Thus, this chapter is devoted to the history of Iran from the latter

Fig. 3.1 In memory of these martyrs of the revolution on a billboard at one of the main highways in Tehran

Fig. 3.2 Young Ayatollah Khomeini and Tayyeb Haj Rezaei along with quote from Tayyeb about his loyalty to Khomeini. Tayyeb is considered to be a martyr of the revolution—killed in 1963 during the period of the last Shah of Iran

part of the twentieth century to the present in order to understand and contextualize the topic under investigation: accounts of same-sex desires in contemporary Iran. In other words, it is necessary to focus on the past and how it influences the present, weaving together important elements of sexuality and gender governance in Iran.

In terms of discourses on sexuality and same-sex desire, there are both discontinuities and continuities between the past and the present, between the period of the Shah and the post-revolutionary Iran. In that respect, some discursive themes of the past continue in the present. They are in many ways reproduced by the contemporary Islamic regime, which has replaced the modernist/secular logic of the Shah period with religious arguments/rhetoric, in its disavowal and regulation of sexual minorities. This disavowal will be explored further in this chapter by engaging with important historical sources and accounts that speak to the historical contingencies of the emergence of same-sex desire and the category of "the homosexual" in Iran. We incorporate into this account the political and social history of Iran from the latter part of the twentieth century until the present. Drawn into the discussion of sexuality and same-sex desire, the historical contingencies will be helpful to understand better the accounts of same-sex-desiring/gay Iranian men under quite specific conditions of sexuality governance, regimes of representation, and self-formative/self-fashioning potentialities of Iran today. This has, among others, been emphasized by Mark Blasius (2013) who postulates the importance of incorporating interpretive frames that speak to matters of historically situated conceptions of sexual personhood, justice, and the ethos of governance (at both the state and individual levels). Thus, by drawing attention to the historical nuances with regard to sexuality and sexual governance in Iran, we adhere to a non-orientalist perspective, which entails working against the basic tenets of orientalism in which the complex cultures of the East are, through the process of Othering, often simplified (Said 1978).

ERASURE OF THE MEMORY OF HOMOSOCIALITY: FROM PRE-MODERNITY TO MODERNITY

For many Iranians, the classical poems of Hafez, Rumi, Sadi, and Khayyam are beloved and held in high esteem. They hold special meaning for Iranian people, being considered almost sacred, and, as such, could be said to be part of the nation's soul. In many ways, the poems act to unify different layers of society. These poems speak directly to their reader about themes such as love, beauty, and unity with god. When recited aloud one feels the power of their message, which gives them a religious and mystical character. They transcend time and space, transferring their reader into another world: for some they take them into the "garden of heaven," for others into the "garden of mystic lovers," as Rumi speaks about in one of his short poems.[1] Some of these classical works are part of the curriculum in Iranian schools. They are read and recited regularly by school children, connecting the present to the past. They also give solace to many Iranians in times of distress or sadness. Roxanne Varzi (2006) in her ethnographic study on Iranian youth, media, and martyrdom recounts how the poems of Hafiz literally saved the life of her uncle after he was imprisoned following the Islamic revolution for being a member of the leftist Tudeh party.

When he was in prison, he regularly recited some of Hafez's poems in order to cope with the situation, find solace, and maintain his peace of mind. For every poem he recited, he tied a knot from a string of his shirt: "That knotted string was like prayer beads, a tie to sanity; tying a knot to remember a poem kept me from thinking of the horrors happening around me" (Varzi 2006, p. 3). In the end he got out of prison after an old man informed the revolutionary guards that he was praying and had renounced Marxism and embraced Islam. Varzi's uncle then evaluates Hafiz's impact on him: "Every knot was a Hafiz poem that freed me from the confines of prison by taking me away. ... He [Hafiz] teaches us how to rise above obstacles. ... He preserved my mind and took it to a beautiful place while my body was kept captive" (Varzi 2006, pp. 3–4).

Indeed, Hafiz speaks of beautiful places in his poems, singing night-ingales, roses, and beauty. He also talks about love and in some of his poems the male is constituted as an object of same-sex desire and love. In fact, there exists a rich vocabulary of homoeroticism and same-sex love in classical Persian poetry, as has, for example, been explored by Cyrus Shamisa in his book, *Shahed-Bazi*. In 2002, the book was ordered off the shelves by the Iranian authorities because in it Shamisa discusses homosexuality and same-sex love in Persian poetry, even going so far as to say: "Persian literature is essentially a homosexual literature" (quoted in Afary and Anderson 2005, p. 156; see also Parsi 2015, January 14). In light of this, it is understandable that these poems have inspired many gay-identifying Iranian males, and, as in the case of Varzi's uncle, helped them to rise above obstacles in their daily lives; to transcend time and space to a place where same-sex desire is depicted as something natural and beautiful, as pure love, irrespective of sex or gender, as can be seen in the following lines from a poem by Hafez: "And men and men, who are lovers, and women and women, who give each other light."[2] Thus, Hafiz, Rumi, and other classical Persian poets provide some gay-identifying Iranians with some acceptance and solace, as they can identify with the homosociality and same-sex love of the past, which in contemporary Iran is forbidden and not officially recognized at all. Arman expressed the following about Hafiz and the meaning of Persian poetry for him:

I was so excited a few years ago when I read it [a poem by Hafiz about a love for a sweet boy] for the first time. I could barely believe what I was seeing. It [the poem] is about homosexual love. It was very sweet and heart warming for me, because it was giving me the history. That this has always been in the world and even in our culture there have been stories and poems for it [homosexual love]. It was really awesome.

Thus, Hafiz gives Arman some hope, and a connection to the homosociality of the past. Some of Jón's other informants also mentioned how the poems of Hafiz and Rumi made an impact on them and even helped them in coming to terms with their sexuality. Some of them even used quotes from those poems to justify or argue that same-sex love had always been part of Iranian culture, and that the current situation was only an exception to the rule; a period that would in due time come to an end. Then everybody would be allowed to enter "the garden of mystic lovers," which does not distinguish or discriminate between gender, sex or sexual orientation. In other words, the "garden of mystic lovers" can be considered as a "queer space"—a space of the Other.

This brings us then to pre-modern times, the actual cultural context of the Persian classical poetry, and the time before the advance of modernity, as well as foreign influences, on Iranian society in the latter part of the nineteenth century. During that time, sexuality in Iran was not organized according to a heteronormative binary system for differentiating heterosexuality from homosexuality in identity category terms. Rather, as indicated by Katarzyna Korycki and Abouzar Nasirzadeh (2014), engagement in same-sex practices for men was governed by a very different regulatory and ethical system of social statuses, designated along three quite distinct lines: (1) age, (2) whether one was a giver or receiver of sexual pleasure, and (3) moral precepts governing sexual conduct in private and public domains of one's life. The beardless, young, adolescent male, referred to as the *amrad*, was an object of homoerotic love and constituted a specific sexual group in pre-modern times, with such understandings of homoerotic attachments finding wide expression in the classical Persian literature. Thus, a binary notion of sexuality, which defines homosexuality as being set in contradistinction to heterosexuality, did not organize the enactment of same-sex desire (Afary 2009, p. 87).

Embedded in the pre-modern hierarchical same-sex relations were regulatory systems of heteronormativity, which govern the terms of such relations, as Janet Afary (2009) points out. For instance, she claims that same-sex relations were considered acceptable only if the older man was married and that such relationships remained discreet (Afary 2009, p. 86). Moreover, within such a system of homoerotic same-sex relations, the adult man was required to assume the active dominant position in the relationship as a *giver* of pleasure: "A dominant man who penetrated both women and boys 'was just as masculine as those who penetrated women' and was regarded as 'hyper-masculine'" (Rowson 1991a, p. 71, cited in Afary 2009, p. 86); a common understanding that is still evident in Iran and in other Middle Eastern cultures today. However, an adult man who continued seeking sexual submission (*ma'bun*) was considered to be a "pervert," and also became an object of the medical gaze as a specific category of person (Afary 2009). In this regard, Afary points out that, while the *ma'bun* married and had children, he was still considered to be suffering from a disease and a loss of masculinity as well as honor. Such men were also distinguished from what Afary terms, *mukhannathun*, which refers to a man who desires to "resemble a woman in his delicate limbs and soft skin" (Afary 2009, p. 86).

Furthermore, Korycki and Nasirzadah argue that this division of sexual space, as demarcated by a classificatory system of different sorts of same-sex-desiring male subjects and their objects of desire, was built around different class and social positions and statuses involving slaves and servants as receivers of pleasure. The accommodation of same-sex desire and its enactment was evident in bathhouses, military and clerical schools without moral approbation. However, Korycki and Nasirzadah (2014) point out that the regulation of homoerotic desire and its enactment were governed by norms related to moral codes of conduct in private and public realms: "Heeding Islamic prohibition of homoerotic love, adult males were expected to marry. Once they did, they were considered to have fulfilled their public obligation and they were allowed to pursue desire and pleasure in private—as long as they did not do so excessively" (p. 6). Here it needs to be emphasized that although homoeroticism and the enactment of same-sex desire were indeed permissible within certain limits or tolerated according to certain grids of intelligibility for hierarchically classifying certain male types and statuses, this did not necessarily equate to a recognition of sexual and gender justice.

In the late nineteenth century, as Iran moved from pre-modern to more modern and contemporary times, a shift occurred in the politics of same-sex desire. Korycki and Nasirzadeh identify the demarcation of a newly reconfigured heteronormative space as a hallmark of modernization at the hands of reformist elites in nineteenth-century Iran. This relied on casting same-sex desire as deviant and erasing the memory of homosociality from the public sphere. Korycki and Nasirzadeh (2014) point out that this historical moment was tied to the impact of European colonial influences—loss of Iranian territory to Tsarist Russia and loss of control over the economy to British imperialist forces—which resulted in an identity crisis driven by calls for rejection and reformulation of Iranian traditions. It was under such conditions, influenced by modernizing influences from the West, that women's segregation and wearing of the veil came to be seen as signs of "Iran's backwardness," and the means by which to explain the tendency for Iranian men to engage in same-sex relations, and, hence, the refashioning of such practices as unnatural (Korycki and Nasirzadeh 2014). Thus, the realization that the enactment and expression of same-sex desire was repudiated and considered a vice by Westerners led to denying its pervasiveness by equating the desire for *male love* of an *amrad* with a "frustrated desire" for a woman. Such rationality came to inform a reframing of an existing (alternative) discourse, locating the source for inciting homosexuality among men in the absence of women in the public sphere. The result was the reconfiguring of new forms of heterosociality and heteronormalization premised on the repudiation of same-sex love and the insertion of the unveiled woman into a gender-desegregated public sphere (Afary 2009).

After Reza Shah founded the Pahlavi dynasty and came to the throne in 1925, he initiated extensive reforms with the aim of modernizing Iran. His role model was Mustafa Kemal Ataturk (1881–1938), who was during that time transforming Turkish society. The reforms consisted of aggressive projects, which were applied not only to the army and the economic sphere of society but also to the cultural sphere, with the aim of changing the customs and traditions of the Iranian people. Marriage became a civil, rather religious, institution and the Shah instigated a policy that outlawed veiling and mandated western modes of dress (Korycki and Nasirzadeh 2014). Moreover, the enactment of same-sex desire prevalent in the eighteenth century was expunged, and any references to the homoeroticism of the past, for example, in classical Iranian poetry, were erased. The argument was that same-sex love and homoeroticism should not be tolerated in a civilized and modern nation such as Iran. Thus, Reza Shah, himself a homophobe according to the historian Abbas Milani (2011), further heterosexualized the Iranian public sphere, a development that started in the latter part of the nineteenth century.

In September 1941, the rule of Reza Shah came to an end, when he was forced by the Allies to abdicate due to his alleged support of the *Third Reich*. Mohammad Reza Shah Pahlavi, aged 22, succeeded his father and became the last Shah of Iran. To begin with, the young Shah lacked self-confidence and spent most of his time writing and discussing poetry with his friend Ernest Perron, whom he had met during his school years in Switzerland (Milani 2011). In fact, the relationship between the Shah and his friend Perron in some ways resembled the homosocial behavior of the past, which the former Shah had tried so much to repudiate from Iranian cultural memory. Perron, who often dressed in a campy style and appeared rather effeminate, did little to hide his homosexuality. They became best friends when the crown prince attended Le Rosey boarding school in Switzerland (Milani 2011). Their friendship gradually grew, and when the crown prince returned to Iran in 1936 he took Perron with him, who lived in the official palace until his death in 1961. Gradually rumors started to spread about the homosexual nature of their relationship. This view was particularly put forward by the enemies of the Shah, and after the Islamic revolution in 1979, a best-selling book was published by the revolutionary regime: *Ernest Perron, the Husband of the Shah of Iran* (Zonis 1991, p. 118). This remains the official interpretation of events in the Islamic Republic to the present day. Some of my informants even mentioned the alleged homosexuality of the last Shah in our talk, drawing mostly on accounts from their parents, who were often referring to the more liberal views espoused during the period of the Shah.

The rumors about the Shah being homosexual draw attention to how accusations of homosexuality are used politically in Iran, both in the past and present, to Other and demonize one's enemies. In fact, the Shah used the same means when he ordered conservative newspapers under his control to describe Khomeini as a homosexual and a drug addict in 1978. This invoked strong protest within Iran and marked the beginning of the Islamic revolution. Thus, in terms of same-sex love or relationships, there are both discontinuities and continuities in the public discourse, from the late nineteenth century onward. On the one hand, there was an effort to erase homoeroticism from the cultural memory; it was expunged and rendered legible as a repudiated desire or condition belonging to the past or rather a pre-modern time. Consequently, accusations of engaging in same-sex relations have often been used to discredit individuals, such as with the case of the last Shah of Iran and Khomeini. On the other hand, some aspects of homosociality survived into modernity in spite of the hetero-sexualization of the public sphere, the relationship between Perron and the Shah being an example. Whether they were actual lovers or not is not the main concern here, but more the way their friendship evolved, which connects the homosociality of the past to the present—a loving relationship between two males, whether purely platonic or a mixture of both. This dialectic notion of the discontinuities/continuities of the past within the present can be further spotted following the Islamic revolution, which re-established a strict separation of the genders within the public sphere, as well as the obligatory veiling of women. At the same time, same-sex sexual practices were not only erased from the public memory but also criminalized, and those individuals who engaged in same-sex practices were in danger of being physically erased. Moreover, homosexuality was depicted as a Western disease, foreign to Iranian culture. These ideas about the corruption of the West and its impact on Iranian youth, *Westoxification*, were promulgated before the Islamic revolution, and became part of the revolutionary rhetoric and grammar, both during and after the Islamic revolution, which we will now turn to.

OCCIDENTOSIS: A PLAGUE FROM THE WEST

In 1962, the scholar, activist, and novelist Jalal Al-e Ahmad (1923–1969) published the book titled *Gharbzadegi* in Farsi (Algar 1984). In the English version the title is translated as *Occidentosis: A Plague from the West*, which reflects quite well the main arguments presented in the book and how Al-e Ahmad compares Western influences in Iran with "a contagious disease, like the plague, like cholera" (Al-e Ahmad 1984, p. 132). Since its publication, it greatly influenced the Iranian intelligentsia and anti-Shah factions, both before and during the Iranian revolution. Moreover, Al-e Ahmad was the only contemporary writer of that time who was praised by Khomeini.[3] Khomeini perceived Al-e Ahmad writings as a call to "authentic Islam" and a struggle against Western influences (Abrahamian 1993). In fact, it can be argued that Al-e Ahmad's analysis and conclusions in *Gharbzadegi* contributed to the dominant revolutionary and post-revolutionary discourse regarding the relationship between Iran and the West, in which emphasis is placed on the authenticity of Iranian culture, immorality, and plague-infused influences spreading from the West (Mirsepassi-Ashtiani 1994). This idea of a toxic Western influence applies particularly to the US, which has been depicted as *Sheytan-e Bozorg*, or the "Great Satan" in Iranian revolutionary/official discourse (Beeman 2005). Thus, the demonization of the US and Westernization in general are referred to by Al-e Ahmad as the "contemporary monster" which has corrupted Iranian youth and culturally alienated its people, making them dependent on Western technology and consumerism (Al-e Ahmad 1984, p. 31). The consequences, according to Al-e Ahmad, have been moral decay and decline of traditional Iranian industries, for example, carpet-weaving.

The concept of *Gharbzadegi*, which is the Persian title of Al-e Ahmad's book and forms his main line of argument, has often been translated in English as "Weststruckness" (Hillmann 1988, p. xv), "plague from the West" (Abrahamian 1993), or "Westoxification" (Keddie 2006, p. 189). Throughout the book the term *Westoxification* is used, when referring to the official discourse within Iran regarding the influences of the West. As referred to above, this discourse is based on Al-e Ahmad's arguments about indiscriminate borrowing from the West, importation of Western values and lifestyle, and imitation of the West (Al-e Ahmad 1984, p. 58). In that sense, the term refers specifically to the toxic influence of the West in terms of its capacity to corrupt the "true" culture of Islam and Iran, and which can result in cultural alienation. An example of the corrupting influences of the West and expressed indirectly by Al-e Ahmad is moral and sexual degeneracy, especially applied to those who have sex outside of Iran and return with a "foreign spouse":

> Those (of either sex) who lost their virginity in Europe or America, who first grew intimate with the opposite sex there. When they return with their foreign spouse, they care nothing for God or man, or they come to see what a terrible mistake they have made. (Al-e Ahmad 1984, p. 120)

The mixed marriage or copulation is one example of "Westoxification" and, according to Al-e Ahmad, should be prevented in order to preserve Islamic authoritarian sexual morality in accordance with the patriarchal, family institution. In fact, the sexual mores and desires of Iranian youth have often been depicted in the official discourse as embodying a fight against Western and non-Islamic values, which need to be resisted at all costs.

In the book *Gharbzadegi*, Al-e Ahmad presents a solution to the harms of modernity and increased influences of the West, which entails a return to the roots of Islamic culture, and as such an accommodation of modernity within the frame of the Iranian-Islamic tradition. Thus, the "cure" for the Western disease is a return to Islamic values. This has been part of the official discourse in post-revolutionary Iran, depicting foreign elements and presumably immoral elements as a "disease," which needs to be contained and "cured." Moreover, the Islamic Republic has in its *raison d'état* and expressions of national interest often drawing on a discourse of authenticity, which can be found in both Al-e-Ahmad's and Ali Shariati's writings.[4] Al-e Ahmad, for example, emphasizes a return to the self (khish), which according to Shiravand has the aim to:

> [R]e-define cultural identity against colonial ideology and imperialist (techno-scientific) onslaught and to realize the 'third way' (rah-e-sevvom), or self-reliance [...], i.e., a specifically Iranian path of autarkic development and state sovereignty informed by the authentic Perso-Islamic past (prior to the Safavid era), and free of toxic imperialist Western influences. (Shiravand 2015, p. 117)

Thus, a discourse of authenticity entails cultivating a national identity by embracing official cultural and religious values, which are depicted as "pure" and underscored by a repudiation of the "contaminated," "toxic" Other. An example of the workings of this discourse, and its official rhetoric, is the ban on teaching English in Iranian primary schools, issued and approved by the supreme leader Ali Khameini in January 2018. The official argument is that learning English early on can expose children to Western "cultural invasion." Instead, according to Iranian officials, primary schools should focus on teaching about Iranian culture (Iran bans the teaching of English in primary schools, official says). As can be seen from this example, the official rhetoric draws on this discourse of authenticity and *Westoxification*. In fact, Iranian authorities have often blamed foreign (Western) forces for many of their problems, whether public protests, economic hardship, or the perceived decadent sexual behavior of its youth. As will be discussed further in this book, the official discourse on same-sex desire draws heavily on the ideas of authenticity, contamination, and this idea of homosexuality as a disease that has been imported from the West. Thus, adhering to "authentic masculinity" in Iran entails being heterosexual and abiding by the marriage imperative. Such discursive framing helps to make sense of official modes of rationality. During the Pahlavi regime it was often argued in the official rhetoric and the media that homosexuality among men could be attributed to the absence of women in the public sphere and, hence, as a consequence of enforced gender segregation and veiling of women. Thus, in order to counter these arguments strict measures were taken by the Islamic Republic to repudiate homosexuality and to create a counter-discourse, which placed the roots of homosexuality within Western societies. In that sense, same-sex desire/ love was postulated as foreign to Iranian culture and any remembrance of it needed to be erased from the collective memory of the nation. Thus, as will be explored further in the next section, with regard to the official discourse on same-sex love/homosexuality, the Islamic Republic has demonstrated continuity with the logic and arguments of the Shah regime, but also discontinuity by adding the religious-moral rhetoric/logic to the previous discourse on same-sex love.

THE LAST YEARS OF THE SHAH AND ESTABLISHMENT OF THE ISLAMIC REPUBLIC

Although the cultural elite in Iran had made considerable efforts, from the late nineteenth century onwards, to erase homoeroticism/homosociality (same-sex desire) from the cultural memory of the nation as a part of modernizing society—discussed in the previous sections—it was still tolerated and practiced under the rule of Mohammad Reza Pahlavi, the last Shah of Iran. Same-sex sexual practices (homosexual practices) were not punishable by the civil law, although it was neither recognized nor generally accepted. In the 1970s, in cities such as Tehran, there existed a small but active gay subculture (Afary 2009). Afsaneh Najmabadi, quoting a report from 1954, talks of a lively entertainment scene in particular neighborhoods of Tehran, such as Sahr-i-nau, which was considered to be the Tehran's red-light district and where a variety of cafés, restaurants, and nightclubs were located (Najmabadi 2014, p. 130). Non-heteronormative male bodies, both those who desired same-sex sexual encounters, as well as those who could be defined as "woman-presenting" males, often frequented these venues. Thus, as pointed out by Najmabadi, "Gay Tehran" in the 1970s was rather inclusive of a wide spectrum of non-heteronormative males who did not fully act within the grids of the heterosexual matrix; in other words, performing gender at odds with the dominant norms (Najmabadi 2013, 2014). In that sense, "Gay Tehran" in the 1970s was quite diverse and did not only consist of individuals who had adopted the Western gay identity label. However, the gay media in the West mostly seems to have emphasized the homosexual nature of the Tehran "gay scene" in the 1970s, describing the scene as a "gay paradise." Moreover, Western accounts thereupon often bore the mark of romantic orientalism, in which the oriental homosexual Other is depicted as exotic and highly sexualized (Najmabadi 2013; Said 1978). Thus, the notion of a sexual paradise in Iran, seen from the Western gay gaze, can be framed within the orientalist discourse of the exotic Other.

Najmabadi quotes Jerry Zarit, who visited Tehran right before the Islamic revolution and wrote an article in a gay magazine in October 1979, which he titled: "The Iranian Male—an Intimate Look." In many ways, the title itself draws on an orientalist discourse, where the exotic Iranian male is an object of the white man's gaze and exploration, even conquest as can be understood (read) from the following quote from the article: "Iran was for me, and others like me, a sexual paradise. In terms of both quantity and quality it was the most exciting experience of my life" (quoted in Najmabadi 2014, p. 120). What is also interesting is that the article was translated into Farsi and published in the gay diasporic Iranian journal *Homan* in 1991, 12 years after its first publication in the US. Thus, as argued by Najmabadi, these kinds of publications depicted gay life in Iran/Tehran before the revolution in progressive and liberationist terms, but this changed dramatically after the Islamic revolution. The question thus remains whether the Islamic revolution can be seen as a darkness that descended over the non-heteronormative male culture in Iran and marked a brutal end to it? As Najmabadi has argued, the "tale" is more complex than that, and by focusing on only one aspect of that particular "tale"— the "brutal end" of gay Tehran during the beginning of the revolution— blurs "important continuities and different sorts of discontinuities" (Najmabadi 2014, p. 120). In other words, in terms of "sexual freedom" and same-sex practices, the dominant discourse portrays the Islamic revolution as bringing an end to an urban gay culture in the making. However, it can be debated how "developed" that culture indeed was, and how liberal society viewed same-sex practices, especially considering that the previous decades of modernization had seen the erasure of homoeroticism/homosociality from the cultural memory. Moreover, many gay-identifying males kept their identity hidden from society, even before the revolution, and in that sense, the establishment of the Islamic republic did not change their situation, as they continued to hide their "true inner self." At the same time, as will be discussed later on in this section, the revolution opened up the possibilities for trans identifying individuals, who gained legal recognition, as well as some financial support for gender reassignment surgery, a procedure decreed illegal and unethical by the Medical Council of Iran (MCI) in 1976 (Najmabadi 2014). But such spaces were still highly regulatory and policed, being demarcated by the heteronormative limits imposed by a form of Islamic jurisprudential governance that is driven by a logic of the repudiated homosexual subject. As we have argued elsewhere, the official recognition of transsexuality was constituted in compliance with Islam as state policy in Iran and became a site for rein-scribing the *othering* homosexuality as a morally reprehensible form of criminal behavior and sexual perversion. Given the conditions of emer-gence for officially sanctioning transsexuality in Iran under which *gayness* has become an important means for distinguishing and differentiating Male-to-Female (*MtF*)-*ness* (Najmabadi 2014, p. 300), it is important to note that such *dividing practices* rely on an incitement to and proliferation of discourses about the "cultural abjection of 'gay'-ness under the sign of *kuni*,"[5] with all of its regulatory and disciplinary effects for endorsing moral prohibitions and "religious-legal sanctions against same-sex behav-iours and practices" (Najmabadi 2014, pp. 138 and 274; Martino and Kjaran 2019).

Shortly after the toppling of the Shah's government in February 1979, measures were taken by the revolutionary authorities to purify society, for example, by closing down establishments, such as bars, cafés, and night-clubs, that were considered to be "spaces of corruption." Moreover, men and women charged with prostitution and sodomy were publicly executed. Lesbian feminist Kate Millet, who in her book *Going to Iran* describes her impression regarding the measures introduced by the revolutionary gov-ernment, is quoted by Afary and Anderson with regard to the public exe-cutions of homosexuals: "As for the homosexuals, they were shot right in the road, judgement took seconds" (quoted in Afary and Anderson 2005, p. 112). In fact, public executions of men accused of being homosexuals were frequently reported in Western gay media and according to Afary and Anderson (2005), at least 16 executions for sexual violations, among them sodomy, took place in February and March 1979 (see also Najmabadi 2013, 2014).

When the Italian journalist Oriana Fallaci interviewed Khomeini in September 1979, she confronted him about these executions for alleged sexual violations:

Fallaci: All right, but I did not necessarily mean the tortures and the Savak[6] killers; Imam. I meant those who were executed and had nothing to do with the regime, the people who are still being shot today for adultery, or prostitution, or homo-sexuality. Is it right to shoot the poor prostitute or a woman who is unfaithful to her husband, or a man who loves another man?

Khomeini: If your finger suffers from gangrene, what do you do? Do you let the whole hand, and then the body, become filled with gangrene, or do you cut the finger off? What brings corruption to an entire country and its people must be pulled up like the weeds that infest a field of wheat. I know there are societies where women are permitted to give themselves to satisfy the desire of men who are not their husbands, and where men are permitted to give themselves to satisfy other men's desires. But the society that we want to build does not permit such things.

Fallaci: Imam, how is it possible to compare a Savak murderer and torturer with a citizen who exercises his sexual freedom?

Khomeini: Corruption, corruption. We have to eliminate corruption.
(An Interview with Khomeini 1979, October 7)

As can be seen from the interview excerpt, Khomeini and Fallaci use different terms and expressions when referring to non-heterosexual behavior. Fallaci, for example, uses words such as sexual freedom and homosexuality—commonly used words in the liberationist discourse in the West during that time—whereas Khomeini talks about "men satisfying other men's needs," which he equates with infestation, and *corruption*. As a matter of fact, in the interview Khomeini invokes some of the discursive themes and metaphors used during and after the Islamic revolution with regard to sexual deviance, such as same-sex practices, homosexuality, or sex out of wedlock. Drawing here on the discourse of *Westoxification* (see previous section) and the need to purify Iranian culture, these morally corruptive acts are compared to dangerous and contagious diseases or infection, such as gangrene. Thus, it can be argued that the Islamic Republic invented itself as a nation-state rhetorically through this kind of moral discourse: Othering the West and the Pahlavi dynasty, depicting both as morally corrupt. According to Korycki and Nasirzadeh, this resonated with many Iranians, who despised the Shah with whom they had come to associate a Western induced form of permissiveness, as evidenced by the presence of same-sex practices among the members of the elite close to the Shah (Korycki and Nasirzadeh 2014). Moreover, the regulation of women in terms of their bodies, and strict gender segregation of public spaces, as well as the criminalization of same-sex practices, had the aim of purifying society and bringing it into harmony with its true Islamic self. It is in this sense that the figures of the *new* segregated woman and the criminalized homosexual were invoked through religious-moral discourse that spoke to a very specific idea of cultural authenticity (Korycki and Nasirzadeh 2014). Furthermore, the introduction of Shari'a and the Islamic penal code after the revolution was used to enforce and administer a social and moral regulation of same-sex desire and sexuality in general, with significant implications for sexual governance and the policing of private morality.

In Iran, at this time, under new Islamic laws, male same-sex sexual practices came to be designated as *lavat* and were considered a criminal offense for which execution may be administered—a situation that continues to this day (Jafari 2015). What is also significant here is the attention of the Islamic penal code to the taxonomy and grids of classification for specifying and differentiating same-sex physical acts as a basis for metering out the *appropriate* punishment for the *crime* committed. Acts such as "lascivious kissing," "being naked under the same cover," and "rubbing of the penis against thighs" were, and still are, all specified as *crimes* resulting in 60, 99, and 100 lashes respectively if charged, with the punishment of execution for the ultimate homosexual *crime* of penetrative anal sex (Korycki and Nasirzadeh 2014). However, while the focus was on classification of *deviant* sexual acts, these regulatory systems, as Korycki and Nasirzadeh (2014) point out, were instrumental in creating a subject category of *the homosexual* as a moral deviant and, hence, "an irredeemable other" (p. 9). It is also important to point to the gendered dynamics and politics at play in the differentiated treatment of and response to lesbian women. For example, the punishment for female same-sex acts, referred to as *mosahegeh* in the Iranian penal code, is more lenient than in the case of *lavat*, with the death penalty being prescribed only after a same-sex act has been proved in court for the fourth time (Bucar and Shirazi 2012). Elizabeth M. Bucar and Faegheh Shirazi (2012) argue that this difference in the penal code indicates "a greater concern with male homosexuality as a challenge to sexual patriarchal heteronormativity, as well as a possible space for a private lesbian identity" (p. 430).

Coming back to the early days of the Islamic Republic, the 1980s was a difficult time not only for those who identified as gay but also for *woman-presenting males*, according to the Iranian transgender activist Maryam Mokala. Whereas those who identified as gay could hide their sexual orientation, which for many had already been a reality before the revolution, it was more difficult for *woman-presenting males* to hide their identity and adapt to the new situation. According to Najmabadi, being a *woman-presenting male* during the 1980s: "not only carried the stigma of male same- sex practices, [these individuals] also transgressed the newly imposed regulations of gendered dressing and presentation in public" (Najmabadi 2014, p. 161). Thus, during the first years of the Islamic revolution, those males who transgressed gender normativities ran the risk of being arrested on charges of prostitution and moral corruption. Najmabadi has argued that one of the key effects of these policies was the "categorical bifurcation of gay and transsexual" (Najmabadi 2014, p. 161). Such dividing practices, between the trans women (*woman-presenting males*) and the "deviant" homosexual were further confirmed with the official recognition and avowal of transsexuality and the Islamic state's sanctioning of sex reassignment surgery (SRS) in the mid-1980s. Then, Khomeini issued a *fatwa* (religious ruling) endorsing SRS for transsexuals (Najmabadi 2014). It marked a definitive moment, both in terms of its implications for the legitimation of the transsexual subject and the policing of same-sex sexuality and desire, particularly for gay-identifying men in Iran. However, the legibility and recognizability of the transsexual as a category of person, rendered comprehensible through its bio-psycho-sexological-medical compliance with Islam, led to an irruption of a discourse around homosexuality and the need to separate out transsexuality from an association with same-sex practices (Najmabadi 2014, p. 180). Thus, being transsexual became a more socially acceptable way of being than being homosexual, and gayness (same-sex practices) became an important means for distinguishing and differentiating Male-to-Female (MtF)-ness (Najmabadi 2014, p. 300). These sanctions continued in the 1990s and have remained up to the present day.

POST-REVOLUTIONARY IRAN: GAY AS AN IDENTITY CATEGORY

Varzi has pointed out that the aim of the Islamic revolution was, and still is, to create good "Islamic citizens," irrespective of whether they are considered to be faithful Muslims or not (Varzi 2006, p. 146). In other words, the Islamic regime places great emphasis on the outer layer of society, the surface or *zaher*, in terms of Islamification. As Varzi has argued, the inner layer, the soul or *baten* of its citizen, is less important in the eyes of the regime as long as citizens act "Islamic" when they enter the public sphere. However, as Varzi has further argued, one cannot ignore the impacts, both direct and indirect, of "the project of Islamification on the part of many secular youth" (Varzi 2006, p. 133). Islamic values are channeled through the educational system (textbooks and the curricula), segregation of public spaces (see Fig. 3.3), as well as numerous images relating to Islam and martyrdom in public spaces (see Fig. 3.4).

Thus, the generation of young urban Iranians born after the Islamic revolution is in a continuous struggle in managing their private identity and "collective public identity." This tension especially applies to those secular young Iranians living in the northern part of Tehran, which are more affluent or "posh," and where there is a concentration of cafés, restaurants, and shopping malls, where young people meet and socialize (see e.g., Khosravi 2008). In terms of sexuality and sexual practices, the children and grandchildren of the revolution, heterosexual and non-heterosexual alike, are in the process of (re)defining their sexual selves vis-à-vis the official discourse on sex, sexual orientation,

Fig. 3.3 Poster in Tehran subway stations saying: "Men are not allowed to enter the assigned section for women passenger. Please do not break the God's/ethical regulation"

Fig. 3.4 Martyrs of the revolution. These images can be seen overall in cities and towns in Iran

and sexual interaction between the genders. In other words, they are carving out a sexual space, or participating in a "sexual revolution" (Mahdavi 2008) in their own ways, within the limits of the official Islamic jurisprudential regime, which demands that they follow particular Islamic rituals concerning behavior, practices, appearances, and dress code (Mahdavi 2008, p. 138).

For non-heterosexual Iranians, there is an even greater split between their "public identity" and their private one, particularly for those who do not adhere to the strict binary gender regime in their appearance, clothes, or attire. This applies to young, non-heterosexual Iranians in every social class, and who often experience homophobia and lack of support from their families—irrespective of them being raised in secular or religious families—as will be discussed in later chapters. Despite this, they are redefining themselves and carving out their own sexual space, whether on various social media application platforms or meeting at particular cafés. Moreover, non-heterosexual Iranian males are adopting the Western category of "gay" as a self-identification (see further discussion in Chap. 6). Korycki and Nasirzadeh (2014) frame such a shift in positive terms and suggest it cannot be rendered intelligible simply in terms of the imposition of Western norms of sexual governance and appropriation. On the contrary, it can be argued, that gay sexual identity—having its roots in the emancipatory discourse in the West—has the potential means of providing the Iranian gay subject with the capacity to refuse their official criminalized, abjected, and vilified status as sexual and moral deviants.

The circumstances leading to such liberalizing conditions of modernity in Iran are identified as emerging in the late 1990s with the election of Seyyed Mohammad Khatami (fifth president of Iran, 1997–2005) who initiated some reforms and political changes, which among other entailed: Increasing the freedom of the press, gender equality, expanding the rights of ethnic minorities, and improving relations with the West (Abrahamian 2012; Korycki and Nasirzadeh 2014, p. 10). However, Korycki and Nasirzadeh indicate that many of his reforms were thwarted due to a fragmentation of the Iranian state that permitted hard-line conservatives to block his progressive interventions. Such liberalizing moments were also accompanied by a considerable backlash leading to further surveillance, repression, medicalization, and criminalization of homosexuals under the presidency of Mahmoud Ahmadinejad (president 2005–2013). In fact, scholars such as Ziba Mir-Hosseini and Vanja Hamzic (2010) indicate that these conditions have a historical legacy and trajectory that have been shaped "in the context of the factional politics of the ruling elite, the structural tension between the theocratic and democratic elements and institutions in the post-revolutionary regime, and pressures from civil society" (Mir-Hosseini and Hamzic 2010, p. 84)—tensions which have continued under Hassan Rouhani's (elected president in 2013) governance.

Korycki and Nasirzadeh claim that a space for addressing human rights opened up under such conditions of Khatami's rule. These conditions, they argue, provided fertile ground for "the linking of human rights to gay rights found in the Western discourse and growing links to the West through cyberspace," thereby increasing the availability of positive modes of self-identification (Korycki and Nasirzadeh 2014, p. 11). Thus, rather than casting the *gay* international movement in terms that limit its influence to a missionary neocolonial zeal for liberating the queer subaltern subject in the global south, Korycki and Nasirzadeh see such Western influences as providing "ready-made positive markers of identity" for *same-sex-desiring* subjects inside Iran. Such self-identificatory categories are employed in subversive ways, as a means by which to counter the derogatory references to their sexuality in the Persian language. In addition, in response to the charges that they have simply appropriated a Western import of gayness, Korycki and Nasirzadeh state that queer Iranian activists inside Iran have simultaneously constructed "new Persian words" to explain, in more positive terms, same-sex identification: *hamjins-gara'i* (same-sex love, same-sex desire, same-sex orientation) as a counter to *hamjins-bazi* ("same-sex play," same-sex lust) (Korycki and Nasirzadeh 2014, p. 11). This new terminology and referents for same-sex desire were promoted by queer/gay activists and subjects inside Iran as a means by which to disrupt the grid of intelligibility for constituting and *Othering* sexual minorities "as non-authentic Iranians"—discussed further in Chap. 6 (Korycki and Nasirzadeh 2014, p. 11). As Sami Zeidan (2013) argues, the "universalizing of gay terminology, which is often condemned as Western hegemony, can in fact have a local liberatory function" (p. 213).

*   *   *

Pre-modern Iranian society was not organized according to a heteronormative binary system for differentiating heterosexuality from homosexuality in identity category terms. In fact, sexuality was in many ways "fluid," and both women and young men were seen as an object of desire. As we have illustrated in this chapter, Persian literature provided many examples of the celebration of homoeroticism and same-sex love and desire. However, although homoeroticism and the enactment of same-sex desire were indeed permissible within certain limits or tolerated according to particular grids of intelligibility for hierarchically classifying certain male types and statuses, this did not necessarily equate to a recognition of sexual and gender justice. In the late nineteenth century, as Iran moved from pre-modern to more modern and contemporary times, a shift occurred in the politics of same-sex desire and love. Same-sex desire was cast as deviant and against the notion of a modern and civilized society. Heteronormativity was seen as a hallmark of modernization at the hands of the reformist elites. This also applied to changes in marriage as an institution: Polygamy and temporal marriages—practices common before the end of the nineteenth century—were repudiated by the ruling elites. Instead marriage was conceived of as companionate. The Pahlavi dynasty continued the heteronormativization of society and introduced some "progressive" family law, for example, divorce laws (Afary 2009). Homosexuality, same-sex desire, and gender non-conformity was further marginalized. In fact, gender reassignment surgeries were banned in the 1970s. After the Iranian Revolution and the establishment of the Islamic Republic, the official discourse on same-sex love/homosexuality incorporated some of the logic and arguments of the previous Shah regime, but also added the religious-moral rhetoric/logic to the previous discourse on same-sex love. As we have shown in this chapter, *Westoxification* continues to be employed in official discourse, particularly when referring to contemporary youth culture or those who do not comply with the officially sanctioned norms on sexuality, gender performances, or body aesthetics. These "Weststruck" individuals are seen as "toxic" and "inauthentic," among them gay-identifying men, who since the establishment of the Islamic Republic have been further marginalized through religious-legal sanctions against same-sex behavior and practices. However, as will be discussed in Chaps. 5–8, gay-identifying men have carved out their own private/public spaces, and resisted both the moral/religious discourse governing the repudiation of same-sex desire and the dystopic discourse on victimization of the Iranian gay subject, mostly portrayed in the Western gay media, as will be discussed in the next chapter.

NOTES

1. Rumi: The Book of Love Poems of Ecstasy and Longing.
2. Ladinsky (2003).
3. According to some sources, the Iranian authorities issued a postage stamp in his honor, which in fact signals his admission into the pantheon of Iran's revolutionary heroes (see Abrahamian 1993).
4. Ali Shariati was one of the main ideologues of the Islamic Republic, and one of its founding fathers. He had, for example, great influences in drafting the first constitution of the Islamic Republic of Iran, and in his book *On the Sociology of Islam* he argues for self-sufficiency and independence from the West (see Shariati 1979).
5. *Kuni* or *kooni* derives from the word *kun* which means ass or asshole. It is an offensive Persian term denoting specifically the disparaging act of anal sex between men. In English, the derogatory word "faggot" could be equivalent to "kuni/kooni."
6. SAVAK (Sazamane Etelaat Va Amniate Kechvar) was from 1956 to 1979 the domestic security and intelligence service of Pahlavi dynasty. It was feared by the opposition and dissidents for its brutal methods and inhuman treatment of prisoners.

References

Abrahamian, E. (1993). *Khomeinism. Essays on the Islamic Republic*. California: University of California Press.

Abrahamian, E. (2012). *A History of Modern Iran*. Cambridge: Cambridge University Press.

Afary, J. (2009). *Sexual Politics in Modern Iran*. Cambridge: Cambridge University Press.

Afary, J., & Anderson, K. (2005). *Foucault and the Iranian Revolution. Gender and the Seductions of Islamism*. Chicago: Chicago University Press.

Al-e Ahmad, J. (1984). *Occidentosis: A Plague from the West* (R. Campbell, Trans.). Berkeley: Mizan Press Berkeley.

Algar, H. (1984). Introduction. In *Occidentosis: A Plague from the West* (J. Al Ahmad, Ed. and R. Campbell, Trans.). Berkeley: Mizan Press Berkeley.

An Interview with Khomeini. (1979, October 7). *The New York Times*. Retrieved from https://www.nytimes.com/1979/10/07/archives/an-interview-with-khomeini.html.

Axworthy, M. (2013). *Revolutionary Iran. A History of the Islamic Republic*. London: Allen Lane / Penguin.

Beeman, W. O. (2005). *The Great Satan vs. the Mad Mullahs. How the United States and Iran Demonize Each Other*. Chicago: University of Chicago Press.

Blasius, M. (2013). Theorizing the Politics of (Homo)sexualities Across Cultures. In L. M. Weiss & M. Boisa (Eds.), *Global Homophobia I* (pp. 218–245). Chicago: University of Illinois Press.

Bucar, E. M., & Shirazi, F. (2012). The 'Invention' of Lesbian Acts in Iran: Interpretive Moves, Hidden Assumptions, and Emerging Categories of Sexuality. *Journal of Lesbian Studies, 16*(4), 416–434. https://doi.org/10.108 0/10894160.2012.681263.

Hillmann, M. C. (1988). Introduction. In J. Al-e-Ahmad (Ed.), *By the Pen* (pp. ix–xxiv). Austin, TX: University of Texas.

Jafari, M. (2015, July 25). Islamic Jurisprudence-Inspired Legal Approaches towards Male Homosexuals. In *Lesbian, Gay Bisexual and Transgender Rights in Iran: Analysis from Religious, Social, Legal and Cultural Perspectives* (pp. 19–25). International Gay and Lesbian Human Rights Commission. Retrieved from http://iran.outrightinternational.org/wp-content/uploads/LGBTRightsInIran_EN.pdf.

Keddie, N. R. (2006). *Modern Iran: Roots and Results of Revolution*. Boston: Yale University Press.

Khosravi, S. (2008). *Young and Defiant in Tehran*. Philadelphia: University of Pennsylvania Press.

Korycki, K., & Nasirzadeh, A. (2014, January 1). Desire Recast: The Production of Gay Identity in Iran. *Journal of Gender Studies, 25*(1), 50–65. https://doi.org/10.1080/09589236.2014.889599.

Ladinsky, D. (2003). *The Subject Tonight Is Love. 60 Wild and Sweet Poems of Hafiz.* New York: Penguin.

Mahdavi, P. (2008). *Passionate Uprisings. Iran's Sexual Revolution.* Stanford: Stanford University Press.

Martino, W., & Kjaran, J. I. (2019). The Politics of Recognizability: Giving an Account of Iranian Gay Men's Lives Under Repressive Conditions of Sexuality Governance. *International Journal of Middle East Studies, 51* (1), 21–41.

Milani, A. (2011). *The Shah.* London: Macmillan.

Mir-Hosseini, Z., & Hamzic, V. (2010). *Control and Sexuality: The Revival of Zina Laws in Muslim Contexts.* London: Women Living Under Muslim Laws.

Mirsepassi-Ashtiani, A. (1994). The Crisis of Secular Politics and the Rise of Political Islam in Iran. *Social Text, 38,* 51–84. https://doi.org/10.2307/466504.

Najmabadi, A. (2013, May). Genus of Sex or the Sexing of Jins. *International Journal of Middle Eastern Studies, 45*(2), 211–231. https://doi.org/10.1017/S0020743813000044.

Najmabadi, A. (2014). *Professing Selves: Transsexuality and Same-Sex Desire in Contemporary Iran.* Durham, NC: Duke University Press.

Parsi, A. (2015, January 14). Iranian Queers and Laws. Fighting for Freedom of Expression. *Harvard International Review.* Retrieved from http://hir.harvard.edu/article/?a=9885.

Rumi: The Book of Love. Poems of Ecstasy and Longing (transl. by Barks, C.). (2002). Harper-Collins e-books. Retrieved from http://sino.mk/wp-content/uploads/2015/02/Banks-Coleman-Rumi-Book-Love.pdf.

Said, E. (1978). *Orientalism.* London: Routledge.

Shariati, A. (1979). *On the Sociology of Islam.* Berkeley: Mizan Press.

Shiravand, S. (2015). *Sovereignty Without Nationalism, Islam Without God. A Critical Study of the Works of Jalal Al-e Ahmad.* Unpublished doctoral thesis, p. 117. University of Alberta, Department of Sociology, Edmonton.

Varzi, R. (2006). *Warring Souls: Youth, Media, and Martyrdom in Post-Revolution Iran.* Durham and London: Duke University Press.

Zeidan, S. (2013). Navigating International Rights and Local Politics: Sexuality Governance in Postcolonial Settings. In M. L. Weiss & M. Boisa (Eds.), *Global Homophobia* (pp. 196–217). Chicago: University of Illinois Press.

Zonis, M. (1991). *Majestic Failure. The Fall of the Shah.* Chicago: University of Chicago Press.

CHAPTER 4

The Construction of the Iranian Gay Subject Outside of Iran

As discussed in Chap. 3, before the Islamic Revolution in 1979, the US pink (gay) press had published articles about "gay" life in Iran.[1] These accounts often depicted Tehran as a "gay paradise" and were told from the perspective of the Western gay visitor, who often framed his account around the exotic oriental sexual other: the beautiful and highly sexualized Iranian male he encountered during his visit. However, after the Islamic revolution, these types of accounts went from portraying Tehran as a "gay paradise" to portraying it as a "gay hell," depicting Iran as a dystopia for gay-identifying individuals—a "deadly" place where gays are executed by the authorities on regular basis. Thus, it can be argued that the construction of Iran as one of the deadliest places for gays and lesbians has been the *leitmotif* in many articles published by the international gay/pink press since the establishment of the Islamic Republic. Not denying the fact that gays, as well as men who have sex with men, are and have been executed since the establishment of the Islamic Republic of Iran, reported by various NGOs (see e.g., Human Rights Watch 2005), the reality and the embodied experiences of gay-identifying Iranian men is often more complicated and multifaceted (discussed in Chap. 5) than the one depicted in the Western (gay) media. There, the focus has more or less been on "gay execution," which has become the dominant discourse, and is reflected on the Internet, as can be seen when searching on Google using the keywords "gay execution" preceded by different country names. For Iran "Gay execution" produced the highest number of search results:

© The Author(s) 2019
J. I. Kjaran, *Gay Life Stories,*
https://doi.org/10.1007/978-3-030-12831-9_4

414, compared to Saudi Arabia: 1, Russia: 0, and Uganda: 277.[2] Thus, these accounts in the gay/pink international press, framed around an emancipatory Western narrative, cast the Iranian gay/lesbian subject "as awaiting rescue" from state homophobia and in danger of being killed at any moment (Shakhsari 2012), not giving nuances to the embodied experiences of gay-identifying men inside of Iran, who themselves are a heterogeneous group, experiencing state homophobia and persecutions differently, depending on their social position and geographical location. In other words, these accounts have been told from one perspective, where the focus is more than often on the victimization of sexual minorities in Iran, not taking into account their agentic self, and how they find ways to pursue their personal life, and resist the official discourse of homophobia and hate.[3] Hence, as the narrative goes, the only option for gay and lesbian Iranians is to leave Iran and move to the utopian global north in order to live freely and openly, and finally be themselves. Other perspectives are rarely incorporated into the Western emancipatory narrative, such as how gays and lesbians, and other sexual and gender minorities in Iran constitute themselves as gendered, sexual, and erotic subjects/agents, and even find ways to construct meaningful lives within the religious-legal limits set by the homophobic theocratic state.[4] Thus, some further analysis is required, particularly in light of the absence of a consideration of the accounts provided by Iranian sexual minorities themselves and their knowledge claims about sexuality governance in Iran (Kjaran and Martino 2017; Martino and Kjaran 2019)

As these accounts in the international gay/pink press have contributed to the formation of the dominant discourses in the West regarding the livability and the current situation of Iranian sexual minorities, it is important to analyze them and juxtapose them with the accounts of gay-identifying men living inside Iran, as I am concerned to do in this book. In this chapter, however, I mainly engage with the media discourses about Iran in selected online gay/queer/LGBTQ publications (journals) from 2013 to 2015 (see Table 4.1).[5] Two dominant discourses can be identified in these publications: Firstly, the discourse of victimization; and secondly the discourse of binary oppositions—between the "utopian" global north and the assumed "dystopian" Islamic Republic of Iran—in terms of sexual rights and livability for sexual minorities. In the next two sections, I will discuss in more detail these dominant discourses, which raise important political questions of misrepresentation in the reporting of the current situation of sexual minorities in Iran, and thus drawing

Table 4.1   Media sources

	Number of articles found on Iran from 2013 to 2015	Readership[a]	Location
OUT	7	200,000	US
Advocate	8	185,000	US
TheGayUK	2	360,000	UK
Attitude UK	3	75,000	UK
DNA magazine	0	135,000	Australia
PinkNews	17	N/A	UK
Total	37		

[a]The numbers of readership are taken from GETA website (Gay European Tourism Association), and they are aimed for marketing purpose—for those who want to advertise in a gay magazine

attention to the need to incorporate more nuanced analysis and reporting on the situation of gays and lesbians in homophobic states such as the Islamic Republic of Iran.

VICTIMIZATION

The discourse of victimization draws on various discursive themes. One theme is death, executions, and other physical punishments of sexual minorities in Iran. It is a recurrent theme and runs like a red thread through most of the online publications analyzed. I provide examples of such representations, focusing mostly on the "death theme," while also incorporating other discursive themes into my discussion, as well as reflecting on why this theme is so dominant in the discourse on victimization of sexual minorities in Iran. The "death theme" appeared in almost 80% of the online material analyzed (in 29 articles/news items of 37 in total), either being mentioned briefly as background information or as the main topic of the news item/article. Two news reports had this theme as their main topic of discussion with the following headlines: "Experts Predict: Iran Will Remain Deadly" and "Unconfirmed Reports That Iran Hanged Two Gay Men for 'Perversion'" (Weinthal 2014, March 14; TheGayUK 2014, March 4). These headlines exemplify how the press often uses dramatic (sensational) rhetoric in their media coverage as a part of their discursive strategy: "Deadly" and "hanged" are words that are emphasized and catch the eye in these two headlines.

Another discursive strategy is to tell the story from unilateral perspective, for instance not giving credit to political reforms in Iran or with regard to improved diplomatic relations to the West. An example of this is an article in the *Advocate*, published in March 2014, which discusses two reports about the situation of "LGBTs" in Iran. The author comes to the conclusion that "despite a new president's overtures to the contrary, Iran will remain a deadly place for LGBTs" (Weinthal 2014, March 14). Here the author is referring to Hassan Rouhani, who became president in August 2013 and was re-elected in 2017. He is considered to be a moderate and a reformist. Since he became president, Iran's diplomatic relations with the West, particularly Europe, have improved considerably. However, the author, citing various reports and other testimonies, argues that Rouhani's promises of reform have not resulted in improving the situation of LGBTs. This is partly right, and after his first term in office, the official policy with regard to sexual minorities remains the same. However, the atmosphere within Iranian society became a bit more relaxed, as he worked on improving diplomatic relations with the West—inspiring a hope to many of my gay informants.

I experienced this when I was conducting my fieldwork in 2015. Some of my informants also concurred that Rouhani had made a difference. Arash, for example, said: "Now things are better for us gays. Manjam [dating app] is for example not filtered anymore and we have a bit more freedom." Mehrdad on the other hand said: "The situation has not changed a lot after Rouhani was elected and the situation of gays is the same. The society, the people are still very conservative concerning these issues." As can be seen from these two quotes, Mehrdad and Arash seem to disagree with regard to the positive effects on Iranian society after Rouhani was elected president. Both of them however emphasized later in our interview that the situation of gays, especially in Tehran, is not as bad as often described in the foreign press/media. The authorities are not systematically persecuting gays and other sexual minorities, often reported in the Western media, and the reality is more complicated than immediately meets the eye, as Mehrdad mentioned. In other words, it is often more the society and the family that is putting pressure on sexual minorities in Iran rather than the authorities, although it needs to be emphasized that the frame of references is set through the religio-official discourse which disavows homosexuality and demonizes same-sex desires. This I will discuss further in Chap. 5.

Ethnographic vignette—Having chicken soup with a former
Sepah commander

I arrive in Mashad, after a three-hour taxi ride from Bojnord, late in the afternoon. It is the middle of August and the heat is overwhelming. Payman, one of my informants in Bojnord, had set me up with one of his relatives who is supposed to pick me up from the taxi stand and take me to a guesthouse. Mashad, second most populous city of Iran, is a chaotic city, especially in the center around the shrine of Imam Reza, the Eighth Shi'a Imam. It is often full of pilgrims that come to visit the shrine. I step out of the taxi, a bit tired but excited to explore the city and meet my informants here. I had only been given a vague description of my "caretaker" in Mashad and start to look around to see if I can see someone that might fit his profile. While I am looking around, a young man appears and greets me politely. "I am Kia, a relative of Payman, welcome to the holy city of Mashad." We then find a guesthouse and set up a time to meet the day after—for a visit to the holy shrine of Imam Reza. The day after, I meet Kia and his wife and they take me to the shrine. They have been married for nine months and recently bought a small flat outside the city center. They are both in their 30s. Kia works at the agricultural office in the city and his wife takes care of the home. They invite me for a lunch at their home after our visit to the shrine. Their flat is small, but cozy and comfortable. Kia and me take a seat in the living room while his wife starts preparing the lunch, chicken soup with some pasta. We start talking about Iran, politics, society, and how they live and view Iran. Both participate in the conversation and sometimes Kia goes into the kitchen to help his wife. "Our dream is to go to India—we both like to travel, and we see the current situation as an opportunity." Here they are referring to the presidency of Hassan Rouhani and the forthcoming nuclear deal, which would "hopefully open the country more," says Kia. "I was a commander in the *Sepah* [Iranian Revolutionary Guard] when I was younger. My father was a high-ranking commander there so it was easy for me to enter the *Sepah* brigades. Neither of us are religious, we are modern and we want changes in our country. I always vote and last time I voted for Rouhani, because I believe that he will introduce some changes in this country." I'm a bit surprised when

(*continued*)

(continued)

Kia tells me this as I had always connected the *Sepah* with repression/oppression, dogmatism and religiosity. But now I am eating chicken soup with Kia, ex-*Sepah* commander, and he's giving me a totally different impression of Iranian politics and its polyphonic nature. This ex-commander in the revolutionary elite brigades is a modern man, not religious, and sometimes even critical towards the authorities.

Referring to the "expert discourse," which consists of reports about the situation of human rights in Iran or the accounts of gays and lesbians, who have fled Iran, is a widely applied discursive strategy in the online publications I accessed. So is the application of the gay identity label, which is often used when reporting about arrests, raids, or executions of sexual minorities. It is somehow assumed that the person involved identifies as gay, and as such, should be incorporated into the gay emancipatory discourse of the West. In other words, Western sexual identity categories are often "forced" upon the Iranian sexual other in these reports in the pursuit of "sameness." According to the logic of the politics of recognition, the Iranian sexual other is "subsumed in the Same," he is like "us" in the West, part of the global "gay family" (Long 2009). Josep Massad has discussed this kind of epistemic violence by the "gay international" in his book *Desiring Arab*, in which he argues the following:

> The categories gay and lesbian are not universal at all, and can only be universalized by the epistemic, ethical, and political violence unleashed on the rest of the world by the very international human rights advocates whose aim is to defend the very people their intervention is creating. (Massad 2007, p. 41)

Thus, by using the sexual identity labels, gay or lesbian, when reporting about the situation of sexual minorities in Iran, the pink press is not only universalizing these identity categories but also constructing an object of its own discussion: A gay/lesbian subject which needs to be liberated, instead of being understood and supported. Furthermore, the aim is to appeal to the gay reader in the global north and convey a message of the persecution of his gay "brethren" in Iran, by drawing on the discourse of the international/universal brotherhood of gays in the fight for gay rights globally. Appealing to solidarity of our gay brethren internationally is admirable and an indication of how interconnected and globalized the contemporary gay lives (cultures) are. However, those same reports need to be contextualized and given a bit more nuanced analysis, bearing in mind that maybe the Iranian non-heterosexual subject does not want to be liberated by the West. Not all of them feel persecuted and some of them might want to do things on their own account, and thus not ascribing to the emancipatory discourse of the West. In other words, we should not solely depict Iranian sexual minorities as passive objects of the international gay liberation movements, but also as agentic subjects who resist and use various strategies to exist within the limits of homophobia, persecutions, and harassment of the Iranian state and society.

In terms of my participants/informants, most of them had adopted the gay identity category, and many were aware of the global gay culture and gay international activist movement. However, their identity was not fixed, and it often depended on the context and the fact that in Iran one needs to negotiate one's identity within the strict limits set by both family and society. Thus, as Judith Butler (1991, pp. 13–14) points out, "identity categories tend to be the instruments of regulatory regimes, whether as normalizing categories of oppressive structures or as rallying points of a liberatory contestation of that very oppression." This was indeed felt by my participants, feeling the need, on the one hand, to identify with the global gay culture, but on the other hand, also experiencing the heteronormative pressure from society, which compelled them to act and behave as straight.

The theme of death, killing, and hanging of "gays" portrayed in the pink press is rarely raised in the account of my informants who identify as gay and live in Iran. When I asked some of them about the emphasis of the death theme in these reports, most of them contested the true nature of these reports and emphasized other issues regarding livability for sexual minorities in Iran. Mehrdad expressed his thoughts about these issues in our talk:

> In Tehran, you can be gay and nobody will kill you [laughter]. Even if they know that you are having sex within the privacy of your home they cannot arrest you. Even in Islam the rule is that four adult men must see you in [an] act of sex before the authorities can arrest you and take you to court. So it's not easy to hang you or kill you for having sex with men. I search on the Internet for news about executions of "gays" and I never see anything about

that. I am not a supporter of the regime and I am not a supporter of Islam, but on these issues I must be honest, you know?

In Mehrdad's account, Tehran is depicted as a rather "safe" place for gay-identifying men and those who desire their same sex, at least in comparison to other parts of Iran. In fact, many of my informants depicted other parts of Iran, especially the rural provinces and towns, as being more homophobic and "backward" in terms of attitudes toward sex and sexuality, dress and attire, and interaction between the genders.[6] It could thus be argued that, by denying or minimizing the persecution and execution of sexual minorities, Mehrdad and some of my informants are protecting the self in order to cope with harsh reality of gay life in Iran. In any case, this counter-narrative with regard to death and persecution, a theme often cited in the gay/pink press, needs to be taken into account, in order to incorporate a more nuanced picture of gay life in Iran. It is not all about persecution and horror but also about love, friendship, relationship, and sexual encounters, as will be explored further in Chap. 5.

Arash, one of my key informants, also cites this discourse about the cosmopolitan and progressive nature of Tehran, and other larger cities in Iran, when we discussed on Telegram the execution of Hassan Afhsar (19-year-old) in Arak, in April 2016 (see *The case of Hassan Afhsar*):

Arash: The authorities say that he raped another boy two years ago, when he was 17 and the boy he raped was 15. The younger boy is free and he reported the rape to the police. But this is the story the authorities put forward. I am not sure if it is true because Arak is a small city. So maybe he was just gay and he did not rape anybody. But maybe the authorities are telling the truth. And if someone rapes another person he should be executed—there is [no] difference if the victim was a boy or a girl. Rape is a rape.

Jón: So this would never happen in Tehran?

Arash: No, not for being gay—maybe if rape was the issue. If the authorities wanted to arrest gays and kill them they would just go into the parks or where gays are cruising. It would be so easy. Maybe I see it a bit [...] more [in] positive terms but I would not think this could happen in big cities like Tehran. Even in cities like Shiraz, this would not happen. There, gays meet in parks and coffee shops, just like here in Tehran. But it is mostly for the middle and upper class gays, I mean these cafés. And now we have a new café in Tehran, which is called *Rangin Kaman* (Rainbow café) ☺.

In talking about the execution of Afhsar (see The case of Afhsar Hassan), Arash draws attention to the arguments often put forward by the Iranian government that the individual in question was not executed because he was "gay" or had consensual sex with a man, but because he was accused of and found guilty of rape. Arash cast doubts on these arguments by referring to it as the "story of the authorities," and in that particular case, he keeps the possibility open that maybe Afhsar was in fact executed because he had sex with another man or identified as gay. However, as can be read between the lines, Arash also tries to minimize these events, by drawing attention to the exemptive nature of Afhsar's case: He was executed in a small provincial city of Arak, where its inhabitants occupy lower social position and are not as educated /informed as those who live in the metropolitan Tehran. In other words, Arash emphasizes that this would rarely happen in Tehran. Thus, his narrative gives us a bit more nuanced and perhaps detailed account of the persecutions of sexual minorities in Iran, drawing attention to how geographical location can be a factor in deciding between life and death of sexual minorities.

The case of Afhsar Hassan

Afhsar Hassan was hanged in a prison in the city of Arak, in Markazi province, on the 18th of July 2016. He was convicted of *lavat-e be onf* (forced male to male anal intercourse), which he supposedly committed when he was 17 years old. Still being a child at the time of the offense, he should not have been convicted to death, which contradicts international law and agreements on the protection of children that strictly prohibit capital punishment against those who are under the age of 18 at the time of committing the crime. Moreover, he was not granted the basic right of a fair trial (Amnesty International 2016, August 2; Human Rights and Democracy for Iran (n.d.)). In the coverage of his case in the Western media Afhsar Hassan was said to be gay and became an object of interest by the international press and the gay activist community in the West (see e.g., Grindley 2016, August 5; Trew 2016, August 4). However, as already discussed, the case of Afhsar draws attention to other factors, such a geographical location, social position, and class, something that was rarely mentioned in Western reports on the case.

The question then remains what are the underlying reasons for the often exaggerated and misinformed framing of the situation of sexual minorities, mostly gay men, in Iran in the Western (gay/pink) media? As argued by Martino and Kjaran (2019), and in line with Long (2009) and Rastegar (2013), these accounts are often driven by a particular political agenda, where the focus is on queer recognizability and rights, as well as universal liberation of gays and lesbians. The West is seen as a "queer utopia" and depicted against the "dystopic Islamic-fascist" states of the Middle East, particularly Iran. Thus, the "hypervisibility" of the victimized and oppressed Iranian gay subject in the Western media, is according to Sima Shakhsari (2012), and further argued by Martino and Kjaran "motivated by certain orientalist impulses and a civilizational logic of 'Iranian backwardness'" (Martino and Kjaran 2019, p. 5). By saying that, I am not diminishing the good intention of the pink/gay press in their criticism of how the Islamic Republic of Iran treats sexual minorities, which is without a doubt and has be reported widely as being in breach with international agreements and human rights accords. Nevertheless, the point I want to make here is that by not attending to the nuances and context of the embodied experiences of Iranian gays living inside of Iran, runs the risk of misrepresentation, and unilateral discussion on sexual minorities living in Iran (or in non-Western societies) from the perspective of Western gay emancipation. It will neither help sexual minorities inside Iran, nor initiate any changes on the part of the Iranian government, as these arguments/reports can be rejected as being part of an imperialist project of the West. Here one needs to bear in mind that Iran has in the past had its share of the West meddling in its internal affairs, often under the disguise of modernity or by drawing on the human rights discourse. Such was the case in nineteenth century when the British government was fighting against the slave trade in the world by referring to the inhuman and barbaric nature of slave trade societies to which Iran (Persia at that time) belonged. Thus, as champions of humanity and being an anti-slave society, the harbinger of freedom, the British gradually expanded their control over the Persian Gulf and gained hegemony in the region (Janet Afary, personal communication, January 4, 2019). In other words, human rights discourse, in this case the abolitionist discourse, was used to expand the imperialist and nationalist project of the West in the Middle East. I will discuss this further in the next section and frame the accounts in the Western media and the pink/gay press within the logic of homonationalism/homoorientalism, which has been resuscitated by the war on terror and increased Islamophobia in the global north.

THE DISCOURSE OF BINARY OPPOSITIONS

The discourse of binary oppositions fueled by an orientalist logic is widely used in the online material analyzed. In Table 4.2 I provide some examples of the oppositional discursive pairs used in the news reports, which have the aim of pitting Iran against the West/global north in terms of the situation and (mal)treatment of sexual minorities.

Through these binary oppositions, the Iranian homosexual is constructed as a victim in need to be saved, who is defined in relation to, and set against, the West's vision of having already achieved an emancipated gay utopia. Iran on the other hand is depicted as a gay dystopia, a necropolis for sexual minorities, whose only option for sexual freedom and "being themselves" is to escape to the West. In fact, many of these news reports tell the story of an Iranian sexual refugee, seeking asylum in the West because of sexual persecution in their homeland. These narratives are often structured in the same way: They begin by describing what the refugee/asylum seeker endured, due either to his family or the authorities, when he lived in Iran. Often there is a reference to the "death theme" discussed in the previous section. The journalist either discusses it generally, or it is presented as a first-person account from the perspective of the refugee: "They killed my boyfriend and would have killed me. Being gay is a death sentence in Iran" (Duffy 2015, April 28). Reported in the

Table 4.2 Binary oppositions

The West	Iran
Life	Death
Freedom	Oppression
Utopia	Dystopia
Progress	Backwardness
Civilized	Uncivilized
Modern	Archaic
Democracy	Theocracy/tyranny
Secularism	Religious extremism
Gay rights	Gay hell
Safe haven for sexual minorities	Necropolis for sexual minorities
Happy gays/gay pride	Sadness and misery
Gay friendly	Homophobic
Developed	Undeveloped
Cosmopolitan	Provincial/pre-modern
Tolerant	Barbaric

PinkNews, this quote is from Mehdi Kazemi, and it appeared in a leaflet, distributed in connection to a political campaign of a British parliamentarian, who supposedly saved his life by helping him when he applied for asylum in the UK some years previously. In fact, the case of Mehdi Kazemi became front-page news in *The Independent* with the headline: "A life or death decision" (Verkaik 2008, March 6). His story had a happy ending and he was eventually granted asylum in the UK. In fact, stories of gay or lesbian refugees presented in the pink press often draw on the discourse of "happily ever after," in which the protagonist pursues a new and happy life in the West, finally being able to live openly and freely. In that sense, adopting an "authentic" gay, lesbian, or queer identity is often depicted as being only a possibility within Western grids of intelligibility. Again, these reports do not attend to the fact that gays living in Iran is a heterogenous group, occupying different social positions and class. Thus, some might perceive Iran as a dystopia and want to move to the "utopic West" and adopt an "authentic" gay identity, whereas others might find life in Iran to be fulfilling.

The sanctuary of the gay utopia in the West for persecuted gays and lesbians in Iran is the topic of another news report in the *PinkNews*, bearing the headline: "Iranian lesbian couple marry in Stockholm." The news report tells the story of an Iranian lesbian couple "who are both from the oppressive Islamic state" and who escaped to Sweden, where they "held their wedding ceremony [...], during Stockholm Pride" (Duffy 2014, August 20). The story has the same structure as the previous one, in which the couple escapes their home country and in the end finds happiness in Sweden. It also draws on the discourse of certain binary oppositions that invoke certain orientalist understanding of the persecuted gay subject in Iran: Freedom versus oppression, pride versus shame/hiding, gay rights (symbolized in the gay marriage) versus repression.

Although many gays and lesbians living in Iran experience oppression, persecution, and shame because of the official homophobic rhetoric, not all of them do so. As I will discuss in next chapters, some of my informants constructed their own liminal queer spaces, where they experienced individual freedom temporally and could be themselves. In other words, they tried to redefine individual freedom in a similar way as some Muslim women have done with regard to wearing the veil, emphasizing ethical relationality in terms of their embodied choices/decisions, one which attends to communal perspective as well as personal. By doing so they resist the dominant discourse that being "free" is to ascribe to the Western version of individual freedom and choices (Fernando 2010). Moreover, as Lila Abu-Lughod (2013) has drawn attention to, there is a difference between Western and non-Western understanding of autonomy, which needs to be recognized in order to acknowledge the agency of Muslim women, in their decisions and choices to wear the veil. Same applies for gay-identifying Iranian men, and for many of my gay informants the concept of individual freedom was experienced differently, and did not, for example, entail expressing one's sexuality openly, keeping in mind the strict segregation between the private and public space. In fact, some of them even said that they had "something" in Iran, more opportunities for sexual encounters, support of friends, and interactions with their family, than they would have in the "utopic" West. This draws attention to the heterogeneous nature of the experiences of sexual minorities in Iran, which cannot be constructed simplistically in terms of binary oppositions, often evident in the pink/gay press in the West.

The story of the Iranian lesbian couple also frames gay rights in the West within the institution of "marriage," taking place during pride festivities. Thus, it can be argued that this kind of discursive strategy draws on homonormative discourses, as well as on the liberal human rights discourses, which have more than often emphasized an equivalency between legalizing "gay marriage" and ensuring human rights. Lisa Duggan has argued in her book *The New Homonormativity: The Sexual Politics of Neoliberalism* that the discourse of homonormativity fits well into the neoliberal discourse, which emphasizes individual freedom, privatization, and a depoliticized subject of consumption. Moreover, as Duggan has argued, the discourse of homonormativity "does not contest dominant heteronormative assumptions and institutions—such as marriage, and its call for monogamy and reproduction—but upholds and sustains them" (Duggan 2002, pp. 179). Thus, putting it differently, the workings of homonormativity are transforming sexual difference into sameness by, for example, expanding the limits of the heteronormative institution of marriage. This particularly applies to the privileged and highly visible sexual other, mostly white middle-class gays and lesbians (See here Ahmed 2002). However, the sexual "other others" remain on the margin of society and are not included as "good citizens" in the nation-state and its institutions.

Coming back to the accounts provided by Iranian sexual refugees in the pink press, Shakhsari has contextualized them as feeding into a broader geopolitical orientalist agenda that has been resuscitated by the war on terror. She states that some diasporic queer Iranians have taken advantage of the opportunities provided by such circumstances for "securing immigration and visa opportunities to Europe and North America" and through acts of "self-entrepreneurship" have inserted themselves as representable subjects within a transnational imaginary that is grounded in Western liberatory and civilizational frames of reference (Martino and Kjaran 2019):

> The shift to homopolitics involves not only the Iranian opposition groups, but also a select number of Iranian disaporic queers who have historically been excluded from the heteronormative imaginations of the nation and thus willingly take the opportunity to insert themselves into national imaginations in diasporic reterritorializations. In the process, while the modern heteronormative binaries of gender and sexuality are reified, the Iranian homosexual is produced and deployed as the marker of freedom in civilizational discourses and practices that divide the world into binaries of liberated/repressed, free/unfree, and democratic/theocratic. (Shakhsari 2012, p. 27)

The "civilizational discourses," referred to by Shakhsari, in which the world is divided into binaries of good/bad, civilized/uncivilized, become evident in the discussion about Israel, and how the pink press depicts it as a "gay oasis" or "gay Mecca" in comparison to Iran and other neighboring countries. Several articles and/or opinion pieces appeared from 2013 to 2015 in the material analyzed, in which support was given to Israel and its official policy in the region, but also rejecting the nuclear deal between the West and Iran as it could threaten, not only the security of Israel but also gays and lesbians in the West. The arguments put forward in these articles, more often than not, draw on a homonationalist discourse, in which incorporation of the "respectable" and "good" gay and lesbian subjects into the nation-state is used to justify exclusion of the "other others," particularly Muslims and (im)migrants (Puar 2007).[7] These "other others" are then portrayed as being homophobic, barbaric and uncivilized.

Moreover, the homonationalist discourse is not only applied within the nation-state to create boundaries between "us," the civilized, and "them," the uncivilized, but also at the international/transnational level in order to distinguish between states that have not legalized any kind of recognition of same-gender couples or that still criminalize homosexuality, and those that are considered to be gay friendly, and are therefore progressive, modern, and civilized. Thus, the intersection of sexual, national, and international politics appears in the media discussion/pink press regarding

Israel and its neighbors. I now provide an example from the online material analyzed about the workings of homonationalism and how the "other others" are (mis)represented as homophobic, extremist and barbaric.

The following quotes are from an opinion piece that appeared in the *Advocate* on July 9, 2014, with the headline: "Why LGBT People Around the World Need Israel. Israel acts as an example of a pro-LGBT society in a part of the world where sexual and gender minorities are often persecuted":

> The fact is that Israel is absolutely critical for our nation and for the security and stability of the Middle East. We cannot afford for Israel to be anything but strong and secure, and this is particularly true for the LGBT community here in America and around the world. [...] They seem to have forgotten that Israel is the only country in the Middle East that has stood up for human rights, particularly those of women and gays, time and time again [...].
>
> Yes, there are a few other Middle Eastern countries where homosexuality is no longer a crime (Jordan, for instance), and they should be recognized. But none of them have stood up as strongly for us as Israel. [...] For Israel to be so principled in its convictions and in its willingness to fight for us, while surrounded by countries such as Iran, where homosexuality is punishable by death, is a testament to Israel's commitment and character.
>
> Unless we want the Middle East to turn into an absolute free-for-all controlled by extremists who want to kill us and turn women into their slaves, then we need to do everything we can to protect Israel and stand in solidarity in any way we can. Not only is it in our interests, but Israel deserves it after all it has done for us. (Mason 2014, July 9)

This opinion piece in the *Advocate* exemplifies some of binary oppositional logic (see also Table 4.2) and homonationalist discourse often used in the discussion about Israel and sexual minorities. For example, the author uses "we" (meaning the LGBTs and West/global north) against "them" (the "barbaric" Muslims) as a discursive strategy throughout the article in order to draw attention to how the interests and security of the global LGBT community, particularly in the West, intertwines with the security and continued support for Israel: They (Israel) are fighting for "us" (the LGBTs), against countries such as Iran, where "homosexuality is punishable by death." Israel is thus depicted as the frontline fighter for human rights.[8] Accordingly, if it were not for Israel, the Middle East would be controlled by extremists who would enslave women and kill "us," the gays. Here the author aligns the alleged maltreatment of women with that of homosexuals.

As Puar has argued, the "Woman Question" is now being supplemented with the "Homosexual Question" as a "barometer of capacity for sovereignty" (Puar 2010). Here the homosexual question not only supplements the woman question, but it is used to create a sharper distinction between the civilization of the West (including Israel) and the "uncivilized" and "barbaric" Middle East, of which Iran is depicted as the main antagonist.

*   *   *

In this chapter, I have discussed how the modern Iranian gay subject has been constructed outside of Iran. The discourses reproduced by Western (pink) media on same-sex desires have mostly been framed around victimization and the persecution of gays within Iran. These reports have rendered the gay subject within Iran solely as a victim and in constant danger of being killed or persecuted. Not denying the fact that gays, as well as other sexual and gender minorities, are persecuted in the Islamic Republic of Iran, reported by various NGOs, the reality and the embodied experiences of gay-identifying Iranian men is often more complicated and multifaceted than the one depicted in the Western (gay) media. By saying that, I am not diminishing the good intention of the pink/gay press in their criticism of how the Islamic Republic of Iran treats sexual minorities, which is without a doubt in breach with international agreements and human rights accords. Nevertheless, the point I want to make here is that by not attending to the nuances and context of the embodied experiences of Iranian gays living inside of Iran, runs the risk of misrepresentation, and unilateral discussion on sexual minorities living in Iran (or in non-Western societies) from the perspective of Western gay emancipation. Although not being a "gay paradise" in terms of livability and sexual rights, Iranian gays try to find ways of accommodating their desires within those limits set by the legal-social and historical context of today's Islamic Republic of Iran. Ultimately, the central question, which will be explored further in the following chapters, is, as Martino and Kjaran have pointed out in their previous publications, "the political ramifications and exigencies that are implicated in how individuals are constituted and constitute themselves as gendered, sexual and erotic subjects/agents, which requires some deciphering of the regimes of sexuality governance that demarcate legitimate sexual citizenship and personhood in differing cultural, geopolitical contexts" (Martino and Kjaran 2019; Kjaran and Martino 2017; Blasius 2013, p. 220; Long 2009; Najmabadi 2014).

NOTES

1. The pink press is used here as a synonym for various online publications that are directed toward the LGBTQ community.
2. The search on Google with the keyword "Gay executions" was conducted on the April 4, 2018.
3. I use the term "sexual minority" for those individuals whose sexuality/sexual orientation differs from the majority of the surrounding society. The term incorporates a variety of sexual identity categories, such as men who have sex with men, bisexual individuals, gays, and lesbians.
4. Here it needs to be emphasized that I am not denying the fact that gay-identifying Iranian men and those who have sex with men have been executed on the basis of their sexual activities/orientation during the time of the Islamic Republic. In fact, various human rights reports indicate that executions of sexual minorities take place in Iran, although the official explanation rarely mentions "sodomy" as a cause of the death sentence. Rather, my aim here is to address the polyphonic nature of the discourse in order to try to understand more fully how gay-identifying Iranian men are constructed, not only by their local context or by themselves but also through the international discourse in the Western gay/pink press.
5. I started this research project by collecting online data in 2013. In 2015, I went to Iran three times to conduct my fieldwork. I have therefore limited the discussion about the gay/pink online publications to this period.
6. Long (2009), in his discussion about the case of Makwan, where he, for example, refers to a "small town-vendetta" influencing his conviction.
7. The concept of homonationalism was developed by Jabir K. Puar (2007) in her book *Terrorist Assemblages: Homonationalism in Queer Times*. Although some scholars have raised some criticism regarding the concept and its applicability (see e.g., Zanghellini 2012) it is in my view still a valuable concept in analyzing the rhetoric and discourse in the pink press in relation to sexual minorities in Iran.
8. I am not denying that LGBTQ rights are well established in Israel today, manifested, for example, in laws on same-sex marriage and other progressive policies/laws on sexual/gender equality. However, the argument I am making here is that these progressive laws and developments within Israel in terms of LGBTQ equality have often been used politically, especially by some right-wing parties, both within and outside of Israel, in their rhetoric against Muslim societies, Islam, and Iran particularly, drawing on the homonationalist discourse, and depicting these societies as backward and barbaric (see e.g., Schulman 2012).

REFERENCES

Abu-Lughod, L. (2013). *Do Muslim Women Need Saving?* Boston: Harvard University Press.

Ahmed, S. (2002). This Other and Other Others. *Economy and Society, 31*(4), 558–572. https://doi.org/10.1080/03085140022000020689.

Amnesty International. (2016, August, 2). *Iran: Hanging of Teenager Shows Authorities' Brazen Disregard for International Law.* Retrieved from https://www.amnesty.org/en/latest/news/2016/08/iran-hanging-of-teenager-shows-brazen-disregard-for-international-law/.

Blasius, M. (2013). Theorizing the Politics of (Homo)sexualities Across Cultures. In L. M. Weiss & M. Boisa (Eds.), *Global Homophobia I* (pp. 218–245). Chicago: University of Illinois Press.

Butler, J. (1991). Imitation and Gender Insubordination. In D. Fuss (Ed.), *Inside/Out: Lesbian Theories, Gay Theories* (pp. 13–31). London: Routledge.

Duffy, N. (2014, August 20). Iranian Lesbian Couple Marry in Stockholm. *PinkNews.* Retrieved from https://www.pinknews.co.uk/2014/08/20/iranian-lesbian-couple-marry-in-stockholm/.

Duffy, N. (2015, April 28). Gay Iranian: Lib Dem Simon Hughes 'Saved My Life' and Helped Me Escape the Death Penalty. *PinkNews.* Retrieved from https://www.pinknews.co.uk/2015/04/28/gay-iranian-lib-dem-simon-hughes-saved-my-life-and-helped-me-escape-the-death-penalty/.

Duggan, L. (2002). The New Homonormativity. The Sexual Politics of Neoliberalism. In R. Castronovo & D. D. Nelson (Eds.), *Materializing Democracy: Toward a Revitalized Cultural Politics* (p. 179). Durham and London: Duke University Press.

Fernando, M. L. (2010). Reconfiguring Freedom: Muslim Piety and the Limits of Secular Law and Public Discourse in France. *American Ethnologist, 37*(1), 19–35.

Grindley, L. (2016, August 5). Teen Executed for Gay Sex in Iran Is Latest in Long Trend. *Advocate.* Retrieved from https://www.advocate.com/world/2016/8/05/teen-executed-gay-sex-iran-latest-long-trend.

Human Rights & Democracy for Iran. A Project of the Abdorrahman Boroumand Center. (n.d.). *Hassan Afshar.* Retrieved from https://www.iranrights.org/memorial/story/-7843/hassan-afshar.

Human Rights Watch. (2005, July 26). *Iran: End Juvenile Executions.* Retrieved from https://www.hrw.org/news/2005/07/26/iran-end-juvenile-executions.

Kjaran, J. I., & Martino, W. (2017). In Search of Queer Spaces in Tehran: Heterotopias, Power Geometries and Bodily Orientations in Queer Iranian's Men Lives. *Sexualities.* https://doi.org/10.1177/1363460717713383. Published online.

Long, S. (2009). Unbearable Witness: How Western Activists (Mis)recognize Sexuality in Iran. *Contemporary Politics, 15*(1), 119–136. https://doi.org/10.1080/13569770802698054.

Martino, W., & Kjaran, J. I. (2019). The Politics of Recognizability: Giving an Account of Iranian Gay Men's Lives Under Repressive Conditions of Sexuality Governance. *International Journal of Middle East Studies, 51* (1), 21–41.

Mason, J. D. (2014, July 9). Why LGBT People Around the World Need Israel. *Advocate*. Retrieved from https://www.advocate.com/commentary/2014/07/09/op-ed-why-lgbt-people-around-world-need-israel.

Massad, J. (2007). *Desiring Arabs*. Chicago: The University of Chicago Press.

Najmabadi, A. (2014). *Professing Selves: Transsexuality and Same-Sex Desire in Contemporary Iran*. Durham, NC: Duke University Press.

Puar, J. K. (2007). *Terrorist Assemblages: Homonationalism in Queer Times*. Durham, NC: Duke University Press.

Puar, J. K. (2010, July 1). Israel's Gay Propaganda War. *The Guardian*. Retrieved from https://www.theguardian.com/commentisfree/2010/jul/01/israels-gay-propaganda-war.

Rastegar, M. (2013). Emotional Attachments and Secular Imaginings: Western LGBTQ Activism on Iran. *GLQ: A Journal of Lesbian and Gay Studies, 19*(1), 1–29. https://doi.org/10.1215/10642684-1729527.

Schulman, S. (2012). *Israel/Palestine and the Queer International*. Durham/London: Duke University Press.

Shakhsari, S. (2012). From Homoerotics of Exile to Homopolitics of Diaspora. *Journal of Middle East Women's Studies, 8*(3), 14–40. https://doi.org/10.2979/jmiddeastwomstud.8.3.14.

TheGayUK. (2014, March 4). Unconfirmed Reports That Iran Hanged Two Gay Men for 'Perversion'. Retrieved from https://www.thegayuk.com/unconfirmed-reports-that-iran-hanged-two-gay-men-for-perversion/.

Trew, B. (2016, August 4). Tehran Hangs Teenage Boy for Being Gay. The Sunday Times. Retrieved from https://www.thetimes.co.uk/article/tehran-hangs-teenage-boy-for-being-gay-7t2pv97mq.

Verkaik, R. (2008, March 6). A Life or Death Decision. *Independent*. Retrieved from https://www.independent.co.uk/news/uk/home-news/a-life-or-death-decision-792058.html.

Weinthal, B. (2014, March 14). Experts Predict: Iran Will Remain Deadly. Two Reports Indicate That Despite a New President's Overtures to the Contrary, Iran Will Remain a Deadly Place for LGBTs. *Advocate*. Retrieved from https://www.advocate.com/world/2014/03/14/experts-predict-iran-will-remain-deadly.

Zanghellini, A. (2012, June 6). Are Gay Rights Islamophobic? A Critique of Some Uses of the Concept of Homonationalism in Activism and Academia. *Social and Legal Studies, 21*(3), 357–374. https://doi.org/10.1177/0964663911435282.

CHAPTER 5

Ethical Relationality and Accounts of Gay Iranian Men

In this chapter, I draw on interviews taken with gay-identifying Iranian males. I take up a particular Foucauldian analysis and work mainly with Foucault's ideas on the technologies or practices of the self, discussed in Chap. 2. I find these ideas helpful in addressing questions of gay embodiment and embodied experience, as well as in exploring the different ways gay-identifying Iranian men navigate their lives. In other words, how do they, in spite of both official and social disavowal and repression of same-sex desire, live out their lives and find ways to embody a gay identity and/or express their same-sex desire within the grids of masked existence? Thus, the aim of this chapter is to draw attention to the intersection of resistance, strategies, masking/unmasking of desires, and identity construction of being gay, while living under particular socio-legal conditions that exist today in Iran. These resistive actions and different strategies can be understood as a part of practices of the self, which I define here as taking care of the self. However, as Michel Foucault has pointed out and I have discussed in Chap. 2, practices of the self also involve gaining knowledge of the self and the need to express the truth about one's self in a confessional manner. In other words, knowing and confessing about oneself is a part of how subjects are constituted and how they constitute themselves within particular power relations and contexts. Ethical relationality is about engaging in the processes of subjectification. In this chapter, I give empirical examples of how gay Iranian men constitute themselves, for example, by "knowing about oneself"—becoming gay—and how they are constituted

© The Author(s) 2019
J. I. Kjaran, *Gay Life Stories*,
https://doi.org/10.1007/978-3-030-12831-9_5

by dominant discourses of gender and sexuality. By providing different accounts of gay existence in Iran, the aim of this chapter is to juxtapose the one-dimensional discourse presented in the West of the victimized Iranian gay male, discussed in Chap. 4. Although living a masked existence, in the sense of not being able to "come out" in the Western meaning of the word, there are both possibilities and opportunities, and also hindrances and dangers, to having sex and being gay in the Islamic Republic of Iran.

KNOWING ONESELF—ADOPTING A GAY IDENTITY

Gaining knowledge of the self and coming to understand oneself as a sexual being, which in the case of most of my informants meant adopting a gay identity, involves various practices and techniques. Drawing here on Foucault, by knowing oneself, one is in fact transforming oneself "in order to attain a certain state of happiness, purity, wisdom, perfection, or immortality" (Foucault 1988, p. 18). These practices of the self can be seen in Arslan's narrative. After he became aware of being somehow "different," he began to gather information about everything related to his state of being. He found information mostly on the Internet and also through gay-themed movies, such as *Brokeback Mountain*. In fact, gay-themed movies inspired many of my informants and filled them with some hope. Arash expressed how the movie *Milk*, which is about the first openly gay public official in history, inspired him:

> I saw the film Milk about Mr. Milk and it was an amazing day for me. I discovered myself and I said, hey I am not alone, there are other people like me on the other [side] of the world. I [began] to search online and in Yahoo messenger, chat rooms, and I [saw] other people who are like me.

Thus, Arash found out that he was not alone with these kinds of feelings. In fact, he found a gay community online, which he "entered" for the first time when he realized that he was different. I will come back to the online gay community in Iran in Chap. 8, and how important it is for gay-identifying Iranian men to gain social and moral support, which they normally don't get from their families or the society in general.

The discourse of difference, which entails constituting oneself as being different from societal norms, is often cited in the narratives of my informants. Arslan mentioned it in his narrative, finding out that he was somehow different. So did Nima: "I found out that I have a difference inside my heart. [...] They say it is against Islamic rule. I found my sexuality because I felt different. But it was against my religious ideas at that time so I had some difficulties dealing with it." Nima and Arslan had both internalized the discourse of difference, which constituted their ways of sexual being and identity. Moreover, as Nima mentions in his narrative, he experienced some inner conflict between his sexuality and his religious ideas. Indeed, religious ideas and traditional values, directly or indirectly, affected all of those I met and spoke to during my fieldwork. Most of them did not define themselves as religious and rarely prayed or went to the mosque. However, they often referred to religion or traditional values, or both, as a decisive factor in their relationship and communication with their families. Even my informants who come from families that are not religious, are educated, belong to the upper middle class, and live in the northern part of Tehran, had difficulties in gaining support and being themselves, as their parents were under the influence of the official discourse of disavowal of homosexuality, in which gay subjectivities are outside the grids of recognizability. Judith Butler argues that "norms condition the possibility of recognition" (Butler 2005, p. 33), which, in the Iranian context, can refer to religion, traditions, and societal values. In the case of Arash, his parents, who are secular and well educated, reacted negatively and with fury when they found out that he was gay. His father took him to the legal medical office in Tehran (*Pezeshki Ghanooni*) and told the officer on duty that his son was sick, drawing on the discourse about the "sick homosexual," and that he should either have treatment or be punished. Luckily for Arash, the officer told his father to take his son back home and try to help and support him. However, after this, nothing remained the same for Arash and his father, for his father could not accept that his son was "different," and constantly expressed anger toward him. Since then, there have been continuous conflicts between Arash and his father. Aradalan had a similar story to tell:

> My father discovered that I had a relationship with a guy. He was furious and kicked me out of the home. I did not have any place to live so I went to my sister's home. I did not tell my sister the real reason so after awhile I went to my friend's home. I lived there for six months. After six months, my mother asked me to come back home. I did so. But when I came back to our home my father did not look at me. I was no longer his son. I cried when I saw my parents. After that, I [no longer] have a good relationship with my

father; I only talk to my mother. My parents are so religious. My mother still loves me but she does not accept the fact that I am gay. But my father, no way, if it was in my father's hand[s] he would kill me. I see it in his eyes that he [doesn't] want me around.

In his narrative, Aradalan states that if his father would have it his way, he would kill him. Shahram Khosravi has pointed out how filicide (killing of the son) and father-son conflict are deeply rooted in Iranian cultural memory. For example, in the famous Iranian epic poem by Ferdowsi, *Shahmameh* (Book of Kings), there is the story of Sohrab who is killed by his father Rostam. Moreover, according to Khosravi, some expressions in Persian draw on that cultural memory and have the aim of establishing the superiority of the father over his son (Khosravi 2008, p. 133). The father is the head of the family and has the power, even to decide upon life and death, over other family members, particularly if they show disrespect to the honor of the family. Thus, the cultural memory of the "son-killing complex" is still kept alive in contemporary Iran, although, today, it is more symbolic of the authoritative figure of the father in Iranian households, rather than being taken literally as a common practice.[1] Thus, the narratives of Arash and Aradalan give an example of the symbolic patriarchal power still very much visible in Iranian households, and map out the conflicts that can arise between father and son, especially if the son adopts a sexual identity outside the grids of recognizability. Given this, it is sometimes better to put on a "straight mask," as will be discussed in the next section.

> *"I find one small reason to be happy and let that be enough for me"*
> *Arslan*
> Arslan is in his 20s. He is studying English literature at the University of Tehran and speaks perfect English. He also works alongside his studies, teaching English to children. He lives with his parents and an older sister. He has not told his parents and sister about himself because he knows that they would never accept it, in fact it would "crush them." "They are not religious but they have some beliefs. So being gay is exactly against their beliefs." Arslan mentions that his parents do not know what it is to be gay, as it is not common knowledge among ordinary Iranians, especially the older generation.

(*continued*)

(continued)

"The idea of being gay is newly introduced to Iranian people through the Western media." Arslan has, for example, tried to reach out to his sister. "I've tried so many indirect ways, such as talking about movies, news and other stuff." However, she has always reacted negatively, and he has thus come to the conclusion that he could never open up his feelings to her. "She believes they're perverts [referring here to gays]." He used the same tactic with one of his best friends and realized that he could tell him about his sexuality and feelings. "He was ok with it and he told me that he had noticed some clues before, for example, I never had any girlfriend[s] before." After telling his best friends, he revealed his sexuality to some of his closest girlfriends, who accepted him as he is. "Two of my best friends are girls and we hang out all the time, they are 100% cool with everything." When they hang out, they like to go to malls, go shopping, and visit coffee shops. Arslan started to date a guy in high school; it was his first love, but they were not in a formal relationship. They had some difficulties because their teacher found out that they were holding hands. "He made fun of us and it was hard to deal with other students for a few days." But after some days, everything went back to normal and nobody suspected that they were gay or were dating each other. I asked Arslan why nobody had any suspicion about the true nature of their relationship: "The good thing here in Iran, is that people have no idea about gays. They think it's just a silly thing teenagers might do. They don't look for gay people among ordinary [*sic*] people. They think a gay man must look and act like a girl. And even if they see something like two guys holding hands or even kissing in public, they just ignore it." Arslan is here referring to the "gay look" and the intersection of sexuality and gender performances, in which being gay is always associated with femininity in the Iranian/Middle East context. Arslan has been in three relationships; the longest one lasted one and a half years. After they broke up, his ex-boyfriend started to date a girl. Arslan assumes that he is bisexual. They are still in contact with each other and meet occasionally for a coffee and chat. When Arslan was coming to terms with his sexuality, he did a lot of reading and also watched some gay-themed movies such as *Brokeback Mountain*. "You are different, so

(*continued*)

(continued)

you need to know why you are different. So I start[ed] [to read] about it and get more information, which gives me more understanding." However, Arslan admits that it can sometimes be difficult to be "different from other people," especially because you need to lie every day and put on a mask. There are also a few people you can talk to about your feelings and desires. It is therefore not easy to identify as gay in Iran: "They [meaning here the society and the family particularly] really put us under a lot of pressure! And I really wish I were born in another country considering my situation. But it's not that bad!! I'm proud of being gay! I am more than ok with it. I wouldn't wish to change that cause it has taught me a lot of things that I wouldn't know had I not been gay." Arslan is aware of how he is constituted as a gay subject by the dominant religious-legal-socio discourse in Iran, and he has, in order to transform the self, accepted his subject position—being not recognized and living with a mask: "You get so used to it that you even believe it yourself. So most of the time, you don't feel the mask." Instead, he is "proud of being gay" and embraces the challenges it has brought him—it is a learning opportunity and it gives him some kind of distinction. When I asked if he was happy and would continue living in Iran, he replied: "I am not a sad person. I find one small reason to be happy and let that be enough for me."

STRAIGHT MASKS—GAY IDENTITY

In *Black Skins, White Masks*, Frantz Fanon draws attention to how the black subject has internalized the dominant discourse of the white society. According to its logic, blackness is equated to "wrongness" and darkness, whereas whiteness is associated with light and "rightness" (Fanon 2008, p. 146). These racial imaginaries have had deep influences on the black subject, causing her/him to experience inferiority and even self-hatred. The fact that she/he lives in a white society, in which the hegemonic norms and values are "white-centered," the only way for her/him to regain humanity, and be recognized as an authentic subject, is to put on a white mask by emulating those same norms, language, and values of her/his oppressor. Fanon's arguments in *Black Skins, White Masks* can easily be applied to the situation of gay-identifying Iranian males. As can be read from Arman's narrative, he experienced inferiority and fear in his interaction with the homophobic straight society, and in order for him to gain recognition and become an authentic subject within that society, he had to hide his real identity. In other words, he had to put on a straight mask and perform the straight script. Part of the straight script is related to performances of gender, as any deviation from the script of masculinity can be read as being gay or sexual other. Arman, for example, tells of how he grew a beard and tried to change his voice, by making it sound more "manly."

Ali Reza had also internalized the dominant discourse of what was expected of him in terms of behavior and gender performances. He did not have high self-esteem and felt the urge to change his bodily performances in order to fit in: "I am imperfect, I am born that way. I need to correct my voice, how I speak, and other things such as my hand movements, so I can become more manly." Thus, to fit in, Arman and Ali Reza played their role according to the dominant male gender script in the "theatre of the straights"—disciplining their bodies and behavior, such as lowering their voice, and acting, talking, and walking in a more "manly" manner. In other words, to avoid being read or signified as being gay, they performed (hetero)masculinity. Thus, in line with Butler, through their performativity of (hetero)masculinity, they took on a particular role, but that same role constituted and set limits to their gay identity and existence (Butler 1990). For them, (hetero)masculinity did not match with their "true" identity; it was only performative, and thus did not express their internal reality or any truth about themselves.

Putting on a straight mask not only serves to hide your sexual identity from family and friends but is also a strategy to live in a society where being gay and having same-sex desire are often connected with a disease or a criminality (pedophilia). Ali Reza had, for example, internalized the discourse of the "sick homosexual," saying that he was born "imperfect"— meaning that he regards himself as somehow different and at odds with the dominant norm. In fact, as discussed in the previous section, the discourse of difference was recurrent in the narratives of all my informants, indicating that they had internalized their inferior status vis-à-vis the straight society. However, they also tried to resist the discourse that labeled them as sick, citing a discourse counter to the official one. Arman, for example, drew on the biological discourse and essentialist logic of being born gay, when he explained his sexuality to his mother. In fact, most of my informants talked about their sexual identity from an essentialist perspective, being born gay, which, in many ways, helped them to come to terms with their sexuality and construct themselves as sexual beings vis-à-vis the official discourse on homosexuality. Thus, according to that logic, being born gay or different in terms of sexuality should therefore be tolerated and recognized by the authorities, because it is biological (genetics) and cannot be changed.

Homosexuality and same-sex desire are labeled as sick and abnormal in the official discourse, and are rarely mentioned within the Iranian mediascape. In that sense, what is not named does not exist, as Mahmoud Ahmadinejad made clear in his speech when he visited the US in 2007. However, the Iranian public is gradually being exposed to gay characters through Western media, which are received through satellite disks or streaming from the Internet. Arslan mentioned the influence of the foreign media with regards to sexuality in our talk and was hopeful that one day there would be changes and more tolerance for the Iranian gay community:

> BBC Farsi, Western TV shows such as Modern Family, and movies. They [Iranians] are gradually getting used to it and maybe soon they will accept the fact that this [being gay] exits. I think the next generation will accept this more. My generation is starting to accept this already and I have for example friends at the university that are OK with it. I have not told them about me but they have talked about it [gay issues] and seem to be fine with it.

Hiding their gay identity both in public and within the realm of the family is a reality that most gay-identifying Iranian males face. In other words, they are experts in putting on an act and performing their role according to the "straight script." In that sense, they are not only aware of how they are constituted by the dominant discourse—modes of subjection—but they also find ways to navigate between different roles in the "theatre of the straights." In the next section, the focus will be on how gay identity is played out in the game of sex in cities like Tehran, in which straight masks are taken off or put on interchangeably.

You are like a statue, you are just alive
Arman

Arman is in his 20s. He finished a bachelor's degree in engineering some months ago. He is thinking of whether to continue his studies or not. However, he has had thoughts about emigrating: "I want to, but I love my family, my mother." Indeed, Arman has a good relationship with his mother, who has raised him single-handedly after his father passed away when he was six years old. He has told her about his feelings and that he identifies as gay: "Fortunately she accepts it because she is not religious, she is open minded, and educated. I explained my feelings to her and told her that it is something natural, not a disease or mental disorder. She said that 'I like you the way you are because you are my son.'" However, it remains a secret between Arman and his mother, and the other members of his family do not know that he identifies as gay: "They will not understand it, so I prefer not to talk about it. I prefer to keep it as a secret in my heart until I die." Thus, in order to "pass" as straight, Arman, in line with other informants, had to put on a "straight mask": "I try to act like [I am] straight. I am always acting among my friends and my family members. For example, when you are with your 'straight' friends you have to say 'wow, that is a beautiful girl,' you know, you have to act." Arman found out that he was "different" when he was in high school. Since then, he has tried to discipline himself in order to blend in and pass as straight. He describes himself as sensitive and emotional, and because of that he was often mocked and bullied during his high school years: "A real man should not [be emotional] and should be strong and not cry easily." Arman recounts when his neighbor made fun of him and called him a "sissy": "I was very angry and called her a bitch. I even tried to beat her but her husband stopped me. When you are as sensitive as me, being called names really hurts." In order to avoid that kind of a situation, Arman worked on himself and started to behave more in accordance to the dominant gender script: "I grew [a] beard and got a tougher voice, you know, [a] more manly voice. I also tried

(continued)

(continued)

to act and behave more like a man, you know, try to be another guy [rather] than [the one] I really was. Maybe then less people will judge me and mock [me]." Arman is, therefore, very aware of his appearance and behavior. He is cautious and is not active on the Tehran underground gay scene, as he does not know whom to trust there. He has a couple of gay friends, and sometimes he goes to gay parties. In fact, he feels more at "home" with his gay friends/acquaintances: "When I am among gays, I am more comfortable because I know that they are like me, they would never bully me and they would understand me. But when I am with straight people, I have always this fear that they might mock me, make fun of me." Hence, Arman has little trust when it comes to "straight" people, and he feels uncomfortable in their presence. He is, however, grateful to have his mother who understands him and supports him. He also considers himself to be lucky to live in "one of the best" neighborhoods of Tehran: "People [here] are more educated and classy. They are not going to make fun of you and injure you. I have this fear when I have to go to other cities, to other parts of Iran, that I will be hurt or injured. For example, when I was sent to Fars province for my workshop, I was very frightened because I did not know what they might do, the rural people. Hence, I acted very manly and talked tough like a real man so no one would notice my difference." Arman defines himself as a gay activist—mostly doing his activist work online. I will come back to gay activism in Chap. 6. Through his activism and communication with gays abroad, he is aware of what is going on in the world with regards to the situation of gays and gay rights. He is not optimistic that life in Iran will change for the better—in fact, he does not see his gay existence being inside of Iran: "What kind of life is it when you have to hide yourself your whole life, wear a mask. You are like a statue, you are just alive, you are just living, nothing else. It is not a life, it is at least not something I call a life." (Fig. 5.1)

(continued)
Fig. 5.1 Contemplating, waiting

SEX IN THE CITY: HAVING GAY SEX IN TEHRAN

"It is mostly all about sex and that's what turns me off," said Arslan, when I asked him about the "gay scene" in Tehran. In fact, I have often heard from my informants and friends that it was rather easy to find a sex date, and most of them were rather active on various gay dating apps. Thus, as in other large cities in the West, the underground gay scene in Tehran was rather focused on sex. Its members identify with and use Western labels in terms of sex role preferences, such as *bottom* (receptive partner in anal sex), *versatile*,[2] or *top* (penetrator in anal sex). These categories often become part of their gay identity, as can be seen from the narratives of Afshin and Saaed. Moreover, adopting the role of the bottom, the recipient in anal sex, is often associated with femininity in Iranian (gay) culture. Both Afshin and Saaed took on that role and were considered to be "gay looking," which meant that they acted in an effeminate way and had rather "flashy" appearances. Nima said, when I asked him about the "gay look," that in Iranian culture "you should not be a flashy person, it's not good to be too fashionable, you should not expose your sexual life to everybody." For Nima, a "flashy person" is someone who might use make-up, eyeliner, dress according to the latest fashion, and perhaps behave somehow at odds with the dominant discourse of (hetero)masculinity. What is also interesting in Nima's account is how he indirectly refers to the traditional spatial division into the private and public spheres—*andaruni* and *biruni*. Accordingly, you should not expose your sexuality or sexual life within the public sphere, as this kind of exposure should be kept private: symbolically, inside of you, but also spatially, inside of your home.

Moreover, this kind of "flashy" behavior runs against the official discourse on modesty, which applies both to dress and to appearance. In fact, the limits of bodily appearance and "official aesthetics" are being contested by the generation born after the Islamic Revolution, who are defying the official discourse on modesty and adopting more of a Western look in terms of fashion and appearance—becoming more "flashy." In line with the official Islamic aesthetics, veiling and not exposing yourself to others within public spaces applies both to men and women, and aims to desexualize the body. Thus, according to Khosravi, "[m]odesty in appearance and behavior... operates both as a symbol of Islamic order and as a mechanism for maintaining it, in a combination of self-regulation and external control" (Khosravi 2008, p. 48). The internalization of the "official aesthetic and Islamic order" and the intergenerational difference in terms of attitudes toward dress code and appearances are demonstrated in the short dialogue between Arash (in his 20s) and Armin (in his 40s, born before the Islamic Revolution):

Armin: When I was sixteen years old, and if you wore a shirt with short sleeves, you know [a] t-shirt, the police may have arrested you.

Arash: But everything has changed now and the police never give you a problem if you wear a t-shirt. I often wear a t-shirt.

Armin: Still, I am afraid. I am afraid what will happen to me if I would wear a t-shirt. I am afraid the police [mostly morality police or Basij] will arrest me, hold me for one night and even beat me.

Arash is a representative of the generation born after the revolution, who has experienced fewer restrictions in terms of how to dress and act in public. Khosravi (2008) has, for example, in his ethnographic study on Iranian youth, documented this intergenerational shift in attitudes regarding dress, attire, and appearances. He has argued that the young generation is expanding the limits of the official ideology of the Islamic republic, which is grounded in an "aesthetic of the modest self" and a "culture of sadness" (Khosravi 2008, p. 32). This is manifested in "flashy" and even colorful clothes, and in veils being pushed back a bit, with the aim of showing a bit of a hair. In that sense, transgressing the "official aesthetic" and codes of dress and behavior is undertaken by straight and gays alike—and straight guys can be "gay looking" and gays can be "straight looking."

Being "gay looking" and applying make-up are also strategies for some gays I met in Tehran to draw attention toward themselves in order to increase their chances in the game of sex. As Afshin and Saaed indicated in their narratives, applying some make-up "gets you more sex," even with straight guys. Arash and Arslan also mentioned this when I raised this subject. Arash, for example, told me: "making straight guys horny, you need to wear a bit of a make-up and act a bit effeminate. You know, it is often so hard for straight guys to have sex with girls and, therefore, they sometimes have sex with effeminate or gay looking guys." Arslan agreed and said that a "lot of them [referring to straight guys] were following my ass when I was in high school and university." It can be argued that, in their explanations of "straight" men engaging in gay sex, Arash and Arslan unwittingly fall back on the "deprivation" hypothesis, which has been rather prevalent in the discourse in the West regarding male sexuality in the Middle East. According to its logic, the strict gender segregation and lack of female intimacy have caused "straight" men to turn to other men to satisfy their sexual needs (Manchanda 2014). However, it can also be argued that fluidity in terms of sexuality and the object of sexual desire has much deeper cultural roots in Middle Eastern societies. In other words, the strict binary categories of homo/heterosexuality do not fully apply there, not even today in a globalized world of hybrid identities. Furthermore, it can be argued that within the Iranian context, the discourse about the "gay look" draws on the cultural memory of same-sex desire, manifested, for example, in classical Persian poems, in which older men praise love to beardless young men, who are often depicted as effeminate.[3] In fact, some studies from the Middle East context indicate that same-sex desire among "straight" men, especially if the object of desire is a young effeminate boy, is practiced and is even culturally acceptable. For example, in Pashtun societies, so-called dancing boys (*bacha bazi*) have been an object of sexual desire among men for centuries. The Western understanding of a binary identity category (straight or gay) does not fully apply there (Schut and van Baarle 2017; see also The Dancing Boys of Afghanistan).

Thus, drawing unwittingly on this cultural memory, for some gays I spoke to, it was exciting to have the potential to engage in sex with straight guys, something that would perhaps not be possible if they left Iran and moved to the West, as expressed by both Afshin and Saaed. Both of them love "Iranian cocks," which can be interpreted as having more potential in Iran to have sex, both with straight and gay guys, in comparison to their perception of gay life in the West—where the norm has been to think in terms of hetero/homo binary. Moreover, it can also be argued that in their preference for "Iranian cocks," they were indirectly citing the discourse of phallocentric or phallic nationalism: Our men (cocks) are the best, and desiring other/foreign men (cocks) is then considered to be a lack of patriotism. This kind of logic has often been applied to women, for example, during war and occupation, who have slept with the "enemy" or with someone considered to be an outsider, and by doing so, have been judged as having shown a lack of patriotism or even to have committed treason (Goldstein 2003).

Finding a suitable or desirable partner to engage in sex with is regarded as quite an easy task according to my informants, especially if you apply some make-up. However, finding a place for sex is considered to be rather difficult, and as one of my informants put it: "To have a place of your own is like having a goldmine—it means you can have lot of sex." The reason for a lack of privacy is that most young Iranians live with their parents until they themselves establish their own family. This is both because of tradition and practicality, as housing prices are quite high in cities like Tehran. Thus, most of my informants lived with their parents, and struggled to find a place for some intimate moments with their boyfriend or sex partner. Different strategies were used, such as having sex in public toilets, at work after office hours, in gardens during the night, or in cars. Pouria, who is in his 30s and identifies as gay, told me about his first and only experience of car sex:

> I once had sex with my boyfriend in a car. We are having sex and suddenly we realize that there is a police car beside us. They are watching us. It is Ramadan, the holy month, and you should therefore not have any sex whatsoever. The police officers ask us to step out of the car. We zip up our trousers and step out. It was so embarrassing. They start to insult us and threaten us, saying that they will take us down to the station and put us in a jail. We were very scared and I was high at that time, in fact both of us were high, and you know your feelings, your emotions, are stronger when you are high. So I was really scared. How was I going to explain this to my parents? But after a while they let us go. I was really shocked and I will never forget this.

Having sex and being high during Ramadan would have, under usual circumstances, rendered them in jail—or at least a fine would have been issued. However, the police only reprimanded them. Pouria learned from this experience and decided that in the future he would be more careful in terms of choosing the right place for having sex. That was the strategy Arslan employed—being careful, which entailed being patient, finding the right time, and somehow accepting those restrictions, which constituted his sexual existence:

Arslan: It does annoy you and you feel that you don't have any privacy, even in your own city. It is hard but you cannot do anything about it. What are you going to do? You cannot change the society over night.

Jón: How did you and your boyfriend then manage, I mean if you wanted to have sex and be intimate?

Arslan: We just waited for the right time. We would call each other whenever we had privacy at home.

Most of my informants had considerable knowledge about sex and having sex. Many of them were aware of the risks involved in terms of STDs, and generally they used condoms during sex (see discussion on HIV and condoms in Chap. 7). Most of them got their information about sex/having sex either from porn, on the Internet, or though gay friends. Ali Reza, who is in his 30s and identifies as gay, realized that he liked guys more than girls when he discovered some downloaded porn-movies on the hard drive in his brother's computer. Arslan also learned about his sexuality by getting information from various Internet sites, including porn sites. During one of our regular meetings/chats, we had some discussion about porn and STDs:

Jón: You sometimes watch porn?
Arslan: I do! ☺
Jón: Often[?]
Arslan: No! Just when I am horny. American porn mostly.
Jón: Gay porn right?
Arslan: Of course!!!
Jón: ☺ Is it easy to access?
Arslan: I don't buy them! I download them. You need to use [a] proxy or VPN to do that here, though!
Jón: Would you say that gays here in Tehran, or the ones you know, are aware of sexual diseases, like HIV?
Arslan: They mostly are! But due to the pressure they're under, they get too excited [about] any opportunity of having sex. They might forget or even don't care about diseases at that moment. We are taught in schools to be careful about these things.
Jón: So gays normally don't use condom[s] when having sex? What is your feeling on this?
Arslan: They do use it, but they're not careful. They might not know how to use it safely.
Jón: Ok I see. And you? You are conscious about these issues?
Arslan: Yeah. I know there's always a huge risk. And I love my life too much to simply let it go to waste.
Jón: So would you say that being gay in Iran, having sex and so on, is not that dangerous, or what is your feeling regarding risk and staying safe?
Arslan: It is not completely safe! But the amount of risk you take is in your hand[s]!

Arslan mentions "risks" involved when having sex. He also informed me of what kind of strategies he uses to minimize those risks and to protect himself. Firstly, as he mentions in our chat, he always uses condom. This is not always the rule, as he indicates in our chat. Due to a lack of privacy and not having access to a "place" for sex, when the opportunity finally comes, some guys get "too excited" and forget to use the condom. Or they do not have it on them, because sex at that moment was not planned—the opportunity just came at the last moment. Secondly, he always meets potential sex-dates in public places a couple of times before he decides to engage in sex with them. In that sense, Arslan is very careful, and he wants to have control of his life, as he knows that any mistakes can have drastic influences on his life. Arman is also very careful and is not active on the Tehran underground gay scene:

> I have only had sex ten times and I am now 25 years old. I am very careful and I am afraid of dating guys here, you never know.

Although Arslan emphasizes that the risk you take is "in your hand[s]," and Arman tries to be careful in terms of dating guys, the fact remains that it is not always easy to spot the dangers and risks involved when having sex in Tehran. It is often a matter of luck, as, for example, in the case of Pouria, when he was having sex in his car with his boyfriend. Others have not been so lucky, even though they have been careful and avoid taking risks. Armin told me about one of his friends who was blackmailed and robbed by his sex partner. In fact, having sex with older guys and then blackmailing them, for example, by taking photos or videos during sex, is, according to my informants, often a source of income for poor straight guys, mostly living in the southern part of Tehran. This kind of practice was rather common in many Western countries in the recent past, for example, in the UK and Germany, during the time when homosexuality was criminalized (Beachy 2015). As a matter of fact, it is often forgotten how recent these changes are in the West regarding gay rights and recognizability, especially when drawing attention to the situation of gays in Iran, and comparing it to the Western notion of achieved gay utopia.

My informants often referred to being sexually harassed, especially during their time in high school. Some of them also mentioned that they had heard stories of gays being raped when they went on a sex date. Two of my informants had the experience of being raped. The following story is from Nima, which he told me when we met in Tehran in February 2015:

I was around twenty years old. Once I was chatting on Yahoo with a guy who said that he was two years older than me. He told me to come to his home to have sex. I went to that place and met him but after some minutes another guy came into the room. They held me down and raped me, both of them, using [a] cola bottle, sticking it into my ass. I remember that both of them were drug addicts, I mean I could smell that they were using grass or something like that. I don't know whether they were straight, gay, or bisexual but I felt during the rape that they were enjoying it; they somehow got aroused sexually from this. After the rape I could not go to the police and tell them that I had been raped. I was going to have sex with a guy and that is of course illegal in Iran. Today, I am still suffering from that injury. After this incident I could never again have anal sex. This has had really bad effects on my life. For long time I went to a psychologist for a treatment and he tried to help me. He was however not very good at that and in order to try to make me feel better he said to me that on the one hand you are injured [physically] but on the other hand has this injury caused you to abstain from hard sex [anal sex] and it might protect you from HIV or something like that. This was supposed to reduce my pain! I should just be positive! Well at least they did not kill me or film the rape. I have heard stories of gays being raped and then killed. I have also heard that gays have been raped and filmed in order to blackmail them.

Nima's story provides insight into to the darkest pockets of Tehran gay life—a life pursued underground without any official or social recognition. Not being recognized as a subject, being constituted by the dominant discourse as an abject, has its repercussions for most, if not all, gay-identifying Iranian males, when having sex or going out on a date: They need to navigate between risk and (sexual) pleasure, danger and desire. The individuals presented in this section found some ways to overcome those barriers. They were aware of their existential limits in terms of sex and sexuality and had no other option but to accept their subject position, constituted by the official legal and religious discourse. However, they employed different strategies in order to make their life meaningful, have sex, go on a date, or spend intimate time with their boyfriends. In that sense they all tried to transform the self in a Foucauldian sense, within the liminal space of their gay existence.

"I love Iranian cocks"—"I love Iran"
Afshin and Saaed

I meet Afshin and Saaed on a sunny afternoon in February 2015. I go there with Arash, who had set up the meeting. We meet in front of one of the main exhibition halls in Tehran. The theme for the exhibition is tourism in Iran. Afshin is 20 years old and is studying psychology at the University of Tehran. He works alongside his studies in tourism. He is wearing jeans, a trendy cotton jacket, and the latest Nike light/air colorful shoes. His eyebrows are well maintained, and he wears a little bit of make-up. When I ask him about it, he says: "I use make-up to get more sex, to have sex with straight guys. You put [on] a bit of a make-up when you, for example, come to this place [exhibition hall] and you will find three men that will have sex with you. If you put [on] heavy make-up you might find ten men, and if you wear women's clothes, you get much more." Afshin identifies as gay, and when I ask him about it, he adds also his sex role preferences: "I am vers [versatile] but more bottom [passive recipient during anal sex]." Arash interrupts our chat: "Lets wait until this religious woman goes away because she might call the police." A good reminder for all of us, to be a bit more careful during our conversation—to lower our voice and be less expressive. Afshin is active on various dating apps such as *Hornet* and *Grindr*, and he shows me his rather revealing profile picture there. Arash also sees it and says that he is a bit "gay looking" in the picture. Afshin replies: "Yes, I am ok with it. I am gay looking and I don't have problem with it. I [have] never had any problems with the police because of it." Thus, for Afshin, being gay in Iran, especially in a large city like Tehran, does not seem to cause him any problems. However, his family does not know that he is gay and, when his parents raise the issue of marriage, he tells them that he is still too young and that he does not want to get married. So far, they have accepted that. Afshin sometimes likes to cross-dress, and when he does that he uses his "feminine" or cross-dressing name, Razia. Because of this, some of his friends as well as his doctor think that he is transgender/transsexual and should therefore get an operation. He sometimes feels this pressure and mentions that one of his friends had the operation,

(continued)

(continued)

both because he identified as transgender and because of the rights associated with that particular subject position. However, Afshin has no desire to reassign his sex: "I don't want to change my sex. I love my body as it is. I love my cock. I don't need an operation." He emphasizes that he has no problem staying in Iran and has never thought about emigration: "I love Iranian cocks [laughs]. I am enjoying my sexuality and sex here in Iran. I like it because it is not important for me what other people think or if they are judging me somehow."

Saaed is 28 years old and, like Afshin, works in tourism as a tour guide. He has a calm appearance, wears jeans, and has a trendy cap on his head. He is not as talkative as Afshin. I ask him about how he identifies in terms of sexuality: "I don't know if I am gay or trans-sexual. I don't know [laughs]. My behavior [meaning appearance and acting] is trans, but my sexuality, I am gay, versatile, maybe more bottom." Saaed is here referring to fact that he, like Afshin, likes to cross-dress. Once he went driving with his friends in full drag: "Once I was drinking a lot and [went] out with my friends in a car wearing [a] woman's dress. We stopped at a gas station and then everybody looked at me when I stepped out of the car [laughs]. But nothing happened." Thus, Saaed agrees with Afshin that normally he does not have any problems with the authorities. Once police stopped him because he was wearing too much make-up. However, he was not taken to the police station because he offered to give the police officer a blowjob (oral sex). "For me it was no problem. He treat[ed] me like a human being and was good to release me. I did not have to spend the night at the police station." Saaed's parents know that he is gay because he became very depressed when he broke up with his boyfriend and had to spend some time in the hospital. The doctor who was treating him told his parents about him and that they should support him. After that they have supported him and he lives with them. He has his freedom, and when asked if he wants to leave Iran, he says: "I only go abroad on vacation—I love Iran and I want to stay in Iran."

NOT BECOMING A "REAL" MAN: MARRIAGE AND CONSCRIPTION

The obligatory military service—conscription (*sarbazi*)—on the one hand, and the institution of marriage on the other hand, often came up in the narratives of my informants. The sole thought of having to serve in the armed forces for 18 months or more, or entering into a heterosexual marriage, often caused them stress and anxiety. Thus, most of them tried to employ some strategies, either to avoid undertaking these social obligations or to find some ways to make them more bearable. In other words, adjusting their gay identity and same-sex desires in order to meet these social obligations, which are often discursively constructed as a test of manhood—male rites of passage—symbolizes the transition into adulthood and the society of men (Lehtonen 2015). In terms of marriage, the pressure mostly came from family members, as getting married and establishing your own family is, in Iranian culture, still considered to be an important duty—marking a transition from childhood into adulthood. In fact, irrespective of gender, at a certain age, you are expected to settle down and marry—terminating your life as a single person, and moving out of your parents' house and establishing your own home. Najmabadi has pointed out that "getting married was, and continues to be, a life-cycle social expectation, without which one does not become an adult in others' and possibly in one's own perception" (Najmabadi 2014, p. 123). Thus, most of my informants felt the power of what Najmabadi (2014) has defined as the *marriage imperative*: A form of pressure from family members to marry, but also an important part of the *heteronormalizing obligation* (p. 123). Men, compared to women, normally feel the force of the marriage imperative later as it is more socially acceptable for males to defer their marriage to a much later age (Najmabadi 2014, p. 271). Thus, most of my informants started to feel real pressure to get married when they were reaching their 30s. However, all of them were aware early on of their social obligation to find a girl and settle down, as can be read from Pouria's narrative. His relatives constantly reminded him of his *heteronormalizing obligation*, wishing that he would marry sooner rather than later. Thus, the pressure to get married or enter a heterosexual relationship is a recurrent theme that gay-identifying men and women in Iran speak about, and which they have to take into consideration when navigating between their gay identity and the straight social environment.

In that sense, many of my informants talked about the need to account for themselves and invent stories as a foil for their gay sexuality in order to temporally ease the pressure from their families to find, or rather to present, a suitable opposite-sex partner in marriage. Arslan, for example, mentioned that he told his parents that he was still too young and wanted to pursue university studies before getting married. Ali Reza also found some excuses to avoid the pressure of the marriage imperative:

Ali Reza: They [my parents] are looking for a wife for me. They are looking for a good girl for me to marry.
Jón: What do you tell your parents?
Ali Reza: That I first need to finish my military service.
Jón: After that you should get married?
Ali Reza: Yes.
Jón: You think you can somehow say no, avoid the marriage?
Ali Reza: I have many girlfriends but I cannot have sex with them.
Jón: Because you like men?
Ali Reza: Yes.
Jón: But what are you going to say to your parents when they find a girl for you to marry, after your military service?
Ali Reza: I don't know.

As can be seen from our chat, Ali Reza's strategy is to defer his future marriage until after his obligatory military service. He knows that his parents can accept it as it is considered to be one's duty to serve in the armed forces and become a "real" man. Being 26 years old and still studying at the university, he will not have to finish his military service any time soon and will therefore be able to postpone his marriage at least for some years to come. However, when I ask him what he will do after he finishes his military service, he doesn't have an answer—he simply does not know. He might continue postponing his marriage by finding some new excuses, as mentioned by many of my informants: I need to find a good job and earn some money, the girls proposed by the family are not beautiful enough, not rich enough, not educated, and so on. In the end, the family might just give up finding a suitable future wife and ease the marriage pressure. However, this is not always a solution to the problem, and sometimes the family set their sons an ultimatum. Najmabadi gives, for instance, an example of an MtF (Male-to-Female)-identifying individual who was faced with two options, death or marriage, of which she chooses the latter in the end. In her case, the family assumed that by entering a heterosexual marriage, she would be cured of her gender non-conformity (Najmabadi 2014, p. 271). Thus, the marriage is often used as a "cure" to force those who do not conform to either gender and/or (hetero)sexual normativities to change their "deviant behavior," and adapt to the heterosexual matrix in which gender, sex, and sexuality are seen as a unity. This also applies to the obligatory military service, of which many Iranian families press their sons to enter, particularly if they are seen as effeminate or if they are assumed to be non-heterosexual. The purpose here is the same—to cure any sexual or gender "deviance" and make men out of them (Najmabadi 2014, p. 271; Connell 2008; Sinclair-Webb 2000).

Mika, who identifies as gay and gender-queer, felt the pressure from family members to enter the military service. He said that during his time there, he tried to be "masculine and act as a man." He was, however, never able to hide his true identity, and his fellow conscripts soon noticed that he was somehow different from the others. This, however, turned into an opportunity for Mika, as he became sought after and found lovers among them. Some of them even kept him under their protection because they really liked him. For Mika, the military service was thus a learning experience and an opportunity to find lovers among his fellow conscripts. Seeing the obligatory military service as an opportunity could also be noted in Ali Reza narrative, in which he perceives it as a solution to the marriage imperative, at least for the time being. Moreover, he does not seem to have a choice other than entering the military service. In the following excerpt from a chat I had with Ali Reza at a gay party in Tehran, he expresses his thoughts about the military service:

Ali Reza: I am finishing my studies, master degree, and I want to go to military service after that because here in Iran, you must do that. I know this will be very hard for me.

Jón: The military?

Ali Reza: Yes, but we can tell the authorities that we are gay and then we get an exemption from the military service. I don't want that. It is bad for my future when I want to work because I will have

	this on my file forever. I will have some problems finding a job.
Jón:	They have a code on the exemption card that says that you are sick?
Ali Reza:	Yes a special code that says I am sick, meaning I am gay.
Jón:	But you don't want to do that?
Ali Reza:	No I don't want that because I will not find a good job in Iran after that. They will maybe check the code.
Jón:	Are you afraid to enter the military service?
Ali Reza:	Yes because I love soldiers in uniform. I don't know, what can I do (laughter)?
Jón:	Many soldiers will be in uniform there.
Ali Reza:	Yes. I don't like to use guns. I am afraid of guns. But I have to do that in the military.
Jón:	So you just have to finish it.
Ali Reza:	Yes.

Similar to Mika, Ali Reza tries to see something positive about his conscription in the near future—"soldiers in uniforms," which he joyfully fetishizes. However, it is clear from his narrative that he has no other choice than to undertake the conscription, both in terms of future job opportunities and also, as mentioned previously, to delay his marriage. Applying for the exemption card is thus not an option, as he does not want to run the risk of being stigmatized. Some of my other informants opted for the exemption card, which I describe in the following ethnographic poem. I base it on my ethnographic data as well as my own feelings and personal interpretation of all the narratives and stories in connection to the topic: "The exemption card."

Ethnographic poem
The exemption card

What is it?
It's a card
Made of plastic
It is not red
Because red is for crazy people
I am not crazy—am I?
It has my picture on it
I cannot smile or look happy in the picture—I need to be serious

It has my number on it—my social security number 1 2 8 9 6 ...
I am a number
It has a code describing my condition
The code states the nature of my condition
I am sick
I am gay
I am sexually abnormal
I am psychologically unfit to serve my country
Unfit to become a solider
Unfit to become a real man

....

How do I get it?

Session after a session with a psychologist
Forensic psychologist approved by the authorities
So expensive—every session is 15.000 toman
Finally I get a certificate of my sickness
It says
I am sexually abnormal
I am unfit to serve
I go to the registration office
I fill out some forms
I go again
I fill out some more forms
I go back in the line
I get a stamp
Interviews with the military authorities
They ask
They examine
I confess
I am gay
I am sick
I like men
I like wearing women's clothes
They ask
They examine
I go home
I feel depressed
I wait
Did the post arrive today?

I wait
Letter
Card is here
Salvation!
Or
Stigma?
I am marked for life
I have a disease
I am unfit to serve
Will I get a job?
Will someone hire a sick person?
I am an abject
I am not a real man
I am gay
I am Iranian

Generally, compulsory military service applies to all Iranian males from the age of 18 to 40, and its duration is, on average, 21 months. However, there are some limited exemptions available, such as being the only son of the family, the sole caretaker of parents/siblings, or having demonstrable exceptional scholastic achievements (Country of Origin Information Portal 2017, November 9). Eligible conscripts can also apply for an exemption on some other grounds, such as disability or mental/physical illnesses. For gay-identifying Iranians, there is also an option to apply for an exemption from the compulsory military service (OutRight Action International 2016, July 28). However, as I indicate in the above ethnographic poem, the process of getting that kind of an exemption card entails undergoing numerous physical and psychological tests and exams, and providing intimate information regarding your personal life. In fact, those gay-identifying men who opt for this kind of an exemption, have to accept their pathological subject position, being categorized as mentally "ill"—"sick"—by the military authorities. This kind of categorization, as well as having to confess their sexual identity, opens them up for more intensified surveillance, official stigmatization, and discrimination (Human Rights Watch 2010; Reaching Out Winnipeg 2013, August 13). Pouria talks about his experience in securing an exemption from mandatory military service:

We have some exemptions [from military service] of which one of them is proof that you are homosexual. [This] means that you have some kind of mental disorder. Military doctors will test and evaluate you psychologically, and after that they interview you again to decide whether you are really gay or not. Actually most of these doctors are not knowledgeable enough. They just know that there are feminine boys, and that these feminine boys are homosexuals. If you are not feminine enough they will not categorize you as homosexual. So most people who go there will act feminine even if they are not. They are wearing certain clothes to make them look feminine. I got this kind of an exemption card easily, but my boyfriend face[d] some problems because they sa[id] that he acts like a "normal" guy, and that he can correct his way of being by undertaking some therapy. Then he can return to leading [a] "normal" life as a heterosexual. But I talked to his mother and I asked her to come to the military medical office and to tell them that her son was like this, that when he was boy he played with dolls, he did these "girlish" things. She came there and she said all these things and after that they gave him the exemption card.

Pouria's account reveals the particular gender dynamics involving deliberate and conscious gender performativity that is at play in securing exemption from military service (Butler 1990). He highlights how the homosexual subject becomes intelligible in the eyes of the state only through the embodied and performative inscription of femininity, which negates any trace of masculinity, the latter also serving as the indicator of a diagnostic basis for ruling out the possibility of being gay (Martino and Kjaran 2019). Such gender performances in terms of diagnosing one's sexuality have also been reported in other Middle Eastern contexts. Oyman Basaran, for example, argues that military authorities in Turkey are directly influenced "by the culturally specific stereotype of homosexuality" in its association with effeminacy as a basis for determining exemption for gay draftees (Basaran 2014).[4] In order to secure exemption, they need to perform their gender in "feminine" ways and are required to declare an affinity for a passive role in sexual relationships. Thus, these state-sanctioned practices regarding what counts as a legible category of person and acceptable sexual personhood cannot be easily disentangled from the culturally inscribed norms of performing one's gender within the grid of a heterosexual matrix (Butler 1990; Martino and Kjaran 2019; Zengin 2016).

"I wish [that] you [will] marry one day"
Pouria

Pouria is in his 30s and lives with his boyfriend in a nice neighborhood in the northern part of Tehran. Their flat is large and nicely furnished. I compliment them on their flat and ask Pouria if they have encountered any difficulties living together as a couple: "Actually we are living in one of the most expensive neighborhoods [in Tehran]. People here are less traditional and not as religious as in other parts of the city, for example in the south of Tehran." However, as Pouria mentioned later in our talk, even here they need to be careful and not draw too much attention to themselves: "I have to be careful about [the] guests that come to my house because sometimes my landlord asks me: 'Why [do] you only invite men/guys to your home? Why don't you have a girlfriend?'" Pouria "came out" to his parents some years ago. "My parents are so traditional but they also have some kind of secular attitude. So when I told them that I am gay they did not accept it but told me that it is your life and you have to decide what you want to do." Hence, for Pouria being gay is an open secret and he rarely talks about his private life with his parents. He never takes his boyfriend for a visit to his parents, and they never ask him about his personal life. "They only advise me to leave Iran and say to me that this kind of life is not accepted here. Especially my father is insisting that I leave." Leaving Iran would not be easy for Pouria as he has a boyfriend who he cares about. However, he admits that he sees no future for himself or his boyfriend in Iran: "I don't like the lifestyle here. I want to be free which is not possible in Iran. Even if I were not gay, it would be difficult to live freely in Iran. However, the gay thing makes everything more difficult." One example Pouria mentions in that respect is the pressure he feels from relatives and friends about having a girlfriend or getting married: "When I started university most of my friends were in some kind of relationship with girls and I felt the pressure to find a girlfriend. I really like girls but when it came to hav[ing] more of a serious relationship I started to find some excuses, like saying she is not beautiful enough, she is shorter than me or she is not rich enough." Hence, similar to other informants, Pouria became an expert in finding excuses to ward off the pressure of having a serious relationship with a

(continued)

(continued)

girl. However, living a double life and constantly trying to conform to the rules of heteronormativity made Pouria feel sad and depressed: "It becomes so depressing and after a while you get so tired having to lie and live with a straight mask. For example, I cannot take my boyfriend with me when I meet my family—for parties or family gatherings. All my relatives have their girlfriends or wives with them and the only thing they say to me is that they wish that I [will] marry one day."

LIVING TOGETHER AS A GAY COUPLE IN TEHRAN

Tehran has undergone enormous changes during the past few decades, and its population has grown considerably. This has pushed up rent, which has made it more difficult for young people to be able to afford to live alone. Thus, for many, the only option to move out of their parents' home is by sharing a rental apartment with a friend of the same gender or by entering into a marriage (Afary 2009). This kind of arrangement is fully acceptable and normally does not raise any suspicion. Thus, for gays and lesbians, living together as a same-sex couple, at least in a big city such as Tehran, is considered to be rather easy, as long as you keep it a secret and do not show affection in public. The gay couple I visited and talked to during my fieldwork confirmed this and said that two young men living together was not seen as strange, taking into account the high rental prices. In fact, for two men or women living together as a same-sex "couple," it is often easier than for heterosexual unmarried couples, and rarely raises any suspicions from neighbors. This is, among other things, due to the strict gender segregation, which facilitates intimacy and homosocial interaction between individuals of same gender, whereas the opposite gender, for example, unmarried "couples," will find it more difficult to interact in public or live together under the same roof. There are, of course, some exceptions to that rule, all depending on the individual situation and the attitudes of the family. But generally, for unrelated individuals of the opposite gender, living together will, in the long run, be problematic, or at least raise the suspicions of neighbors, which may even result in complaints to the authorities (Afary 2009).

Although it is easier for same-sex couples to live together, they are still under the scrutiny of their neighbors. Najmabadi (2014) has pointed out that even in big cities like Tehran, Iranians care about their neighbors and want to know who their neighbors are and what they are doing. This kind "caring" can, in fact, be interpreted as curiosity, an intrusion into your private life. "Iranians are rather curious, especially the neighbors. They think they have the right to know everything about other people's [lives]," Pouria explained when I asked him about his neighbors. It is, therefore, necessary to be careful and discreet in order to not cause the neighbors any "discomfort" or give them an excuse to file a complaint to the local *kumitah* (committee) (Najmabadi 2014, p. 258). In the case of Pouria and his boyfriend, who live in one of the most expensive neighborhoods in Tehran, there are some precautions needed: "My neighbors don't know that I am gay or that we are a couple. I have to conceal it all the time and I have to be careful about my guests who come to my house because sometimes my landlord will ask me why I only invite men to my house. You might find it a bit nosy but this is in fact rather common in Iran." Pouria mentions that he sometimes needs to be careful about whom he invites to his home in order to not raise any suspicions. For example, his guest cannot be too "flashy" or "gay looking," as discussed previously (Fig. 5.2).

Farhod and Basir were also aware of the *panoptic gaze* of their neighbors, especially when they invited friends over. I, for example, noted that during gay parties, guests would arrive in rather formal clothes in order

Fig. 5.2   In love watching the Tehran skyline

not to draw any attention, but then they would change their clothes after they entered the apartment. Mika, who identifies as gay and gender-queer, for example, came in dressed as a man, but then changed his clothes right away in the bathroom, putting on a mini skirt, revealing blouse, make-up, and a wig. I asked Farhod about this, and he confirmed that this was part of the play, keeping a low public profile in order to not raise any suspicions or questions from the neighbors. Thus, even within the confines of their home, they need to be careful and disciplined and censor their behavior and that of their guests.

Living together under the same roof is not always possible for gay couples as both economic factors and age can influence their decision to move in together. Muhammad, who is in his 50s and lives alone in a nice flat in northern part of Tehran, told me that it would raise suspicions if he would have his boyfriend living with him. Although Muhammad is affluent and regularly holds gay parties for his friends, he would have difficulties living with his boyfriend, as it is not expected that two men, after a certain age, will live together. This kind of cohabitation is socially acceptable for younger men or students, out of economic necessity. In fact, Muhammad should, in line with the cultural script, already be married and living together with his wife. Other informants mentioned that, due to lack of economic support from family, they could not afford to move out of their parents' homes and live with their boyfriends. As a matter of fact, most of my informants lived with their parents, and if they had a partner/boyfriend, they only saw him once or twice a week. Moreover, as mentioned previously, finding a place for intimacy was often hard and required them to be both patient and resourceful.

Gender can also play an important role when same-sex couples want to live together, as it is somehow easier for two women to live together than for two men, especially if they are students and young. Leila, a self-identifying lesbian in Najmabadi's study, for example, gave the following explanation for better living possibilities for lesbian couples: "when two men live together and one of them looks effeminate ... neighbors keep them under surveillance" (Najmabadi 2014, p. 258). This does not apply as much to lesbians according to Najmabadi's informant, as it can often be easier to tell a gay appearance than a lesbian one. Thus, as discussed previously, being effeminate is often associated with being gay, and can raise questions from neighbors, and influence the possibilities of cohabitation for those gay couples that do not censor their behavior and act "straight." In other words, gay men living together should not be "gay looking," at least not in public.

"We are only small dots in the universe"
Farhod and Basir
Together for 2 years and 20 days

I went with Arash (my key informant) to the Navad neighborhood, in the center of Tehran. We were on our way to meet a gay couple, Farhod and Basir, who had invited us for a gay gathering later that evening. They had lived in Isfahan before moving to Tehran six months ago. The reason they moved was because life in Isfahan was getting too difficult. "We could not find a good flat there and we had to live in a poor neighbourhood with [a] lot of problems. People there did not have any knowledge about the outside world; they were narrow minded, and religious. For example, when I went to the supermarket some of them came up to me and asked why I was dressed in that way," said Farhod about their experience of living together in Isfahan. So they moved to Tehran, and have been living in this small flat for the past six months. "We can live easily here and nobody needs to know anything about us. It is actually very normal for two boys to live together—I mean we don't get any questions about this," says Basir. The family of Basir knows that he is gay, but only his father knows the true nature of his and Farhod's relationship. His mother only thinks that they are friends. Farhod's family does not know anything about his gay life and thinks that Basir is his roommate and best friend, and that they are living together for economic reasons—to share the rent. Farhod thus regularly gets questions from his family about when he is going to get married. "I tell them that I don't want to get married because I cannot afford it now. I have to get a better job and I tell them that maybe when I am 50 I will consider it. But I am not a person that feels pressured from anything so I don't care what they say." They have had their share of hardships in life, which has put a strain on their relationship. Farhod was arrested and tortured during the 2009 protests, which I will discuss further in Chap. 6. Since then, he has not been able to secure a stable job, and sometimes the money has been scare—despite getting financial support from their families. "It has sometimes been difficult for us and when we have no money left we have to eat dry bread." Farhod has also had some psychological problems related to

(continued)

(continued)

his traumatic experience in prison and being tortured, and for a time he drank too much and smoked cannabis. However, his partner, Basir, always stood by him and supported him when he was feeling depressed. "He accepted me and now we are here. I am working now and our life is getting better," says Farhod. I sensed that they truly love each other, and I felt the care they showed each other, holding hands and giving each other romantic eye contact. They have been together for 2 years and 20 days. They wear matching (identical) rings, which they told me symbolized their engagement. They want to be united and together—whether they move out of Iran or not. "We just hope for the best. We are only small dots in the universe," Farhod said, referring to Stephen Hawking and scientific theories about the construction of the universe and life in general.

Transforming the Self: Emigrate to the West or Live as a Gay Subject in Iran

A recurrent theme in the narratives of my informants is whether they should leave Iran or not. It was often not an easy task to reach that decision and to follow it through, as many factors were needed to be taken into consideration. Moreover, some of them did not want to leave Iran whatsoever and were, in fact, happy with their lives in Iran. Morteza gives an example in his narrative of some of those factors involved, which, in many ways, can be framed within Foucauldian ethics of the self, discussed in Chap. 2. Before Morteza took the drastic decision to leave Iran and his mother, he had worked for many years on his self. He was therefore very aware that he was constituted by certain modes of subjections: the pressure of being a heterosexual son who would eventually get married, for example. Thus, telling the truth about himself and confronting his mother on these issues was, for him, the beginning of transforming the self, as can be seen in the following quote:

Finally, I decided to talk to my mother and tell her everything about myself because she had only heard things about me from somebody else. I however wanted to tell her after 22 years of [lying about] who I was so, I started to talk to her about homosexuality and explain what it meant to be gay.

As can be seen from the quote, telling the truth about his inner self can be interpreted as *parrhesia*, which refers to telling the truth about oneself, not in the confessional Christian way, but more in order to relate to others and become a "subject of truth" without sacrifice of the self. The truth telling was, therefore, a way to expand the limits of his subjectivity, symbolically but also spatially in the sense that he claimed a space for his feelings and identity within his own home. However, for his mother, homosexuality was outside the grids of intelligibility. For her, and in line with the official discourse, homosexuality is a disease and therefore unacceptable. Thus, Morteza decided to leave Iran as the only option left in order to transform the self and find ways of reconstituting the self. In fact, by leaving Iran, he was resisting the homophobic views of his mother and conveying a message to her that if you cannot accept me as I am, you will have to live alone for the rest of your life. In Iranian and Middle Eastern cultural memory, living alone is viewed negatively, as family values and traditions are still held in high esteem, and one should be surrounded by family members (Gregg 2005). Thus, after Morteza left, his mother begged him to come back home, crying constantly and promising him to change her ways.

In terms of practicality, it was rather easy for Morteza to travel from Iran to Turkey, as he was in possession of a passport and did not require a visa. However, for most Iranian gays, getting a passport is often the first obstacle when you decide to leave Iran. Only those who have finished military service (*sarbazi*) or those who get an exemption from it (see previous section) can apply for a passport. Thus, for gay-identifying Iranian men, there are only two options for getting a passport, both of them time-consuming: Do the army draft for almost two years or apply for exemption. However, there are some other exceptions, as discussed in previous sections, which applied to Morteza, being the sole caretaker of his mother. Thus, Morteza did not have to go through the difficult and time-consuming process of applying for an exemption card in order to get his passport. He was also rather young, 22 years old, when he decided to leave Iran, and could therefore easily have been able to start a new life in the West.

Armin, who is in his 40s and identifies as gay, mentioned youth as a factor in terms of emigration:

> The young gays are leaving Iran. That is one of the greatest regrets of my life. I had the opportunity when I was young to move to Canada and stay with my uncle. However, my parents did not want me to go. So I stayed with them. I regret it so much today. It is easier when you are in your twenties to leave—you can start over again. But now, it is too late for me. I['d] have to give up my career here and my education has no value abroad. I just don't have the courage anymore.

Armin clearly connects emigration with being young, and for him it is not an option any more to leave Iran. His transformation of the self entailed accepting his situation and accommodating his gay identify with his social context and the official disavowal of homosexuality. Amin was, thus, very much aware of how he is constituted by certain modes of subjections—such as keeping your sexual identity within your private sphere. What is also interesting and can be seen both in Morteza's and Armin's narratives is their dialectic relationship with their families, causing both of them some *existential splitting* (Kierkegaard 1989): On the one hand, they wanted to stay on good terms with their families and take care of them, feeling the obligation to not leave them alone in Iran. On the other hand, they found it difficult to be themselves around their families as they knew that their sexual identity and desires would never be accepted by them. Morteza tried to confront his mother on this issue, and after she rejected him, he left Iran; however, he came back some weeks later after she promised to treat him better. Armin, on the other hand, did not tell his family about his inner self, but, at the same time, he could not leave them when he had the opportunity to do so when he was younger. Thus, both of them had to apply some tactics to navigate their sexual identity within their social environment—putting on a mask within one context and taking it off in another, or as Morteza expresses in his narrative: "play[ing] out the straight script."

Mehrdad, who is in his 30s and identifies as gay, took a rather critical stance toward those who left Iran. In his view, emigration on the basis of sexuality had in fact more to do with securing a better economic existence in the West: "[It is] not because of the religion or the government, they just say that they are gay to get citizenship in the West." In fact, these arguments have often been put forward by immigration offices in the West, and been used as the basis on which gay refugees have been denied asylum, and in some instances been sent back to their home country. However, Mehrdad also acknowledges that sometimes the pressure from the family can be unbearable, pushing those who do not fit into the heterosexual matrix to move out of Iran. He himself has not experienced that kind of pressure and in fact keeps his life rather private from his family. However, many of his friends have left Iran because of this kind pressure from the family:

> I think they are running away from their families not from Iran, I mean not from [the] government. A friend of mine, who is gay, was pressured constantly by his family to get married and he could not even shave his face because his family is very religious. So he left Iran. However, when I have a chat with my friends that have left, they tell me that they miss Iran and they['d] like to come back. Why? Because it's difficult to live in the West, even in terms of [having] sex, it can be difficult to find your "type" outside of Iran. So many of them wish to come back to Iran, for example, when their family gets older and they can maybe live more of an independent life.

Mehrdad summarizes quite well some of the tasks involved in terms of ethics of being and care of the self. For many gay-identifying Iranians, this mostly means coming to terms with your family and finding tactical means to pursue your life. This might entail leaving Iran due to social and family pressures or putting on a straight mask, which means splitting your existence between the privacy of your desires and feelings, and the social context of family and friends. Both options can be difficult and stressful. Mehrdad, for example, indicates in the quote that leaving Iran is not always the best solution and, as he has experienced through his friends, the "gay" life in the West can be quite difficult and not without problems of its own. It takes time to adapt to a new country, and being there without any support from your family can be difficult. In that sense, the narratives presented in this section exemplify the polyphony of the embodied experiences of gay-identifying Iranian males. These narratives and embodied experiences are not unified and simple, of which the main focus is on leaving Iran for the *gay utopia* of the West, but rather it is a complex process of adjudication of being and becoming, in which keeping a good relationship with your family is weighed against the care of the self.

"I just breathe, I do not have any life here"
Morteza

Morteza is in his 20s. He is an engineer student at the University of Tehran and lives alone with his mother who divorced his father 12 years ago, when he was 11 years old. His father lives in another city, and he sees him once a year for a couple of days. "He does not want to know me. He does not know anything about my sexuality," said Morteza when I asked him about his relationship with his father. Hence, his mother raised him single-handedly. From a young age, Morteza knew that he was "different," and in high school he started to have sexual feelings for boys rather than girls: "I tried to ignore it because of God and family." After he started university, he lived in the dormitory, and there he met his first boyfriend. At that time, he was still very religious and felt some inner conflict between his religious beliefs and the relationship with his boyfriend: "I believed that this [was] wrong. I felt guilty every time we had sex." They became roommates and their relationship developed further. However, they faced some problems, especially due to their surroundings: the stress of keeping it a secret and the constant fear that someone would "find out" about the true nature of their relationship. In addition, they did not know much about relationships and their feelings of same-sex desire: "We did not know anything about homosexuality." This caused them to argue a lot and a couple of times they did so in public, sometimes in front of friends who started to suspect that something was going on between them. Finally, Morteza decided to quit the relationship—it was causing him too much stress and pain. However, his former boyfriend took their breakup really badly and told some of their mutual friends about their relationship: "It was the worse part of my life because my best friend found out that I was in a relationship with [my former boyfriend]. He found out that I am homosexual and he started to ignore me. I had a stressful situation and I really had suicidal thoughts." He told his mother about his depressive state, without referring to the real reason behind it; she found a psychologist for him and he started to attend regular sessions, during which he told his psychologist "every detail" of his life. "I was really a simple [naïve] person, because he was not one [to] accept these things. In Iran, most of the psychologists think that homosexuality is a disease

(*continued*)

(continued)

or abnormality and that it is possible to cure it." Hence, in the beginning, Morteza believed that he could change his sexuality and he tried to follow the advice of his consultant: "He told me that I should sign up for kung-Fu or some martial arts classes. He said that this kind of exercise will make you masculine and stronger, and by doing this you will change your homosexual behavior. I really tried it, but I hated it, so I gave up after attending three martial arts sessions. I came to the conclusion that I cannot change my sexuality or orientation, it is something fixed." Morteza started to read about homosexuality and decided to terminate his session with the psychologist. "That was the start of my disaster." After that the psychologist called his mother and told her everything. "He told her that I was homosexual and that I had [a] boyfriend at the university." The relationship with his mother became tense. "My mother did not treat me well and I started to have arguments with her every day. She told me that she would tell everybody about me and even call the university." Morteza then decided to leave Iran and took a flight from Tehran to Ankara. After having stayed three weeks in Turkey, he returned to Tehran. "I could not leave her and I had no money. I did not know what to do. I could not leave Iran." Although his mother had promised him that things would change, everything stayed the same. "She told me that if you decide to live as a homosexual I would prefer not to see you anymore." Hence, Morteza decided to act out the "straight script." "Now she thinks I have girlfriends and that I have changed. She treats me well now because I am living as a heterosexual and [in] my family nobody knows that I am homosexual." Morteza still wishes to leave Iran: "I don't have any future in Iran. I just breathe, I don't have any life here."

CLAIMING SPACE THROUGH WORKING AT THE LIMIT AT THE SELF

In this chapter, different stories about practices of the self were told from the perspective of my informants, who all identify as gay. The practices of the self entailed both knowing and caring for the self. The "knowing" aspect of the self focused on practices related to coming to terms with your sexuality and adopting a gay identity. In other words, it was making confessions about your sexual or gender identity—telling the truth about your inner self. This was, however, not done in the Christian confessional way, but more in order to relate to others and become a "subject of truth" without sacrifice of the self. The truth telling was, therefore, a way to expand the limits of one's subjectivity, both symbolically and spatially in the sense that most of my informants tried to claim a space for their feelings and identity. In other words, working on those liminal spaces in which you can be yourself. These liminal spaces were both made and remade, depending on time, place, circumstances, and the occasion. I will discuss further the making and remaking of spaces in Chap. 8, specifically in relation to the heterotopic queer spaces created and (re)made by the members of the underground gay community in Tehran. These spaces are outside the traditional normative or dominant institutional spaces of power, which normally constituted their gay existence. Thus, an important part of the process of taking care of the self was to become aware of the various modes of subjection and how one was constituted by those same modes, for example, the pressure of being a heterosexual son who would eventually get married. Thus, in order to make their life meaningful, have sex, go on a date, or spend intimate time with their boyfriends, different strategies were employed, within the limits of their own subjugation. They, therefore, all tried to transform the self in a Foucauldian sense, within the liminal space of their gay existence—whether avoiding the marriage imperative, finding a place for sex, or just establishing some connection to the underground gay community.

NOTES

1. Khosravi refers to Mostafa Rahimi, an Iranian expert on Shahnameh, who has argued that within Iranian culture, there is a "son-killing complex" (see Khosravi 2008, p. 133).
2. *Versatile* or vers is a person who enjoys both sexual roles of topping and bottoming.
3. See discussion on this in Chap. 3.
4. In Turkey as in Iran, those individuals who apply for exemption from the military service because they identity as gay are often discharged on the basis of "psychological illness." This can influence their possibilities of state employment in the future. Even in some cases, private employers have sought information about the military service of their future male employees (see here Human Right Watch 2008).

REFERENCES

Afary, J. (2009). *Sexual Politics in Modern Iran*. Cambridge: Cambridge University Press.

Basaran, O. (2014, March 10). "You Are Like a Virus:" Dangerous Bodies and Military Medical Authority in Turkey. *Gender and Society, 28*(4), 562–582. https://doi.org/10.1177/0891243214526467.

Beachy, R. (2015). *Gay Berlin: Birthplace of a Modern Identity*. New York: Vintage Press.

Butler, J. (1990). *Gender Trouble. Feminism and the Subversion of Identity*. New York: Routledge.

Butler, J. (2005). *Giving an Account of Oneself*. New York: Fordham University Press.

Connell, R. (2008). A Thousand Miles from Kind: Men, Masculinities and Modern Institutions. *The Journal of Men's Studies, 16*(3), 237–252.

Country of Origin Information Portal. Ministry of Internally Displaced Persons from the Occupied Territories, Accommodation and Refugees of Georgia. (2017, November 9). Iran. Exemption from the Compulsory Military Service. Retrieved from http://coi-mra.gov.ge/en/2017/11/09/iran-exemption-from-the-compulsory-military-service-november-2017/#_ftnref10.

Fanon, F. (2008). *Black Skin, White Masks* (C. L. Markmann, Trans.). London: Pluto Press.

Foucault, M. (1988). Technologies of the Self. In L. Martin, H. Gutman, & P. Hutton (Eds.), *Technologies of the Self: A Seminar with Michel Foucault* (pp. 16–49). Amherst: University of Massachusetts Press.

Goldstein, J. S. (2003). War and Gender. In C. R. Ember & M. Ember (Eds.), *Encyclopedia of Sex and Gender. Men and Women in the World's Cultures* (pp. 107–116). New York: Kluwer Academic /Plenum Publishers.

Gregg, G. S. (2005). *The Middle East. A Cultural Psychology*. Oxford: Oxford University Press.

Human Rights Watch. (2008). We Need a Law for Liberation. Gender, Sexuality, and Human Rights in a Changing Turkey. Retrieved from https://www.hrw.org/sites/default/files/reports/turkey0508webwcover.pdf.

Human Rights Watch. (2010). We Are a Buried Generation. Discrimination and Violence Against Sexual Minorities in Iran. Retrieved from https://www.hrw.org/sites/default/files/reports/iran1210webwcover_0.pdf.

Khosravi, S. (2008). *Young and Defiant in Tehran*. Philadelphia: University of Pennsylvania Press.

Kierkegaard, S. (1989). *The Sickness Unto Death* (A. Hannay, Trans.). London: Penguin.

Lehtonen, J. (2015). Going to the 'Men's School'? Non-heterosexual and Trans Youth Choosing Military Service in Finland. *NORMA: International Journal for*

Masculinity Studies, 10(2), 117–135. https://doi.org/10.1080/18902138. 2015.1050861.

Manchanda, N. (2014). Queering the Pashtun: Afghan Sexuality in the Homo-nationalist Imaginary. *Third World Quarterly, 36*(1), 130–146. https://doi.org/10.1080/01436597.2014.974378.

Martino, W., & Kjaran, J. I. (2019). The Politics of Recognizability: Giving an Account of Iranian Gay Men's Lives Under Repressive Conditions of Sexuality Governance. *International Journal of Middle East Studies, 51* (1), 21–41.

Najmabadi, A. (2014). *Professing Selves: Transsexuality and Same-Sex Desire in Contemporary Iran*. Durham, NC: Duke University Press.

OutRight Action International. (2016, July 28). Human Rights Report: Being Transgender in Iran. Retrieved from http://www.refworld.org/docid/58c2b6e44.html.

Reaching Out Winnipeg. (2013, August 13). Gay Men in Iran's Military Can Seek Exemption. Retrieved from https://reachingoutwinnipeg.com/2013/08/13/gay-men-in-irans-military-can-seek-exemption/.

Schut, M., & van Baarle, E. (2017, January). Dancing Boys and the Moral Dilemmas of Military Missions: The Practice of Bacha Bazi in Afghanistan. In A. B. Bah (Ed.), *International Security and Peace Building. Africa, the Middle East, and Europe*. Bloomington and Indianapolis: Indiana University Press.

Sinclair-Webb, E. (2000). "Our Bülent Is Now a Commando": Military Service and Manhood in Turkey. In M. Ghoussoub & E. Sinclair-Webb (Eds.), *Imagined Masculinities: Male Identity and Culture in the Modern Middle East* (pp. 65–92). London: Saqi Books.

Zengin, A. (2016, July). Violent Intimacies. Tactile State Power, Sex / Gender Transgression, and the Politics of Touch in Contemporary Turkey. *Journal of Middle East Women's Studies, 12*(2), 225–245. https://doi.org/10.1215/15525864-3507650.

CHAPTER 6

Iranian Gay/Queer Activists and Activism

The Stonewall Riots that broke out in June 1969 at a gay bar in the Greenwich Village, New York, have in the historiography of the Western gay liberation movement been epitomized as the beginning of sexual (queer) activism and mark the beginning of the gay and lesbian liberation movement (Armstrong and Crage 2006).[1] During that warm June night, drag queens, lesbians, and other sexual "outcasts" fought back and protested the official harassment from the local police authorities that had regularly raided the bar and arrested those queers who looked effeminate or queer (D'Emilio 1992a, 1992b). Over the following years and decades, the Stonewall Riots became a symbol for gay/queer resistance and activism (D'Emilio 2002). Today, it is commemorated in gay pride parades all over the world in which the emphasis is on queer visibility and recognition of sexual and gender diversity: "We're here! We're queer! Get used to it!" (Queer Nation NY 2016).[2] In that sense, the Stonewall Riots marked a rupture in terms of gay liberation and activism, moving away from the previous tactics of the homophile movement which aimed for assimilation, acceptance, and tolerance to more radical methods of gay/queer activism, in which the aim is not only to gain sexual rights and recognition but also to confront and destabilize the hegemonic norms on sexuality and gender performances (Brown 2015). Thus, in terms of the gay/queer resistance and activism, the post-Stonewall discourse came into being, which draws on a mythical liberation narrative and a collective memory of the past struggles (D'Emilio 1992a). Today, it is celebrated globally, not only in

© The Author(s) 2019
J. I. Kjaran, *Gay Life Stories*,
https://doi.org/10.1007/978-3-030-12831-9_6

Western "gay/queer" capitals such as Berlin, Madrid, New York, and San Francisco, but increasingly in the global south, where the nascent gay/queer social movements have in some cases organized pride parades and other social events.

However, the pride narrative celebrating visibility and "coming out" as a political action has not been the main focus of gay/queer activism in all social/cultural contexts in the global south. Naisargi Dave has pointed out, in her ethnographic research on lesbian activism in New Delhi (India), the challenges and dilemmas activists face (Dave 2011). For example, they need to evaluate the limitations and possibilities of identity-based politics in their activist work. Should they, for example, adopt a Western approach to activism, in which the emphasis is on disclosure of sexual identity and the attainment of equal rights? In other words, employ the Western notion of "coming out" as a political action and a strategy. Or should they aim for anonymity and reject predefined sexual identities? As Dave explores further, lesbian groups in New Delhi took different approaches to these questions—some aimed for more identity-based politics, while others opted for more anonymity in their work and activities to "avoid being dismissed as westernized" (Dave 2011, p. 13).

These same dilemmas and strategies have been reported within the Middle East context where queer/gay activist groups need to navigate between disclosure of sexual identities, in line with the Western "coming out" narrative, and the politics of anonymity—putting up "masks" within the public sphere. Jason Ritchie has, in his ethnographic study on queer Palestinian activists/social movements, argued that contrary to their Israeli counterparts, queer Palestinian activists place less emphasis on visibility and recognition of particular sexual identities (Ritchie 2010). In other words, in contrast to the dominant activist discourse in the West, queer Palestinian activists reject the narrative of "coming out of the closet," with the aim of being accepted as visible and fully recognized citizens. As one of Ritchie's informants explained: "[T]here are different kinds of visibilities" (Ritchie 2010, p. 569). In other words, the Western paradigm regarding the politics of visibility—"coming out of the closet" as a political action—is just one aspect of many in terms of queer/gay activism, and cannot be applied to all cultural settings/contexts. For queer/gay Palestinians, as well as Iranians, the emphasis is on creating a community and offering mutual support instead of pursuing a politics based on identities and visibility. Thus, in order to understand the queer/gay activism among Iranian gay-identifying males, I turn again to the Foucauldian ethics of the self, which I introduced in Chap. 2. Accordingly, understanding activism as ethics draws attention to the inventive and creative practices performed in order to transform or change the discourse, and produce spaces of same-sex desire and support within the limits set by the hegemonic religious-political discourse.[3]

This chapter focuses on gay/queer activism among Iranian gay men, living inside of the Islamic Republic of Iran. It discusses what it means to be a gay activist, drawing attention to the socio-cultural context and particular historicity. It draws on interviews with gay-identifying Iranian males who could be seen/defined as activists, fighting for not only sexual rights but also political rights in general. Some of them moved out of Iran because of their activism, while others suffered at the hands of the authorities and were imprisoned. The chapter will also engage briefly with the "Green Movement" in Iran, which emerged during the 2009 presidential election (Dabashi 2011). Here, the emphasis will be on the fact that the movement and the protests in the aftermath of the 2009 presidential election were not only for political rights but also for more personal freedom, including sexual freedom. Many gay/queer Iranians participated in the protests and were members of the Green Movement. The chapter will also address blog sites and other social media sites, which have been widely used by Iranian youth to express their dissatisfaction and voice their protests with authorities (Sreberny and Khiabany 2010). Despite the strict online censorship that the Iranian authorities have in place, these online platforms have also been used by gays, whether activists or not. Thus, these online platforms are discussed in terms of gay activism, as well as their impact in creating a gay/queer social space and awareness of a particular gay community within Iran, which I will further explore in Chap. 8.

"Gandalf Is My God": Becoming a Gay/Queer Activist

Ramtin is in his 20s and lives in Istanbul as a queer refugee. When we met on a warm August afternoon, on my way to Tehran for my second fieldtrip in 2015, he had been in Istanbul for over a year. We sat down close to one of the main landmarks of the city, the Galatasaray tower, where he told me his story over a beer we had bought in a shop close by. His story mostly follows the same patterns as those of my other informants, consisting of inner conflicts, pressure from the family, religious beliefs and upbringing conflicting with sexuality, and putting up straight masks. However, his story is more tragic than those I recounted in Chap. 5, though also full of hope and an example of how you can transform your oppression and suffering into something meaningful. In Ramtin's case, becoming a queer activist and finding strength in his gay friends and activists were his means to survive and find meaning in his life after having endured both physical and psychological violence from his brother and father after they found out about his sexuality. Moreover, when he helped one of his gay friends, an addict and living on the streets, to get to one of Tehran's shadier neighborhoods where he was staying, he was gang-raped by five men and physically abused. However, looking back, Ramtin does not regret having helped his friend:

> I am not that person who doesn't want to help others. It has always been deep in me to help people, even if they have done something bad to me, it doesn't matter. I will give my last money to others in need. That is why I went there and helped my friend. I am happy I did it.

Ramtin's journey into the underground gay community began one morning when he was in a bus heading from his home to Azadi Square:

> I saw someone that felt to be so much similar to me. It was a strange feeling. He came at once and sat besides me and started to talk to me. 'Hi, how are you my lady?' I was shocked and didn't know what to say to him, and then he continued: 'Are you good?' I said: 'What does that mean, my lady?' He said: 'Are you saying that you are not?' 'What does it mean, sister, lady?' I did not know back then. So we talked more and he said: 'Yeah, I am gay like you.' Then I finally found out that I'm gay.

As can be seen from the interview excerpt, Ramtin was interpellated as gay with the words "my lady" (*khanomam* in Farsi)[4] by a fellow passenger during a bus journey. He did not know what this meant at that time but got an explanation from his fellow gay passenger, who also gave him important information where he could meet other "ladies." Hence, Ramtin gradually discovered the underground Tehran gay community and started to attend gay gatherings at a particular "gay" restaurant regularly. But why was he interpellated with the words "my lady" during the bus ride? Was it because he was "gay looking," as discussed in Chap. 5? Or were there some unexplained gay vibes, expressed non-verbally through the *gaydar* that connected them?[5] Ramtin does not provide any explanation for why this happened, but the fact remains that nothing was the same for him after this. He found support and solidarity within the "invisible" gay community of Tehran. He also started to be more conscious and even critical about his social context. In our talks, he talked about how patriarchal and (hetero)sexist Iranian society is, and that he first realized it when he and his mother were physically abused by his father and brother because of him being gay:

> In [a] patriarchal society, a son can beat his mom because he is the man. My brother and father were always beating my mom and me—blaming her for the way I was. My mother was all I had in this life; she was everything for me, and my only supporter.

Wanting to contribute to the Tehran gay community by supporting and helping other gays and those questioning their sexuality, he became an activist. "For me it is not about recognition or being visible as gay, we don't have that here in Iran anyway. It is more about support, building a community and helping others, without thinking about who you are or how you define yourself," said Ramtin, when I probed him further about his motives for becoming an activist and what it meant for him. This is in line with what Ritchie has reported in his ethnographic study on queer activism among Palestinians, in which giving support and building a community as well as taking a critical stance toward a racist/homophobic society form the basis of local queer Palestinian activism (Ritchie 2010). Hence, Ramtin began disseminating information about gay issues to those who were like him some years before the eventful bus ride—unaware of the underground gay community of Tehran and what it is to be gay. Ramtin also got involved in some queering activities which entailed taking photos in public places with either gay symbols, such as the rainbow flag, or slogans about ending homophobia and (hetero)sexism. These pictures were then posted on the gay website *Hamjensgera* with the aim of showing other queers/gays and lesbians inside of Iran that there is a community out there and that we as queers can claim or queer the public space with our presence—although done rather discreetly.[6] These pictures show the rainbow flag and slogans against homophobia in the public sphere: in busses, on the street, and in the hills surrounding Tehran, indicating that sexual and gender minorities are everywhere in public spaces although invisible and not recognized by the official discourse (Day of Fighting against Homophobia and Transphobia in Iran 2012, June). Hence, in line with understanding activism as ethics, Ramtin and his activist friends found means of performing inventive and creative activist works, the "queer photo installations," in order to transform or change the discourse and produce spaces of same-sex desire and support. However, these photo installations and raising of the rainbow flag in public had some repercussions for Ramtin. Shortly afterward, he was arrested and spent some time in jail. Most of his friends, out of fear, stopped staying in touch with him and he felt rather isolated. Around the same time, his mother died. Having nothing in Iran anymore and being branded as a gay/queer activist, he decided to leave Iran and apply for asylum in Turkey, as a gay refugee.

In Istanbul, he has continued his activism. He is much aware of how homophobic Turkish society is becoming and, in that respect, he made a comparison to Iran in our talk: "Turkey is becoming a religious fascist state just like Iran. They are banning everything and it is becoming more difficult to be a gay/queer refugee in Turkey." He, however, tries to confront the situation through activism. For example, he took part in the "illegal" Istanbul Gay Pride in 2015, when the authorities had banned it on the grounds that it clashed with the holy month of Ramadan. Force was used to disperse those who dared to march under the rainbow flag (Caliskan and Dikmen 2015). Thus, with regards to religion in general, Ramtin is very critical, especially toward Islam, as he connects most of his misery and suffering in his home country to oppression from the religious state/society, as well as from his family, who are both religious and traditional. As an indication of his disgust for any religious ideology and dogma, he does not use his actual name anymore as it has a religious (Islamic) connotation. Instead, he uses the name Ramtin after some of his friends started to call him that. He used to pray in his youth and especially after he started to feel "different," but today he has altogether turned away from religion. "Gandalf Is My God," he says when I probe him further on the issue. In fact, he is a great fan of the Tolkien trilogy, *The Lord of the Rings*, and, for him, Gandalf, the white-haired wizard (played by actor Ian McKellan who identifies as gay and has often spoken out for gay/queer rights) and the guardian of the ring, symbolizes something greater than God—the one he was raised up to worship and pray to. Gandalf is, in Ramtin's view, just like God, a fictitious character in a story about the force of good and evil and the attainment of salvation: In Tolkien's trilogy, salvation and inner peace lie within the power of a precious ring, whereas, according to the holy Qur'an, salvation can be reached by praying and adapting your actions, mind, and behavior to Islamic morality. By expressing his beliefs in "Gandalf," Ramtin draws attention to the fictitious character and instability of all religions. In that sense, he is queering religion, a practice which can be seen as a part of ethics of the self: Realizing how one is constituted and finding ways to transform oneself within those same limits, as discussed in Chap. 5. Moreover, by referring to Gandalf and *The Lord of the Rings*, he is also expressing a hope for a better future, in which the magic ring signifies something that is out of reach but still so close. In the case of Ramtin, it is the case of being a queer refugee in Istanbul waiting for the approval of his asylum application in the West. The wait has, however, been long, and it could still take some time until he will be allowed to move to the West, "preferably to Canada," said Ramtin, when I asked him about the country of his dreams. In fact, many gay/queer Iranians end up in Canada with the help of the organization *Iranian Railroad for Queer Refugees*.[7]

BATTLE OF THE WORDS: CLAIMING A DISCURSIVE SPACE WITHIN THE OFFICIAL DISCOURSE ON SAME-SEX DESIRES

Post-structural theorists, such as Judith Butler and Michel Foucault, have drawn attention to the importance of language/discourse in calling identities into being and hence producing subjects/subjectivities (Butler 1990, 1993). In fact, Butler has argued that resistance is limited to the linguistic field. The individual subject can therefore only offer resistance at the discursive level, as discourse confers existence and creates particular realities (Livia and Hall 1997; Butler 1993). Thus, according to Butler, individual subjects have the possibility to resist the discursive power of subjectification and categorization through resignification (Butler 1993). To resignify is, according to Butler, to reclaim particular terms or labels about marginalized groups, which previously had a negative meaning. Thus, early on, discursive or linguist resistance has been part of gay and lesbian activism in the West. The aim was to influence and/or change the dominant views and attitudes toward sexual minorities and to (re)claim the power to define their own reality. For example, the word "queer" was reclaimed by resisting the past stigmatization of that particular term. However, resignification as resistance depends on the social context and the social position of those involved. Not all marginalized groups have the same opportunities to resignify oppressive and stigmatized labels because the effect of resignification intersects with, for example, race, class, culture, and social context.

Inside Iran, gay/queer activists have, since the 1990s, resisted the dominant discourse and negative language on homosexuality. In doing so, they have employed the Western "gay" identity label as a means by which to counter the derogatory references to same-sex sexuality in the Persian language. The most commonly used derogatory term, *hamjins-bazi* (*hamjins-baz* when referring to a person), which translates as "same-sex play" or "player," signifies the immaturity of gay individuals and denies them of any erotic self-determination.[8] *Hamjins-bazi* is used along with other negative referents to homosexuality such as *evakhahar* (sister), which refers to effeminacy and *kooni/kuni* (ass), which denotes the one who assumes the passive role in the act of anal intercourse (Korycki and Nasirzadeh 2014).[9] In addition, in response to the charges that they have simply appropriated a Western import of gayness, queer Iranian activists inside Iran have simultaneously constructed "new Persian words" to explain, in more positive terms, same-sex identification: *Hamjins-gara'i* [10] (as a counter to *hamjins-bazi*) refers to "same sex orientation" (*hamjinsgera* refers to the person in singular), while the term *degardbasshaan e jensi* refers to the notion of "a sexual queer minority" (Korycki and Nasirzadeh 2014, p. 11). This positive self-identification as "gay," coupled with discursive strategies for inventing new terminology and referents for same-sex desire, points to the productive effects of power as it is being mobilized by gay and lesbian activists and subjects inside Iran as a means by which to disrupt discourses that constitutes and others sexual minorities "as non-authentic Iranians" (Korycki and Nasirzadeh 2014, p. 11).

Nima started his activist work when he was 19 years old. At that time, he joined a gay and lesbian activist/advocacy group called the *Persian Gay and Lesbian Organization*, which was founded outside of Iran in 2006 and is today based in Canada.[11] He worked as a deputy for that group within Iran, and his tasks entailed, among others, offering support to his fellow gay Iranians, as well as disseminating information through online publications, particularly by writing blog posts on LGBTQ issues: "I wanted to tell Iranian gays that they are not alone. God does not hate you because you are different." He was also involved in reclaiming and disseminating the word *hamjins-gara'i*, a more positive Persian word for same-sex desire (homosexuality). In the following excerpt, he gives an account of his activism:

> If you ask me what was the greatest achievement of our activities, I would say it was when we introduced the word *hamjins-gara'i* to the Iranian public, instead of *hamjins-bazi*. When doing so, our first step was to establish

connection to VOA (Voice of America), the popular TV channel, which broadcasts from the US in Farsi and is watched by many Iranians. We sent them emails and asked them to stop using the offensive word *hamjins-bazi* and use instead *hamjins-gara'i*. For instance, when the famous film Brokeback Mountain won the Oscar, we asked them to use *hamjins-gara'i* in their description of the plot. After one or two years even the official Iranian radio channels started to revise their use of words, using *hamjins-gara'i* instead of *hamjins-bazi*. Even the official television channel is using the correct term now. It is important to have positive terms in Farsi to describe yourself. For example, if I want to tell my parents that I am gay, I want to have the possibility to do so in Farsi and use a positive word, *hamjins-gara'i*. Today, I am really happy that we were able to accomplish this. You see the results and you become happy, in my case, when I hear that people say *hamjins-gara'i*. Then, inside my heart I feel happiness and I say to myself: I took part in these changes and by using that positive word people no longer connect homosexuality to pedophilia or sickness.

Nima rejects being referred to as *hamjinsbaz*. For him, such a term has connotations that conjure up an image of a pedophile. Furthermore, he would never use that particular term to confront his parents and tell them that he identifies as gay, as they would immediately make association to perverse behavior and being mentally ill/sick. Thus, as Nima points out, the identification with *hamjins-gara'i* opens up new possibilities for Iranian gays to express their feelings and identity in a positive way, and in their own language, without having to employ the Western gay identity label—although most of them still do, and *hamjins-gara'i* is mostly used in more formal speech (Karimi 2017). Nima also draws attention to the fact that, through their activism, they were able to influence the official discourse and terminology in terms of sexual categories, despite the limits to public debate in the Islamic Republic, given the official medico-religious-legal disavowal of homosexuality and criminalization of same-sex relations. As an indication of this, the new penal code now uses the term *hamjins-gara'i* in place of *hamjins-bazi* to describe all same-sex acts including kissing and touching.[12] Thus, Nima's account gives an example of how queer Iranian men have resisted certain norms, which govern how they are discursively constituted in derogatory terms as sexual minorities, and which make visible specific language use as both a site of subjectification and ethical agency involving a degree of self-determination vis-à-vis the realization of one's sexual personhood (Martino and Kjaran 2019).

The Green Movement—A Queer/Gay Perspective

In 2009, Mahmoud Ahmadinejad sought to be re-elected as the president of the Islamic Republic of Iran. His presidency had been marked by profound human rights violations according to international agencies such as Human Rights Watch (Human Rights Watch 2008).[13] Moreover, Iranian society became generally more repressive during his presidency and individual freedom underwent further restriction: "He was not a president, he was a dictator. Saying we don't have gays in Iran, it was false," said Arash when I asked him about his views on Ahmadinejad. Thus, for the younger generation of Iranians, especially in urban centers, who longed for more personal freedom, the election of June 2009 sparked some hope for change, and many of them supported one of the oppositional candidates, the reformist and former prime minister of Iran, Mir-Hossein Mousavi. Thus, when it was announced after the election of June 12 that Ahmadinejad had won by 60% of the votes, Mousavi's supporters took to the streets and accused the authorities of having rigged the election in favor of Ahmadinejad. What followed during the next days, weeks, and months are by far the largest street protests and demonstrations in Iran since the Iranian Revolution in 1979. The protests soon turned into riots and street fights between protesters and security forces and the unofficial militia, the *Basij* units, which used unrestrained force to quell the protests/riots. Hundreds of protesters were arrested and many incurred serious injuries from beatings and brutalities at the hands of the security forces (Hashemi and Postel 2010). A movement was born which took its name from the green symbol used by Mir-Hossein Mousavi's campaign. However, within months, the authorities had secured its position and suppressed all protests/demonstrations. This section will neither focus on the political aspect of the Green Movement nor give an account of the movement itself, but rather draw attention to the fact that many gay- and lesbian-identifying Iranians participated in the protests, not demanding recognition or visibility within the public sphere, but focusing more on personal freedom in general. Pouria, who told his story in Chap. 5, did not take part in the protests, but mentioned that many gays he knew at that time participated because they wanted to "open up society." Arash and other informants also told me that they knew or had heard about many gays who took part in the Green Movement. One of those gay-identifying males who took to the streets during the protests was Farhod, whose story I will now tell.

I met Farhod on two occasions during my fieldtrips to Tehran and stayed with him and his partner, Basir, for a couple of days during my third fieldtrip (see also Chap. 5). I got to know Farhod quite well and gained his confidence. One morning after Basir went to work, we sat down in the living room and had some tea together while Farhod told me how he got involved in the Green Movement. After he started his studies, he became an activist, attending meetings and protests. "When I, for example, was a student in Tabriz [city in the northern part of Iran— Iranian Azerbaijan], I organized meetings and protests against the government. In the end, I was arrested." He was released shortly after, and following that he moved to Tehran. It was right after the election in June 2009, so he joined the Green Movement and continued to participate in protests and actions against the government. There he got arrested again. "I had to stay for one week in hotel Evin," referring to the infamous Evin Prison in Tehran, where most political prisoners and those who have protested against the government are held. After being held in Evin Prison for a week, he signed a statement in which he declared that he would never participate again in any protests against the government/the authorities. "I signed it but I knew immediately after I did so that I could never stop taking part in protest against the authorities. It was just in me to protest and express my views."

He returned to his hometown, Isfahan, and shortly afterward, he was again on the streets protesting. One day, after clashes with the security forces, Farhod saw a police officer punching and kicking a young woman. "I asked the police officer why he was beating a defenseless woman. When he did not stop, I just got furious and helped the woman to get away—hitting the police officer. Then more officers came and took me down." Farhod was brought to the police station and put in a cell, where he was beaten and kicked for some hours. "I just laughed at them and made the victory sign with my fingers. I thought it would be like before, I would be released shortly afterwards." However, at this time, authorities were applying tougher measures against those who dared to participate in the Green Movement protests. Thus, after the initial beatings, Farhod was taken to another cell where he was undressed and tortured for ten hours. "The cell was very cold, one degree inside or something like that. I was shivering. They hung me upside down and started to beat me with clubs and give me [regular] [electric] shocks. I felt like my head was just going to blow. I have never experienced so much pain in my entire life." His torturer wanted him to confess to having used a knife when he attacked the police officer. In the end, he signed the confession: "I would have signed anything at that time. I just wanted it to stop."

Afterward, he was brought to a judge where he was sentenced to six months in prison. "I told the judge that I had been tortured but he did not listen to me." Farhod spent the next six months in a prison cell with a couple of other political prisoners. "One of my cell mates was a mullah and he was always telling us that we need to pray. I told him that it was of no use. Allah is not going to listen to us anyway." Farhod's family did not know about his whereabouts or what had happened to him. Finally, he was able to send them a message when one of his cellmates got released. Eventually he got released, physically and psychologically injured. "I do not regret anything. I am happy today and I see things differently after this experience." Today, Farhod lives in Tehran but has plans of leaving Iran as soon as possible. "I am gay but I am also an enemy of the state. I don't get any work and I cannot build up my life here." When I asked him if he knew about others gays that took part in the Green Movement and protested against the government he said: "Yes I know [a] lot of gays that took part in the protests. I also know that the security forces, for example the *Sepah*, made some false video clips showing gay people in the line of protest. Their aim was to ruin our reputation—saying that the protests were inspired by gays and Western agents who want to destroy Iranian culture."

Farhod's story draws attention to the polyphonic nature of the Green Movement. Different groups and individuals participated in the protests, whether they identified as environmentalist, feminist, or queer, having in common hopes for political change and societal reform (Bashi 2010). His story also informs us about the brutality of the repression on behalf of the Iranian authorities and how those who were arrested had to endure both physical and psychological torture. Farhod still has scars on his body and soul after being tortured after his arrest. He, however, emphasized in our talk that he does not regret having participated and made his contribution to the movement—taking a similar stand as Ramtin, when he helped his friend and was gang-raped. Farhod also draws attention to how the authorities used the image of the gay protester in their official propaganda, as a manifestation of Western liberal values, which they claimed inspired the protesters. Thus, in line with the official logic, the protesters were under the influences of *Westoxification*, discussed in Chap. 3.

Beyond Queer/Gay Visibility and Recognition

In this chapter, I turned to the Foucauldian ethics of the self in order to understand queer/gay activism among gay-identifying Iranian males. This meant drawing attention to inventive and creative practices performed in order to transform or change the discourse and produce spaces of same-sex desire and support within the limits set by the hegemonic religious-political discourse. Three stories exemplify how queer/gay Iranian activists tried to transform the self, influence the dominant discourse on sexuality, and carve out a queer/gay space. Ramtin emphasized the importance of creating a community and offering mutual support to his gay/queer brethren. He also participated in more direct activism through "queer photo installations" in order to transform or change the discourse and produce spaces of same-sex desire and support. Nima also emphasized community building, but also the significance of terminology by creating and introducing a positive word in Farsi for same-sex desire. Thus, the identity category *hamjins-gara'i* opens up new possibilities for Iranian gays to express their feelings and identity in a positive way, and in their own language, without having to employ the Western gay identity label. Moreover, as Nima explained, through this kind of activism, he and his fellow queer/gay activists were able to influence the official discourse and terminology in terms of sexual categories, despite the limits to public debate in the Islamic Republic, given the official medico-religious-legal disavowal of homosexuality and criminalization of same-sex relations. The last story told in this chapter centered on Farhod and his involvement in the Green Movement protests. It draws attention to the polyphonic nature of the Green Movement, in which different groups and individuals participated in the protests, whether they identified as queer, gay, or feminist. In that sense, the Green Movement initiated some hope of political change and increased personal freedom, which were, in the end, crushed with brutal force, ending for many young Iranians all further aspirations for political reform or belief in politics in general: "After the Green movement I don't vote anymore, nothing will ever change is this country," said Farhod, seeing his only option being to emigrate.

Notes

1. Here it needs to be noted that gay liberation movements existed before the Stonewall Riots, both in Europe and North America. It was not the first time that riots against oppression based on sexuality erupted in the US—before Stonewall, there had been riots both in San Francisco and Los Angeles.
2. This slogan was used by the group/organization Queer Nation in the 1990s. Its aim was to eliminate homophobia and increase LGBT visibility.
3. In her ethnographic study on lesbian activists in New Delhi, Dave theorizes activism as an ethical practice, arguing that activism "relies on its own constant interrogation and how moments of closure are the impetus to new kinds of previously unthinkable emergences" (Dave 2011, p. 4).
4. Words with similar connotations and also used among gays are bano (miss or lady) and malake (queen).
5. According to the urban dictionary, "gaydar" is "The ability/gift of being able to detect homosexuality in other people" (Urban Dictionary 2001, December 5).
6. *Hamjensgera* is a website, and the domain *hamjensgera* means homosexual in Farsi (see next section). It has been run since 2010 by an Iranian queer activist, and is hosted outside of Iran, in the US. It caters to those Iranians that identify as LGBTQ, especially young gays and lesbians who are coming to terms with their sexuality. It offers information about LGBTQ issues and has an online forum where it is possible to post questions (email from June 29, 2019, from the manager of *Hamjensgera*).
7. Iranian railroad for queer refugees was founded by Arsham Parsi. It is located in Canada/Toronto and operates exclusively through the Internet. The aim of the organization is to help queer refugees from the Middle East, mostly from Iran, Afghanistan, and Syria, to seek asylum in the West. Parsi explained the name of the organization, which, in fact, also entails its main aim, in an interview I took with him in March 2017: "Historically [there was] an underground railroad […] in the Nineteenth Century, running from the US to Canada, helping slaves from the US to enter Canada, where they gained freedom. We use this terminology because we are actually doing the same thing. We are helping those people who face persecution in Iran or other countries in the Middle East; we bring them to safe countries such as Canada. And actually there is a railroad between Tehran and Istanbul—from there we got this 'name'" (IRQR n.d., Iranian railroad for queer refugees).
8. These terms were popularized and introduced to the Iranian discourse on sexuality by Hasan Hasuri and then by other medical specialists. Hasan Hasuri was educated as neurologist in the US. *Hamjins-bazi* ("same-sex

play," same-sex lust) is a broad term, which refers to actions, rather than feelings or desires (see e.g., Forbes 2016–2017).

9. My informants mentioned these derogatory words, but added the word *obi* to the list, which refers to a person who is willing to sell his ass for money.

10. *Hamjins-gara'i* refers to feelings and desires rather than actions and behavior, and can therefore be used by gay Iranians for self-identification. According to Najmabadi (2014, p. 57), this term first appeared in the Iranian press around 1973 and was then mostly used negatively. It was then, in the 1990s, that gay Iranian activists reclaimed the word through resignification.

11. The *Persian Gay and Lesbian Organization* (now named *The Iranian Queer Organization*) was founded in 2006 by the human rights/queer activist Arsham Parsi. He, however, left the organization and established a new organization called the *Iranian Railroad for Queer Refugees*.

12. *Qanun-e Majazat-e Islami* [Islamic Penal Code], 2013, Article 237. Forbes has also pointed out that the controversial president M. Ahmadinejad made a distinction in an interview between *hamjins-gara'i*, which entails keeping your actions and desires within your private sphere, putting up masks, and *hamjins-bazi*, in which you express your sexuality and desires more openly, as being "out of the closet," so to speak, something that is practiced in the West. Thus, the logic goes, and in line with his argument in the infamous Harvard speech where he denied the existence of homosexuals in Iran, that in Iran, there are no *hamjensbas* (openly gay individuals as in the West), only *hamjensgera* (see Forbes 2016–2017).

13. Whitaker also pointed out in an article in *The Guardian* in December 2010 that during Ahmadinejad's presidency, discrimination and persecution of sexual minorities increased (see Whitaker 2010). However, here it needs to be noted that repressive measures affected everybody during Ahmadinejad's presidency, not only those who identified as gay or lesbian, although some of them might have experienced some further repercussions.

REFERENCES

Armstrong, E., & Crage, S. M. (2006, October 1). Movements and Memory: The Making of the Stonewall Myth. *American Sociological Review, 71*(5), 724–751. https://doi.org/10.1177/000312240607100502.

Bashi, G. (2010). Feminist Waves in the Iranian Green Tsunami? In N. Hashemi & D. Postel (Eds.), *The People Reloaded: The Green Movement and the Struggle for Iran's Future* (pp. 37–41). New York: Melville House.

Brown, G. (2015). Queer Movement. In D. Paternotte & M. Tremblay (Eds.), *The Ashgate Research Companion to Lesbian and Gay Activism* (pp. 73–84). London: Routledge.

Butler, J. (1990). *Gender Trouble. Feminism and the Subversion of Identity.* New York: Routledge.

Butler, J. (1993). *Bodies that Matter. On the discursive limits of sex.* New York: Routledge.

Caliskan, M., & Dikmen, Y. (2015, June 28). Turkish Police Use of Water Cannon to Disperse Gay Pride Parade. *Reuters.* Retrieved from https://www.reuters.com/article/us-turkey-rights-pride/turkish-police-use-water-cannon-to-disperse-gay-pride-parade-idUSKCN0P80OQ20150628.

D'Emilio, J. (1992a). After Stonewall. In J. D'Emilio (Ed.), *Making Trouble: Essays on Gay History Politics, and the University* (pp. 234–274). New York: Routledge.

D'Emilio, J. (1992b). *Making Trouble. Essays on Gay History, Politics, and the University.* New York and London: Routledge.

D'Emilio, J. (2002). *The World Turned: Essays on Gay History, Politics, and Culture.* Durham, NC: Duke University Press.

Dabashi, H. (2011). *The Green Movement in Iran. Edited with an Introduction by* Navid Nikzadfar. New Brunswick, NJ: Transaction.

Dave, N. N. (2011, April 15). Activism as Ethical Practice: Queer Politics in Contemporary India. *Cultural Dynamics, 23*(1), 3–20. https://doi.org/10.1177/0921374011403351.

Day of Fighting against Homophobia and Transphobia in Iran. (2012, June). Retrieved from http://hamjensgera.com/article/33.

Forbes, S. (2016–2017). The Reconstruction of Homosexuality and Its Consequences in Contemporary Iran. *The SOAS Journal of Postgraduate Research*, 10, 25–47. Retrieved from http://eprints.soas.ac.uk/24678/1/07_SForbes_Reconstruction_Homosexuality.pdf.

Hashemi, N., & Postel, D. (Eds.). (2010). *The People Reloaded: The Green Movement and the Struggle for Iran's Future.* New York: Melville House.

Human Rights Watch. (2008). We Need a Law for Liberation. Gender, Sexuality, and Human Rights in a Changing Turkey. Retrieved from https://www.hrw.org/sites/default/files/reports/turkey0508webwcover.pdf.

IRQR. (n.d.). Iranian railroad for queer refugees. Retrieved from http://irqr.ca/2016/.

Karimi, A. (2017, January 19). Hamjensgara Belongs to Family; Exclusion and Inclusion of Male Homosexuality in Relation to Family Structure in Iran. *Identities. Global Studies in Culture and Power, 25*(4), 456–474. https://doi.org/10.1080/1070289X.2017.1286921.

Korycki, K., & Nasirzadeh, A. (2014, January 1). Desire Recast: The Production of Gay Identity in Iran. *Journal of Gender Studies, 25*(1), 50–65. https://doi.org/10.1080/09589236.2014.889599.

Livia, A., & Hall, K. (1997). "It's a Girl!": Bringing Performativity Back to Linguistics. In A. Livia & K. Hall (Eds.), *Queerly Phrased: Language, Gender and Sexuality* (pp. 3–18). Oxford: Oxford University Press.

Martino, W., & Kjaran, J. I. (2019). The Politics of Recognizability: Giving an Account of Iranian Gay Men's Lives Under Repressive Conditions of Sexuality Governance. *International Journal of Middle East Studies, 51* (1), 21–41.

Najmabadi, A. (2014). *Professing Selves: Transsexuality and Same-Sex Desire in Contemporary Iran.* Durham, NC: Duke University Press.

Queer Nation NY. (2016). Queer Nation NY History. Retrieved from http://queernationny.org/history.

Ritchie, J. (2010, October 1). How Do You Say "Come Out of the Closet" in Arabic? Queer Activism and the Politics of Visibility in Israel-Palestine. *GLQ: The Journal of Lesbian and Gay Studies, 16*(4), 554–575. https://doi.org/10.1215/10642684-2010-004.

Sreberny, A., & Khiabany, G. (2010). *Blogistan. The Internet and Politics in Iran.* London: I. B. Tauris.

Urban Dictionary. (2001, December 5). Gaydar. Retrieved from https://www.urbandictionary.com/define.php?term=gaydar.

Whitaker, B. (2010, December 15). From Discrimination to Death—Being Gay in Iran. *The Guardian.* Retrieved from: https://www.theguardian.com/commentisfree/2010/dec/15/gay-iran-mahmoud-ahmadinejad.

CHAPTER 7

The "Sick Gay": Being HIV-positive in Iran

This chapter addresses the intersection of sexuality, gender, and bodies in terms of HIV/AIDS, which, during the last decades, has increased in Iran, particularly in Tehran, due to high numbers of IDUs (injecting drug user). It explores how the discourses on HIV/AIDS have evolved within Iran and how those bodies, who live outside of what can be considered culturally intelligible in terms of seropositivity, sexuality and gender, are constructed. It draws on the Foucauldian analytical framework, as well as Butler's writings on abjection. The Foucauldian concepts of *biopower* and *biopolitics* are employed in the chapter in order to analyze the various power dynamics at work in relation to sexuality, gender, and HIV/AIDS. *Biopower*, "a technology of power centered on life" (Foucault 1991, p. 266), entails the power held by the state/authorities to manage the population, for example, through health-related issues regarding HIV/AIDS, as will be discussed in this chapter. The effects of *biopower* are well summarized in the following quote by Kenneth Plummer, written during the first decade of the HIV/AIDS epidemic:

> With the symbolism of AIDS has emerged a range of institutional practices that aim to increase surveillance and regulation over 'deviances' and 'sexualities', many new agencies have appeared along with many new practices that aim to keep records, classify and order, take tests, watch over, maybe brand and quarantine people on the AIDS spectrum. [...] Small trends can become big institutions; what has emerged in the past few years may very well proliferate and extend [...] establishing firm new structures for the control of 'deviance' and 'sexuality' by the end of the century. (Plummer 1988, p. 46)

© The Author(s) 2019
J. I. Kjaran, *Gay Life Stories*,
https://doi.org/10.1007/978-3-030-12831-9_7

In terms of "institutional practices," Iranian health authorities are no exception, and during the last decades, institutions have been built to monitor, categorize, record, and treat those in danger of infection, as will be explicated later in the chapter. Through *biopower*, politics and policies on health and well-being are enacted. Thus, *biopolitics* has the aim of fostering the health of the general population by isolating or "othering" those that are a threat to its well-being. By doing so, the forces of *biopolitics* necessarily institute divisions within the population, by valorizing certain bodies and delegitimizing others in order to protect the "purity" and health of the general population. This is particularly true in the case of HIV/AIDS, and especially when seropositivity intersects with gay subjectivity. Moreover, as will be discussed in this chapter, *biopolitics* intersects with the concept of *geocorpography*, which denotes how space affects and effects the treatment of bodies, combining geography with corporeality, space with bodies (Pocius 2016).

The empirical data used in this chapter are drawn from my field notes, reports, documents, and several chats I conducted on Telegram with my gay Iranian informers, as well as interviews with those that run one of the main clinics for HIV research and treatment in Tehran. I will draw on these data in the first three sections of the chapter, which explore and contextualize HIV/AIDS in Iran, the operation of the HIV/AIDS research center in Tehran, and being tested for HIV as way of a confession to one's inner self/identity. In the last section, I will give an account of what it means to be both gay and HIV-positive in today's Iran, drawing on an interview with a gay couple, both individuals being HIV-positive. Finally, I summarize the main arguments.

Westoxification: HIV/AIDS in Iran

On December 27, 1982, *Newsweek* published a short article with the title: "AIDS: A Lethal Mystery Story" (Fader 2014, April 24).[1] It quotes the gay activist and playwright Larry Kramer, who said "to be a gay man in New York today is like living in London during the blitz" (cited in Kinsella 1989, p. 92). In September that same year, the CDC (Centers for Disease Control and Prevention) had used for the first time the term AIDS (Acquired Immune Deficiency Syndrome) to define this new disease, which had until then mostly affected gay men (A Timeline of HIV/AIDS (n.d.)). On April 18, 1983, AIDS became a cover story in *Newsweek* with the title: "Epidemic: The Mysterious and Deadly Disease Called AIDS May Be the Public Health Threat of the Century. How Did It Start? Can

It Be Stopped?" (Frydlewicz 1983, April 11). Thus, due to increased media attention, the "deadly" acronym, AIDS, consisting of four letters, was gradually becoming known to the public, not only in the US but also globally, in which being labeled with it meant both social stigma and death. It was the new "plague" of the century. During the following decades, increasing numbers of people became infected, turning this lethal disease into a global epidemic.

Iran was no exception. In 2016, it has been estimated that there were 66,000 people living with HIV/AIDS (PLHIV), and that same year there were 5000 new infections (Table 7.1). The first reported cases of HIV/

Table 7.1 Statistics on AIDS/HIV in Iran, 2000–2016

	2000	2003	2005	2006	2010	2015	2016
Number of reported HIV-cases—cumulative (official statistic)	N/A	5086 (4838 males and 248 women)[b]	9800[c]	13,702[a]	N/A	N/A	32,000
New HIV infections (estimated)[d]	N/A	N/A	8300	N/A	5800	N/A	5000
HIV incidence per 1000 population[d]	N/A	N/A	0.12	N/A	0.08	N/A	0.06
AIDS-related deaths[d]	N/A	N/A	1700	N/A	3300	N/A	4000
People living with HIV (estimated)	N/A	N/A	30,000[c] 48,000[d]	N/A	63,000[d]	N/A	66,000[d]
Estimated HIV-related deaths[e]	600 (400 age 30–49)	N/A	1900 (1300 age 30–49)	N/A	3100 (age 30–492,100)	3900 (2700 age 30–49)	N/A

[a]Fallahzadeh, Morowatisharifabad, Ehrampoosh, 2009
[b]Tavoosi et al. (2004)
[c]Ramezani Tehrani and Malek-Afzali (2008)
[d]http://www.unaids.org/sites/default/files/media_asset/20170720_Data_book_2017_en.pdf
[e]Global Health Estimates 2015: Deaths by Cause, Age, Sex, by Country and by Region, 2000–2015. Geneva, World Health Organization; 2016. Retrieved from http://www.who.int/healthinfo/global_burden_disease/estimates/en/index1.html

AIDS in Iran were during the years 1985 to 1987.[2] This was a difficult time in Iran. The society was still in turmoil after the Islamic Revolution and the new revolutionary regime was fighting its enemies, within society but also externally in a bloody war against its neighboring country, Iraq. During the height of the Iran-Iraq war, often referred to as the "forgotten war," which took place between the two countries from 1980 to 1988, Iranian authorities not only had to defend its citizens against Iraqi missiles, hitting Tehran regularly during that time, but also had to organize its health system and find strategic solutions to tackle a new and hidden "enemy," the HIV/AIDS virus (Karsh 2009; Takeyh 2010). In that sense, the "blitz" referred to by Larry Kramer in the *Newsweek*, was for most Iranian citizen a reality, experienced almost every day during the war, which resulted in high civil casualties.

Due to this, Iranian authorities needed to import blood plasma from France, as its own production did not satisfy the high demand caused by the war. Thus, the official story runs that the roots of the HIV virus in Iran can be traced to contaminated French blood plasma imported during the Iran-Iraq war. This was explained to me by a doctor working at the HIV-center, which I visited during my fieldwork in Tehran. He further added: "When a French minister of health visited Iran couple of years ago he did not even apologize for this." A World Bank Report from 2010 on HIV/AIDS in MENA countries (Middle East and North Africa) also draws attention to the external roots/causes of the initial reported cases of HIV/AIDS in the MENA region. It states the majority of initial cases in these countries "were linked to blood or blood products or exposures abroad" (Abu-Raddad et al. 2010, p. 179), and that in the case of blood products, the majority were imported, which was the case with Iran in the 1980s. In that sense, the roots of the "HIV/AIDS plague" in Iran fit well into the official rhetoric about *Westoxification* mentioned in previous chapters. Thus, in line with the official discourse, HIV/AIDS, along with homosexuality, is considered to be a Western disease, and as such is external to Iranian culture and society. It is something that has its roots outside of Iran, which in the official discourse is "projected" onto external factors, in this case the West and its toxic influences on Iranian youth and culture. Although not as extreme as the official discourse, scientific papers on HIV/AIDS written by Iranian scholars also emphasize external factors when explaining the origins, impacts, prevalence, and causes of the HIV/AIDS virus in Iran.

Table 7.2   Mode of transmission in three MENA countries (min and max value)

	Iran (%)	Lebanon (%)	Saudi Arabia (%)
Injection drug	78/87	6	1.3/2
Homosexual	N/A	15.68/16	2.5/5
Heterosexual	N/A	53/56	37.9/46
Blood or blood products	0.35/1.8	7/8.5	25/26
Mother-to-child	0.5/1	3/4.3	6.5/12

Source: Abu-Raddad et al. (2010, p. 86)

The papers draw in different ways on the discourse about external factors when accounting for the impact, causes, and prevalence of HIV/AIDS
cases in Iran. Some scientific papers argue that the fact that Iran is located
on a major narcotics transit route explains the high addiction rate and
hence prevalence of HIV/AIDS among IDUs (e.g., Fallahzadeh et al.
2009, p. 301). These arguments are also supported by other sources, such
as the *World Bank Report*, which estimate that the Islamic Republic of Iran
has the highest rate of heroin/opium addition in the world, almost 1 in
every 17 people (Abu-Raddad et al. 2010, p. 15). The main reason for this,
according to the report, is increased supply due to the transit route, which
then explains the higher rate of heroin usage. In other words, according to
the World Bank Report, "IDU and HIV are known to follow drug-traffick-
ing routes" (Abu-Raddad et al. 2010, p. 16). Consequently, according to
most sources on the topic, the prevalence of HIV/AIDS infections in Iran
is mostly concentrated among IDUs (Table 7.2). In that sense, the pattern
of transmissions in Iran differs from other countries. For example, in
Lebanon, the prevalence of HIV/AIDS among IDUs is only 6% (Table 7.2).

In comparison to the West, where for the past decades HIV/AIDS
prevalence has been highest among gay men/MSMs (men who have sex
with men), the reported modes of transmission in Iran differ considerably.
In fact, homosexuality or non-heterosexuality is rarely or only vaguely
mentioned in research papers as a mode of HIV/AIDS transmission in
Iran. In other words, this group is either silenced or not mentioned as a
possible target group in terms of HIV/AIDS infections. This is partly due
to lack of data with regards to HIV/AIDS prevalence within that particular group, as its members are a hidden population and therefore not
accounted for in the official statistics. This is particularly striking when it
is taken into account that, globally, gay men/MSMs accounted for 12% of

new infections in 2015, whereas IDUs account for only 8% of new infections (UN AIDS DATA 2017a). However, some papers acknowledge this imbalance in the data, for example, Haghdoost et al. state: "due to the lack of valid information regarding this group, and as they are one of the most hidden populations, we are unable to speak with certainty with respect to the epidemic of HIV in this group" (Haghdoost et al. 2011, p. 236). Thus, it is acknowledged that the rate and prevalence of HIV/AIDS in Iran is underreported, and in fact exact statistical information about HIV/AIDS is often hard to obtain. This is confirmed by the World Bank Report, which emphasizes that MSMs (men who have sex with men) "form the most hidden and stigmatized risk group of all HIV risk groups in MENA" (Abu-Raddad et al. 2010, p. 31).

In terms of risky sexual behavior, which can often go hand in hand with stigmatized and excluded social status, more attention should be given to MSMs and gay males within Iran and other MENA countries. A study from Lebanon suggests that "they [MSMs] often engage in unprotected sex, with 74% of those surveyed identifying unprotected sex as the main reason for seeking voluntary counseling and testing" (Abu-Raddad et al. 2010, p. 201). An Iranian survey on HIV and the HIV risk factors among homeless men having sex with men in Tehran in 2006–2007 indicated that only 19.4% had used a condom the last time they had had anal sex (Abu-Raddad et al. 2010, p. 36). Although not representative of the general MSM/gay population of Iran, these details give some indication of the sexual behavior of men who have sex with men, suggesting that condom use during anal sex may not be very common among MSMs.

This was also what Kasra had experienced during his participation in one of many online gay communities. In the following excerpt, taken from our online chat on Telegram in December 2017, Kasra talks about his encounters with gay Iranian men, mostly online, in terms of sexual behavior and risk:

Jón: How is it with your gay friends—are they aware of HIV? Are they
         as careful as you are?
Kasra: My friends, yes.
Kasra: Other gays?
Kasra: No
Kasra: Not at all.
Jón: Ok.
Jón: You have heard about others gays?

Jón: Or you have experienced it?
Kasra: You mean like have I met a gay guy who is HIV+?
Jón: Yes and how do you know if other gay guys are not careful?
Kasra: I have never met any gay guys that have HIV.
Jón: Ok.
Kasra: But I know that gays in Iran are very careless with STDs.
Jón: Aha.
Kasra: Cumming inside is really common.
Jón: How do you know that? Have you heard about it?
Kasra: I was a part of gay community ☺.
Kasra: I got messages like that A LOT.
Jón: Which gay community? On the Internet?
Kasra: And the number of HIV+ gays is high in Iran.
Jón: Ok.
Kasra: And I just see the ones that are openly HIV+.
Kasra: There is definitely more guys that don't know or don't say that
         they are.
Jón: Ok so you see openly HIV+ gay guys in the online community?
Jón: They tell about their status?
Kasra: Yes, they tell me.

Kasra distinguishes clearly between his gay friends who are careful and those within the Tehran gay online community of which he was member, who are not. In that sense, he draws a line between them and his friends. He and his friends are careful when it comes to sexual practices, and only engage in safe sex, which means using a condom at all times. The majority of other gays within the online community are, on the other hand, reckless in terms of sexual behavior, "cumming inside," and seem not to worry too much about the possible risk of getting infected by HIV or other STDs (sexually transmitted diseases). Arslan also expressed his concerns about the issue in our chat:

> Many gays don't even care about using condoms for hard sex with different guys. And they don't take the [HIV] test. I honestly don't understand them. How some people can be so careless is beyond me! They are crazy!

Coming back to Kasra, he goes on to mention that some members of the online group are rather open about their seropositive status. However, what Kasra and Arslan also draw attention to is the divide within the gay community in Iran/Tehran, in terms of sexual practices and the negative attitudes toward those who are considered to engage in "risky" or "reckless" sexual behavior, termed within the gay community in the global north as "barebacking," meaning anal sex without condoms. Thus, Kasra and Arslan draw here on a particular moral discourse, which some members of the gay community in the global north have embodied in terms of sexual behavior. This discourse draws on homonormativity, which depicts those individuals who "bareback" as irresponsible and a bad representation (image) of the gay community as a whole. In that sense, the moral discourse has the aim of othering those who practice unprotected sex, and categorize their sexual acts as "bad" and "slutty" (Dean 2009; Pocius 2016).[3] Thus, for Kasra and his gay friends, anal sex is only perceived as intelligible when a condom is used, and those who abstain from condom use and practice unprotected sex are "othered."

Condoms are highly available in Iran today, and the Islamic Republic is the largest condom producer in the Middle East (Muir 2002, April 24). This can be traced back to the mid-1980s when the authorities started a campaign in order to reduce the population growth, which was indeed getting out of hand, with an average rate of growth at 3.2% in 1986, one of the highest in the world at that time (e.g., Afary 2009). Condoms and other contraceptives were made highly available and at the end of the 1990s the annual population growth had been reduced to 1.2% (Sciolino 2000, p. 282; Larsen 2001, December 28). This trend has continued and today contraceptives such as condoms are rather easy to obtain in the Islamic Republic of Iran.

Kayhan Bad factory, based 120 miles outside of Tehran, is the largest domestic condom producer, supplying the market with 75% of the demand. On its website they proudly state that they offer "products to maintain the health of family and society" (Kayhan Bad Company homepage 2015). Thus, the focus is on the sexual and reproductive health of the family and society, an aim that goes hand in hand with the official policy of family planning. However, when you explore its products, then it can be assumed that the company is also catering to other needs/target groups. According to their website, they now produce nine brands of condoms, with names such as "Hot condoms," "Happy condoms," "Eros," and simply "Condom," which all come in different colors and flavors. Within each brand, there are different types of condoms. For example, the "Eros" brand offers seven types of condoms, and the "Condom" brand has five types. The "Eros Classic condom" type emphasizes romance between heterosexual couples indicated with the binary gender sign and the beach/holiday atmosphere on its package. The package also draws attention to the HIV/AIDS risk involved in sex by adding the international HIV/AIDS symbol on it. It is emphasized that condoms are not only contraceptives but also protections against STDs, such as HIV/AIDS. On the other hand, the "Condom Rainbow" type would be seen within the context of the global north as connected to LGBTQs—marked by the colorful rainbow and birds flying over it. However, on the description, it reads: "You can surprise her," emphasizing the heterosexual use of the condom. It seems that the "rainbow" symbol refers to the variety of condom colors in the package. In that sense, the rainbow condom falls within the boundaries of heteronormativity.

But what does this variety of condoms tells us about the sexual culture of Iran? One thing is clear, that Iranians, especially young Iranians under the age of 30, accounting for 60% of the population, are, despite official rhetoric, engaged in "a sexual revolution," as argued by Pardis Mahdavi in her ethnographic study on young people, sex, and sexuality in Tehran (Mahdavi 2008). This group is understood to be an active consumer of condoms, which state-sponsored condom producers such as Kayhan Bad are responding to by diversifying their variety of products. In that sense, they are acknowledging the fact that young people find ways to have sex and one way to keep them "safe" is to give them more options in their choice of condoms. However, the question then remains whether young sexually active Iranians are using this large selection of condoms when they engage in sex.

Statistically, it is difficult to give an answer to that question because data is lacking about the sexual behavior of young Iranians, including their condom use. However, the majority of adolescents seem to have knowledge about condoms and their importance with regards to HIV-prevention (Abu-Raddad et al. 2010). Moreover, a study by Tehrani and Malek-Afzali indicates that many young Iranians have relatively good knowledge of the modes of transmission of HIV. However, the survey question in the aforementioned study, about the connection between sex and HIV exposure, did not indicate whether the sex act was safe or not, but rather if "HIV can be transmitted through sexual intercourse with an unknown person," of which 80.3% of the respondent youth answered with "yes" (Ramezani Tehrani and Malek-Afzali 2008, p. 147). Thus, in this context, sex with an "unknown" person could be interpreted as having unprotected sex, as it is not culturally/socially acceptable to engage in sex prior to marriage. A study by Haghdoost et al., however, indicates that young Iranians, especially those who have been exposed to "Western" influences either through travels or living abroad for study or work, are more likely to engage in risky sexual behavior, particularly when they are living abroad, because, during that time, the argument goes, they do not live with their family or they are "actively searching for a certain type of freedom, which has subjected them to risky sexual behavior" (Haghdoost et al. 2011, p. 236).

To sum up the characteristics of the HIV/AIDS epidemic in Iran today, it firstly needs to be emphasized that data is lacking, and reported cases within particular risk groups, such as MSMs/gays, are highly underreported. In Tables 7.1 and 7.2, I have summarized available statistics gathered from different research papers and reports. These numbers are often based on estimation and could therefore, in reality, all be lower or higher. In 2016, according to the UN-AIDS report, it is estimated that there were 5000 new HIV infections. This is relatively high if compared to countries with similar population sizes, such as Germany, which, in 2015, reported 3200 new HIV infections (Unaids 2017b, May 12). Also, in comparison to other MENA countries, Iran along with Sudan ranks on top with regards to new HIV infections (UN AIDS DATA 2017a, p. 151). These new infections are mostly assumed to be related to IDUs. In fact, most reported HIV cases in the Islamic Republic of Iran are traced to IDUs, which, in comparison to Lebanon, is very high, where the main mode of transmission is via heterosexual sex (Table 7.2). However, data is lacking for this factor in Iran, and those cases are most often only reported in connection to when a drug-addictive male infects his partner/spouse.

Biopower and Abjected Bodies: The Imam Khomeini Hospital HIV/AIDS Center in Tehran

The temperature is rising gradually with the start of August, which, along with July, is the hottest month in the city. When I woke up that morning, it was already 27 degrees, and it was sunny with clear sky. I was meeting Arash close to the Imam Khomeini hospital, which is located in the southern part of the city. It is one of the oldest hospitals in Tehran and consists of a huge complex of buildings. Its main and oldest building was constructed during the rule of Reza Shah Pahlavi (ruled from 1925 to 1941), as a part of many reform projects initiated during that time in order to transform Iran into a modern society (Amanat 2017; Nemanipour et al. 2008). In fact, as a symbol of modernity, German contractors undertook the construction of the hospital between 1938 and 1941 (Nemanipour et al. 2008). Hundreds of German technicians and advisers were contracted to work on various projects. During that time, the Shah had close ties with Germany, an effort to reduce and counterbalance past and present influences of both Britain and Russia in Iran. However, by the time the hospital was finished, the allies, Britain and Russia, had already forced the Shah to abdicate and hand over the throne to his son, Mohammad Reza Pahlavi, due to his close links to Nazi Germany. Today, Imam Khomeini is a teaching hospital and the biomedical facility of the Tehran University of Medical Sciences. It is also one of the main centers for treating, testing, and researching HIV/AIDS in Iran.[4]

After I met Arash at a bus stop close to the hospital, we walked together and entered the main gate of the hospital complex. It was already getting quite busy within the compound of the hospital, cars coming and going and people walking in and out of the many buildings located within its limits. We walked through the compound, and soon we were in front of the HIV-center. It is a rather modern building hidden by the many trees within the hospital compound. I noticed, as we got closer to it, that the surroundings became less busy, and somehow more quiet and tranquil. In fact, the HIV-center was in many ways a separate world in itself, not connected directly to any other buildings within the compound, perhaps reflecting the sensitive work done there and the patients/bodies coming there for a treatment and/or testing. In line with Foucault, these bodies are produced as subjects of power through the technologies of testing/treatment, in which the state uses disciplinary and *biopolitical* strategies of *biopower* (Foucault 1990, p. 140; Foucault 1994). In that sense, the center can be seen as a disciplinary space in which confessions about one's identity are made during the process of HIV-testing, but also during treatment for HIV-positive individuals. It is also an official site and part of the health system of the Islamic Republic of Iran, where subjugation and control (regulation) of bodies is achieved through various techniques, which, for example, entail documentation, categorization, and treatment of those diagnosed as HIV-positive. Thus, the HIV-center as a part of the Iranian state health system denotes social and political power over its users. Moreover, within its spatial boundaries, a clear distinction is drawn between the "normal" and "abnormal." In other words, drawing here on Butler's notion of abjections, those individuals who do not act or behave in accordance to the "regulatory norms," due to their HIV status being positive and/or "non-normative" sexual behavior, are denied the status of subjects and become abjects (Butler 1993).

Arash and I entered the waiting room/reception, walking down a couple of stairs. It was a rather small room, with a couple of chairs and tables. Its walls were covered with information posters about HIV/AIDS, possible routes of infections/transmission, and how to protect oneself from it. Shortly afterward, we were greeted by Mr. Dabiri and Ms. Ghorbani. I shook hand with Mr. Dabiri, but when I was going to do so with Ms. Ghorbani, she did not accept my greeting and I noticed that she felt a bit uncomfortable. I then realized my mistake and was further reprimanded by Arash, who explained to me that a man should never offer his hand to a woman who was not his relative. I apologized, and the matter was resolved without any further consequences, as I was a foreigner and a guest, which gave me a bit more flexibility in terms of not strictly following the unwritten rules and customs. Mr. Dabiri works as a biologist and researcher at the HIV-center. He is in his 30s and is bearded and wears glasses. His appearance appeared rather sympathetic. Ms. Ghorbani is a gynecologist and wore a long dress and *hijab*. She was more reserved than Mr. Dabiri, who was quite talkative and open and willing to answer our questions in connection to the work of the center.

He gave us a short introduction about the work done at the center; he began by briefing us about the main target groups of the center: "We mostly treat and help IDUs, sex-workers, MSM and gays." Thus, the focus of the center is on marginalized groups within Iranian society. By entering the space of the center for testing or treatment, one was automatically both categorized and documented as a member of a highly stigmatized and marginalized group. In fact, one had to make "confessions" to a particular identity, group, or behavior, as Arash revealed in the following excerpt from a dialogue, which I conducted with him on Telegram:

Arash: I did not go there.
Arash: Because I don't have trust to them.
Jón: Ok.
Jón: Why did you not trust them?
Arash: Because I don't want them know me as gay in the Health Ministry.
Jón: Ok.

Thus, particularly for gay-identifying men, such as Arash, to enter the center could be difficult, as their identity is not recognized, and their sexual behavior is indeed punishable by Iranian law. In other words, their existence is not officially recognized, and they therefore fall outside the norms of what is considered to be culturally intelligible. Mr. Dabiri and Ms. Ghorbani confirmed this further in our conversation:

> Those two topics, HIV/AIDS and homosexuality are very difficult to discuss in Iranian society. In fact, homosexuality is more frowned on than being HIV positive. That is why it is often difficult for us here at center to reach out to homosexuals and it is our feeling that some members of that group do not know how HIV is contracted. All kinds of myths about the disease are circulating within that group. We have tried to reach out to this group on the Internet and on various apps but it so difficult because the government does not recognize homosexuality and therefore gay males live their lives underground. What is causing us worry is that new infections are getting more frequent among gays and during the last two years it has nearly doubled. We therefore need to find ways to reach out to this group and do more research on homosexuals in Iran. But again all this is so difficult due to the official position regarding these matters.

Another vulnerable group, not mentioned by Mr. Dabiri and Ms. Ghorbani, includes the seropositive women, which draws attention to the gendered aspect of the HIV-epidemic in Iran, Middle East, and North Africa (MENA). This is confirmed in a report published by the World Bank about the characteristics of HIV/AIDS in the MENA:

> Women are especially vulnerable because most risk behaviours in MENA are practiced by men. The majority of women living with HIV in MENA were infected through their husbands or partners, who were mostly not aware of their infections [...]. Seventy-six percent of women living with HIV in the Islamic Republic of Iran were also infected by their husbands, who were predominantly IDUs (Abu-Raddad et al. 2010, p. 61).

The gendered dynamics at play in Iranian and other Middle Eastern societies with regards to health issues and diseases such as HIV/AIDS, in which women suffer and get infected because of the risky behavior of their husbands/partners, draws attention to the workings of patriarchy and (hetero)masculinity in general. In fact, risk-prone behavior is a global phenomenon among men and is in some ways connected to (hetero)masculinity, as, for example, Jeff Hearn (2015) has argued in his research. In Iran, as has been discussed in previous chapters, the impact of (hetero)masculinity on men and boys is quite strong, and any behavior that deviates from the (hetero)masculine norm is frowned upon. Moreover, men who have sex with men (MSM) are also placing their spouses and partners, defined as a bridging population in terms of the HIV-epidemic, at risk of exposure to the disease, as they are often unaware of the possible ways to contract HIV. Mr. Dabiri and Ms. Ghorbani elaborated further on this issue:

> In fact, many Iranians connect HIV/AIDS with those that are on the margin of society, the others, and they are not aware that everyone can be exposed to HIV/AIDS. However, some men that have sex with other men and are married think that they are not at risk of contracting HIV. In fact we are quite worried about this group, especially as they also have sex in heterosexual relationships. In fact, this group is rather large in Iran and it is quite common that men have sex with other men, without identifying as gay. One reason for this could be the segregation between men and women in Iranian society.

The work within the center can be divided into three parts: Firstly, counseling and testing; secondly, research on HIV/AIDS; and thirdly, a support group for those who are HIV-positive. The counseling part of the center is officially called the "Behavioral Disease Counseling Centre." Similar centers are in most major cities of Iran and their "activities are related to AIDS and sexually transmitted diseases" (Iranian AIDS Research Center). Moreover, these centers offer free counseling services, testing, and provision of condoms and clean needles.[5] Thus, these centers are quite progressive in terms of HIV/AIDS prevention, and generally the attitude of the staff is quite liberal and open-minded, as Arslan, who took his test for the first time at the center in 2017, told me in our online chat on Telegram:

> The whole process can be anonymous if you wish. You meet with a consultant first. He is friendly and nice. He asks you about your sex life and whether you use condoms all the time. And I said I do use protection for hard sex all the time, cause I'm too careful. It was a little stressful at first. But I found the whole experience very interesting. And I left the clinic feeling very good after they told me the result was negative.

Health counseling and intervention programs, particularly those related to sexually transmittable diseases, often attempt to control the behaviors of certain "problem" or target groups through the promulgation and legitimation of dominant norms and values, which, as Watney (1988) has argued, can reinforce homophobia and discriminatory practices in relation to HIV/AIDS. Within the Iranian context, the official discourse portrays HIV/AIDS, and especially its intersection with homosexuality, as unacceptable social behavior, which does not conform to the dominant cultural norms and religious values of society. Nima, identifying as gay, mentioned this in our chat on Telegram when he referred to his experience of taking the HIV-test in 2011 in Tehran:

Nima: When I was living in Iran, HIV positivity was equal to being criminal from public opinion perspective.

Jón: Yes.

Jón: And being gay and positive was then seen as really bad?

Nima: Exactly.

The Tehran Affiliate Club is the official name of the "positive" club at the HIV-center. The Family Health Association (Family Planning Association) of Iran launched it in 2005 in cooperation with the Imam Khomeini hospital complex and the HIV/AIDS research center.[6] Its initial aims were to support those people living with HIV/AIDS. Today, the aims of the club are both educational and entertainment, but it also offers free counseling on HIV/AIDS. A support group for HIV-positives regularly meets there, and the club offers them a psychological service/consultation. Arash and I entered the club after our visit to the counseling and testing part of the center. Friendly faces greeted us. Among them is Nasrin, who is in her 40s and who gave us some information about the club and herself. She told us that she is HIV-positive, and her husband had passed away one year ago. She therefore needs to take care of her two children, but works at the "positive" club a couple of times during the week. "This gives me some strength to cope with my difficult situation and interact with people that share my experience," Nasrin told us when we asked her about what the club meant for her. Being a single mother living with HIV, Nasrin's situation draws further attention to the vulnerable situation of many HIV-positive women in Iran (Vahdat and Fattahi 2017, November 29). As mentioned previously, they often contract the disease from their husbands/partners, thus forming a "bridge" between the "general" population and those groups that Iranian epidemiologists have targeted as being at high risk of contracting HIV/AIDS. Thus, for Nasrin and other HIV-positive subjects, being "seropositive" is still highly stigmatized, not only in Iran, but also in many other countries in the global north. However, in Iran, being either gay or a single mother as well as HIV-positive increases one's vulnerability. Particularly for gays, the double stigma of belonging to a sexual minority and being infected by a socially unacceptable disease render them as abjects, as will be discussed further, later in this chapter. Thus, having a place to meet, such as the "positive" club, can function as a mirrored place in the Foucauldian heterotopian sense, discussed in Chap. 2, where seropositive Iranians are able to see themselves reflected, and to be visible or *real* to one another in ways that are not possible in their everyday lives where they are otherwise required to live hidden existences. This experience of finding oneself in the shadows speaks to the mirroring effect that such heterotopic spaces afford (Foucault and Miskowiec 1986). Thus *the other side of the glass* is a space of self-constitution enacted at the site of the "positive" club. However, this space is also highly confessionary and thus disciplinary, where subjects are produced and disciplined through the official medical discourse. This applies particularly to the space of testing and counseling, which I will now turn to and draw on my informal chat on the social media app Telegram with Iranian gay-identifying men who have all experienced HIV-testing in Iran.

Confessions Through HIV/AIDS Testing

The verb to test (or in testing as a present participle) is derived from the Latin verb *testari*, which means to bear witness to or give evidence of something. The process of testing involves truth telling, which can be verified, forced, or given willingly. In any case, being tested is all about power relations between giving a testimony, being tested; and receiving it, conducting the test. Thus, the process of testing draws attention to the various power dynamics involved. In that sense, the nature of testing and indeed giving a testimony, meaning telling the truth or giving evidence about oneself, relates to confessing about one's inner self. Thus, taking a test, in this case a HIV-test, means revealing some truth about oneself, not only with regards to biometrics in the form of a small blood sample but also giving information about one's inner self, related to one's sexuality and/or past sexual practices. These confessions often take place at the doctor's office or at a specific HIV-testing and counseling clinic, such as the HIV center in Tehran. These places, whether in Iran or elsewhere globally, can be seen as confessionary spaces, which, in line with Foucault and explicated in Chap. 2, are disciplinary spaces where *biopower* is enacted and played out. This is not always the case and, in some instances, both in the global north and south, NGOs, such as LGBTQ+ organizations, have themselves offered "safe" spaces for HIV-testing and counseling, and thus reduced the effects of the disciplinary nature of testing. This partly applies to Iran. However, as has been discussed previously, most testing and counseling spaces are run by the authorities and, due to this fact, its "clients" are often suspicious and worried about revealing the truth about their inner self, which I will now turn to.

At the clinic/center, we were offered to take the "rapid" HIV-test. Arash and I both agreed to do it. First, Mr. Dabiri explained about the test and how it functions. A drop of blood from your finger is taken and mixed with some kind of liquid. Then the liquid is poured on to some kind of a meter. After five minutes you know your status. If the line stops at the letter "c," then you are clear, if it goes to number 1 or 2, then you are probably infected by HIV-1 or HIV-2. These were the longest five minutes of my life. I was actually quite sure that I was negative; however, being there within that space and waiting for *the* ruling of the rapid tester made me feel quite stressed. I could just imagine those individuals coming here for testing, being already stigmatized in society for being gay, knowing that if this test will be positive, they will not only be labeled as having one disease, the "gay disease," but also be infected by HIV, which for many gay-identifying Iranians can be a death sentence. All was negative, and the same applied to Arash who also experienced the stress associated with the test. We talked about this after we got out of the clinic—how stressful this was. Mr. Dabiri told me that if the test is positive, one is then sent for an actual blood test and not even told of one's status until after the result of that test. However, as Arslan informed me, if one gets negative results, one is told of one's status immediately.

In light of this, going for the test can be difficult and stressful for many gay-identifying Iranians, and as discussed previously, many do not bother to get tested—not knowing one's status keeps the hope alive that one is still "alright." There is also the fear of the unknown, whether one will be asked lots of questions during or after the test, and particularly whether one will be judged, as Arslan talked about in our chat:

Jón: Why were you hesitant? Nervous?
Arslan: I don't know. Maybe because it was my first time there. And maybe because I had worse ideas about how they might treat you and look at you like you're a whore.
Arslan: But the experience changed that idea completely.

In the end, Arslan felt comfortable at the Imam Khomeini HIV-center, and he was never asked about his sexuality/sexual identity, as he told me later in our chat:

Jón: Do they ask if you are gay or not?
Arslan: No they don't ask you. They don't even imply it.
Arslan: And they don't assume you're gay. I talked to a guy who was waiting for his results. Actually, he talked to me. He asked me why I was there. And I said because I'm too cautious. And he said his condom burst during sex with a girl. I was treated as a heterosexual.
Jón: So he assumed that you were heterosexual and also those that treated you?
Arslan: Yeah. With guys like me, bearded and male-looking, they never even consider you might be gay.

What is interesting in the above excerpt is the implicit gender dimension, discussed in Chap. 5, involved in determining whether you are gay or not. It is somehow assumed that you are heterosexual, as the homosexual category is not recognized in the official discourse. It is somehow suggested within the Iranian cultural context that those who are gay are in many ways feminine and do not look like "real" men, which entails having a beard and acting and behaving manly. In that sense, Arslan fitted into the "heterosexual matrix," at least in terms of appearance and by acting in accordance with the hegemonic ideals of Iranian masculinity when he entered the testing and counseling part of the HIV-center. In fact, performing your gender "correctly" within the confessionary space of the testing/counseling clinics, and whether your sexuality will be assumed or not, was also mentioned by Morteza:

Jón: But would you say that gays are afraid of taking the test. I mean more so than others because of the situation of gays in Iran?
Morteza: No, I don't think so. Who would understand your sexuality unless you say it yourself?
Jón: What do you mean?
Morteza: I mean that they won't find out about your sexuality if you do not say it by yourself or having a strange style!
Jón: And strange style is like?
Morteza: Wearing girlish clothes or make up.

Arman did not have the same positive experience of the official/public HIV/STDs testing and counseling clinics as my other informants had. He expressed more mistrust toward the authorities and was rather aware of the confessionary nature of these official spaces, as can be seen in the following chat:

Arman: I have taken the test once.
Jón: Only once?
Arman: Yes because it's an expensive test.
Jón: It is not free?
Arman: I've heard there are some new places, where you can take the test free. But I don't trust them. Because they would ask many questions before the test.
Jón: What kind of questions?
Arman: Why are you taking it? Have you had dangerous sex? With whom? What is your sexual orientation? I don't like being investigated. It might be dangerous for my job
Jón: So where did you go then?
Arman: You can go to private clinics. They would do it without investigation. But it's not free as it isn't governmental.
Jón: And this private clinic where you did your test they don't ask anything?
Arman: No. They don't make you uncomfortable. Just do it.

As can be seen from our chat, Arman had a different view toward the public HIV/AIDS testing clinics. He is well aware of the confessionary nature of that particular space, and doesn't "trust" the staff there or wants to be "investigated" by them. In other words, he does not want to make confessions regarding his sexual behavior or sexuality. Moreover, as he mentions, this can have consequences for his job security, a fact that many gay Iranians have to take into consideration when they reveal or confess something about themselves. There are numerous examples of gay men being laid off because of their assumed or suspected sexual orientation. In light of that, Arman's worries are understandable as he has a good job within his field of specialty, and does not want to risk it. He therefore goes to a private clinic in order to have his HIV-tests. This also draws attention to how HIV/AIDS, particularly in terms of testing and prevention, intersects with economic and social status. For more discretion and privacy, Arman had to pay a rather high fee for his tests, but he was able to do that because he is in a good, stable job. Thus, differing from most Iranians, whether gay or not, he could afford going to a place for testing where there was no risk of getting exposed in terms of your sexuality/sexual orientation. In this context, the concept of *geocorpographies*, which combine "geography with corporeality, space with bodies," draws attention to the spatial nature of the economic inequalities regarding HIV-testing and privacy. Arman, who lives in the more affluent northern part of Tehran, and has a well-paid job, is in a more advantaged, even privileged, position in comparison to many other Iranian gays that need to get tested at public clinics, and thus might feel more insecure and less willing to go there to check their HIV status.

The *geocorpographies* regarding HIV-testing, the intersection of bodies and spaces, in which some subjects have better options than others, are particularly evident when Iran is compared to the global north. Nima mentioned this in our chat when he compared Iran to Canada: "I do like Canadian HIV test style. You don't need even to say your name!" Thus, in comparison to Iran, Canada, and in fact most countries in the global north, offer free and anonymous tests for HIV, which was not the case when Nima lived in Iran. Moreover, as opposed to Iran, many of the testing/counseling clinics in the global north are run or operated by LGBTQ organizations, without any formal connection to governmental agencies. Thus, gender and sexual minorities trust these "independent" clinics more and feel welcome and secured. In the next section, I will draw further on the concept of *geocorpographies* in terms of living with HIV/AIDS as a gay man in Iran.

"Our Lives Are Miserable Here": Being Gay and Living with HIV/AIDS

It's August 12, and it is getting warmer every day. It is my last day in Tehran for now, as I am flying late in the evening back to Europe. I meet Arash close to my guesthouse located in the vicinity of Imam Khomeini Square. We take the metro to the HIV-center of Imam Khomeini hospital, and our plan is to meet Amir and Hassan, a gay couple who are HIV-positive. We are supposed to meet them at the HIV-positive club, so we head to that section as soon as we arrive to the hospital compound. After waiting for some minutes, Amir and Hassan appear at the front of the entrance. Amir is slim, in his 20s, has well-maintained hair and eyebrows, wears a bit of a make-up, and seems to follow the latest fashion in terms of clothes and style. In terms of Iranian strict gender regime, he would be seen as being "gay looking." In fact, Hassan, confirms this at the beginning of our interview, and emphasizes that this has had some "consequences" for their relationship:

> You know, honestly I can tell you; his appearance is not accepted here. Everybody says bad things because of his appearance. He always had troubles when he went out and I couldn't stand it anymore. I had to tell him to change his appearance.

Hassan tried to change the "appearance" of Amir, in order for him to fit more into the strict binary system of the gender regime in Iranian society. This was vital for Hassan, so they could be left alone, without judgment and hassle from others. In terms of appearances, Hassan is the opposite of Amir. He is in his 30s, and does not seem to take much care of his appearance. He is rather tall and has a rather muscular figure.

Both of them try to smile when we greet each other, but you can feel the sorrow and the sufferings behind their smiles. We enter an adjacent room and sit down. After some small talk, Arash explains what we are doing and that we would very much like to hear their views and experiences, with the focus on being gay and living with HIV/AIDS. Amir and Hassan had met a couple of years ago in Tehran, and have been together ever since, more formally after they both became HIV-positive. Amir takes the blame for their HIV-positive status when he says during the interview that Hassan "got it from me." Hassan holds Amir's hand even tighter when he says that and does not seem to think much about how he got infected. He cannot change his situation now, he says. He used to be a police officer, but when he got diagnosed with HIV, he was fired. He revealed a bit about his job as a police officer during that time and how he tried to guide/help young gays from the countryside coming to Tehran:

> I've helped a lot of them and guided them when they were arrested because I'm one of them, many of them come from small towns and they've just heard about Daneshju Park so that they just go there, they don't know that there is just a swamp.

In the above quote, Hassan emphasizes that he is "one of them" and in that sense he feels compelled to guide those young and inexperienced gays when they come to Tehran, the big city with its many "swamps" and pitfalls, such as the Daneshju Park (see Chap. 8).

Hassan's family does not know anything about his situation, neither that he is gay nor that he is HIV-positive. He is the only son, and thus they have tried many times to find a wife for him, but he has always come up with some excuse and rejects their proposals. Amir's family knows that he is gay. He explains that in the beginning they were "annoying," but they "don't care anymore." Hassan explains a bit further what they mean by not "care[ing] anymore":

> They start denying [the gay person] and stop caring [about him]. With harsh reactions they respond to your different way of life at first by putting some sanctions or limitations on you as a family member and their actions make the gay member feel terrible and empty [emotionally and mentally].

Coming back to the topic of HIV/AIDS and how the disease has affected them, Hassan first gives his views about initial reaction to seropositivity, which he has either experienced or heard about from his gay-identifying friends who are seropositive:

> Psychologically when someone recognizes that he is positive either he commits a suicide or decides to take the revenge of his disease by transferring it to others, which is terrible.

Both Hassan and Amir explained in the interview that there were moments when they had both thought of taking their own life, and that both of them had heard stories about HIV-positive gays not taking any precautions when engaging in sex. Amir particularly feels guilt-ridden, and he perceives that his life prospects are not very good:

Arash: Yeah we've taken him to some places but he [Jón] is leaving tonight and he'll be back in December.
Amir: If I will be alive then.
Arash: Oh, dear, don't say that.
Amir: Yeah, I mean it ☹
Hassan: He's being illusionary that he's dying.
Amir: Because it's a serious situation. I was living my life and I was healthy.
Arash: Do you know that HIV is not a deadly disease anymore? I mean it's not on that list anymore in the United States of America.
Amir: That's America, here's Iran.
Arash: It will be in Iran too, soon. Never lose your hope and technology is improving every day.

The dialogue between Arash and Amir draws attention to the "geocorpographies," or how "bodies and bodily identity are always already constrained or enabled by their placement in space" (Randell-Moon and Tippet 2016, p. vii). As Pocius (2016) has argued, this is particularly true in terms of HIV/AIDS treatment and expectation to live among HIV/AIDS patients. In the US, and the global north, at least for those who are insured, seropositive individuals have wide access to medical care in order to improve the quality of life, turning this once-deadly disease into a chronic one. In the global south, on the other hand, this is not always the case, and many HIV-positive individuals get no treatment at all. Although Iran offers free antiretroviral treatment, Amir did not experience it positively, as indicated by his reactions to the comparison Arash made to the US. For Amir, being HIV-positive is still a "deadly" disease in Iran, not necessarily physically, more so in the sense that you are socially dead, you have no status, being gay and HIV-positive. In other words, you become an abject, carrying the stigma of a "double disease," HIV and being gay.

Hassan elaborated on this theme, and it draws further attention to the abjected status of those individuals that are HIV-positive and "gay looking," as in the case of Amir:

> [Amir] was hospitalized in a mental hospital. There they told me that he was so strange. Since they knew of his HIV-status they kept him in some kind of cage and some of the patients walked around it, watching him like they're in the cinema or the zoo. In the end they sent him to a "normal" room, which was a part of the intensive care unit. Even the nurses there, who are mostly males, always asked me in private, when I went there to visit him, about how I knew him or what's our relationship. Of course they didn't know the term "boyfriend" and it was also not all right to say that we are friends since they would then know about our true relationship. So I told them that we are relatives. Every time they warned me that I should be careful and not shake his hand, kiss him or get too close. He was toxic in their views, HIV-positive. I don't understand this. Their knowledge about this disease is so low that it sucks. I felt sick of them every time even though they didn't know that I'm positive too but I knew how bad it is and that hurts. My only motivation to be there was to take care of him [Amir]. He was crying every night and wanted to commit suicide.

Hassan's description of how Amir was treated at the hospital is both grim and plainly inhuman. Furthermore, the fear among staff members regarding the disease, and as described by Hassan, recollects some of the descriptions from the global north during the initial stages of the HIV/AIDS epidemic when information about the routes of infection was not fully known, and HIV/AIDS patients were considered to be "toxic" (Gardell and Greider 2007). These descriptions, however, contradict some surveys conducted in Iran regarding attitudes toward people living with HIV, and the knowledge of its modes of transmission. According to one survey from 2004, attitudes are generally positive, particularly in the big cities such as Tehran (Montazeri 2005). Moreover, people are generally aware of its modes of transmission, particularly the younger generation (Montazeri 2005). However, these surveys are both limited in scope and in terms of the composition of its participants. Thus, they are unlikely to be fully representative of the general attitude and knowledge of HIV/AIDS in Iran. What also makes Amir's case more complicated and which needs to be taken into account, is that his seropositive status intersects with his "gay looking" appearance. This drew forth prejudices and homophobia among the staff members at the hospital, and they didn't perceive him as a "real person." He was thus not recognized for what he is, a human being, but stigmatized as a sick person in a double sense, infected not only by HIV but also by the "gay disease." He is, therefore, seen as something toxic that cannot be touched or kissed, and within the official discourse, he is rendered as an abject.

We finished the interview with Amir and Hassan, and hugged them for a while before our paths departed. After that Arash and I walk our way to the bus station. Both of us are silent and in a bit of shock after the interview. Arash burst into tears two times during the interview and had to leave the room: "I should not have cried. Maybe he [Amir] thinks that I have pity on him or that I judge him," Arash said when we were walking out of the hospital compound. I told him that nobody thought so during the interview and that hearing difficult experiences can be painful. We continued our reflections and talked about the interview in a small teahouse close to the bus station and tried to support each other emotionally. My thoughts during that time revolved around if I should have stopped the interview rather than putting Arash into this situation. We discussed this at the teahouse, and I asked Arash whether we should have stopped the interview when he felt uncomfortable and I explained to him my thoughts on the issue. He told me that he had learned a lot from the experience and had himself grown as a person. He had experienced something new regarding "gay life" in Iran, and he felt a bit emancipated in the sense that he was doing something good: "This made me feel good in the end. I feel as if I have some purpose and I want to help my fellow gay Iranians." When I asked him more about the interview and what the most emotional part for him was, he referred to that fact that Amir was so young. Maybe he saw himself in him, and what happened to Amir could have happened to him: "I could not imagine how I could cope if I would be positive. Being both positive and gay is terrible in Iran."

On our way from the teahouse, Arash got a message from Mr. Dabiri, the consultant at the HIV-center we met the day before. He had heard about the interview and had asked for a copy of it. Both of us were a bit surprised by this and replied to him that the interview was strictly confidential and that he could not get a copy of it. However, Mr. Dabiri was not satisfied with our reply and insisted on getting a copy of the interview. He was obviously under pressure from his superiors. I started to feel a bit insecure myself and thought about ways to hide the recordings or to destroy them so it would not fall into the hands of the authorities. In the end, Arash was able to calm Mr. Dabiri down and I went to my guesthouse. But then when I was there, Mr. Dabiri contacted me through short messages and repeated his request to get a copy of the interview. Moreover, he asked me to call his superior at the HIV-center, and explain this to him, which I then did. I was able to explain everything to Mr. Dabiri's superior, and the matter was resolved. Still being uncomfortable with the situation, I asked Arash to come to my guesthouse and help me transcribe/translate the interview. We did so for some hours, and I then translated everything into Icelandic. After that I deleted the interview and all the files related to the interview in English and only kept the Icelandic version of the transcription on a USB stick, knowing that Icelandic is not understood so widely. With this, I was trying to secure the confidentiality of my informants but at the same time getting their message out there via the Icelandic version.

This scenario shows how sensitive everything is regarding HIV and being gay in Iran. Even the friendly staff at the HIV-center went on the defense when they heard about the interview with Amir and Hassan, probably being afraid of their superiors, and that some harsh criticism on the system might have been expressed in the interview. Arash and I felt the tension, and it somehow drew us back to reality: that we were somehow walking on "eggshells" and we needed to take even more precautions regarding the research. Moreover, the interview with Amir and Hassan, and what followed, not only draws attention to some ethical questions, which I have tried to reflect on already (see also Chap. 1), but also emphasizes the importance of approaching ethics as a process, a social construct, which one needs to revise through the research process. It also involves cooperation between the participants and the researcher, and all ethical decisions need to be adapted to the research context (Brown and Thompson 1997; Stalker 1998). This particularly applies when the government does not sanction the research, and fieldwork is thus done "underground."

*   *   *

In this chapter the main focus was on how *biopower* operates on different levels in terms of HIV/AIDS, sexuality, and gender. At the societal level and within the official statistics, HIV/AIDS is mostly understood to affect those on the margins of society, for example, IDUs. In fact, homosexuality or non-heterosexuality is rarely or only vaguely mentioned in research papers as a mode of HIV/AIDS transmission in Iran. In other words, this group is silenced and not mentioned as a possible target group in terms of HIV/AIDS infections, which is in line with the official discourse that does not recognize this particular group. As an example of the institutional level of *biopower*, the operation of the HIV-center in Tehran was described and analyzed. It was argued that the center operates mostly for those on the margins of Iranian society, a site for abjected bodies, which are regulated within its isolated space. In that sense, the HIV-center draws attention to how subjects are in general constructed through religio-cultural discourses and practices of *biopower*, especially in terms of sexuality, and other practices, which are assumed to be outside of what is perceived intelligible within post-revolutionary Iranian society. This was also felt at the individual level in terms of being tested for HIV/AIDS. As argued in the chapter, the process of testing draws attention to the various power dynamics involved. In that sense, the nature of testing and indeed giving a testimony, meaning telling the truth or giving evidence about oneself, relates to confessing about one's inner self. Thus, taking a test, in this case an HIV-test, means revealing some truth about oneself, not only with regards to biometrics in the form of a small blood sample but also giving information about one's inner self, related to one's sexuality and/or past sexual practices. The last section of this chapter addressed livability in terms of being HIV-positive and gay. It gives an account of how being gay and seropositive was experienced by Amir and Hassan. In their case, different modalities of power had implications for their life and full civic participatory action. They both experienced prejudices and homophobia, especially Amir, who felt that he was not perceived as a "real person," neither by the medical authorities nor society in general. Instead, he was stigmatized as a sick person in a double sense, not only infected by HIV but also by the "gay disease." He is therefore seen as something "toxic," and within the official discourse, he is rendered as an abject. However, it needs to be kept in mind, that the voices presented here provide only some insight into the livability of gay HIV-positive men in Iran. I therefore do not claim to be giving a representative account of being gay and seropositive in urban Iran, and Amir and Hassan's story is only one of many.

NOTES

1. Two years before the *Newsweek* article was published, *The New York Times* had published an article titled "Rare Cancer Seen in 41 Homosexuals," which can be defined as one of the first news coverage related to the AIDS epidemic. However, *The New York Times* did not feature the epidemic prominently until after the *Newsweek* article/paper (see Altman 1981, July 3).
2. Sources do not agree on when exactly HIV/AIDS was first reported in Iran. Montazeri (2005) states that AIDS was first identified in 1985, Ramezani Tehrani and Malek-Afzali (2008) maintain that it was in 1986, whereas Fallahzadeh et al. (2009) and Tavoosi et al. (2004) claim that the first case of HIV was diagnosed in 1987.
3. Gayle Rubin has written about hierarchy of sexual practices, which can be applied with regards to "barebacking" versus use of condom. According to Rubin's arguments, heterosexual sex in a monogamous relationship is considered to be a "good" sexual practice, whereas other sexual practices, such as non-heterosexual sex, are assumed to be "bad" (see Rubin 1984).
4. Morteza, in a Telegram conversation with the author, 11.25.2017.
5. Morteza, in a Telegram conversation with the author, 11.25.2017.
6. The Family Health Association (FHA) was founded in 1995. It is an NGO which has two main aims: Firstly to provide information to the public, media, religious, and political leaders about family planning, as well sexual and reproductive health. Secondly, to promote sexual and reproductive health needs of young people and adolescents (see IPPF (n.d.). Family Health Association of Iran).

REFERENCES

A Timeline of HIV/AIDS. (n.d.). *Aids.gov*. Retrieved from https://www.hiv.gov/sites/default/files/aidsgov-timeline.pdf.
Abu-Raddad, L. J., Akala, F. A., Semini, I., Riedner, G., Wilson, D., & Tawil, O. (2010). *Characterizing the HIV/AIDS. Epidemic in the Middle East and North*

Africa. Time for Strategic Action. Washington: The International Bank for Reconstruction and Development / The World Bank.

Afary, J. (2009). *Sexual Politics in Modern Iran.* Cambridge: Cambridge University.

Altman, L. (1981, July 3). Rare Cancer Seen in 41 Homosexuals. *The New York Times.* Retrieved from http://www.nytimes.com/1981/07/03/us/rare-cancer-seen-in-41-homosexuals.html.

Amanat, A. (2017). *Iran. A Modern History.* New Haven: Yale University Press.

Brown, H., & Thompson, D. (1997). The Ethics of Research with Men Who Have Learning Disabilities and Abusive Sexual Behavior: A Minefield in a Vacuum. *Disability & Society, 12*(5), 695–707.

Butler, J. (1993). *Bodies That Matter. On the Discursive Limits of Sex.* New York: Routledge.

Dean, T. (2009). *Unlimited Intimacy. Reflections on the Subculture of Barebacking.* Chicago: University of Chicago Press.

Fader, L. (2014, April 24). Newsweek Rewind: 30 Years Ago, Scientists Discovered the Cause of AIDS. *Newsweek.* Retrieved from http://www.newsweek.com/newsweek-rewind-30-years-ago-scientists-discovered-cause-hiv-248566.

Fallahzadeh, H., Morowatisharifabad, M., & Ehrampoosh, M. H. (2009, April). HIV/AIDS Epidemic Features and Trends in Iran, 1986–2006. *AIDS and Behavior, 13*(2), 297–302. https://doi.org/10.1007/s10461-008-9452-7.

Foucault, M. (1990). *The History of Sexuality: Vol. 1. An Introduction* (R. Hurley, Trans.). New York, NY: Vintage Books.

Foucault, M. (1991). *Discipline and Punish. The Birth of the Prison.* London: Penguin.

Foucault, M. (1994). *The Birth of the Clinic: An Archaeology of Medical Perception.* New York: Vintage Books.

Foucault, M., & Miskowiec, J. (1986). Of Other Spaces. *Diacritics, 16,* 22–27.

Frydlewicz, R. (1983, April 11). Newsweek Cover Story Explains AIDS to the General Public. Retrieved from http://thestarryeye.typepad.com/gay/2012/04/newsweek-explains-aids-to-the-general-public-april-11-1983-.html

Gardell, J., & Greider, R. S. W. (2007). *And the Band Played on: Politics, People, and the AIDS Epidemic.* New York: St. Martin's Griffin.

Haghdoost, A. A., Mostafavi, E., Mirzazadeh, A., Navadeh, S., Feizzadeh, A., et al. (2011, January). Modelling of HIV/AIDS in Iran up to 2014. *Journal of AIDS and HIV Research, 3*(12), 231–239. https://doi.org/10.5897/jahr11.030.

Hearn, J. (2015). *Men of the World. Genders, Globalization, Transnational Times.* London: Sage.

Iranian AIDS Research Center (IRCHA). Retrieved from http://ircha.tums.ac.ir/index.jsp?fkeyid=&siteid=95&pageid=5319#.

IPPF. (n.d.). Family Health Association of Iran. Retrieved from https://www.ippf.org/about-us/member-associations/iran.

Karsh, E. (2009). *The Iran-Iraq War.* New York: The Rosen Publishing Group.

Kayhan Bad Company (homepage). (2015). Retrieved from http://kbdco.com/.

Kinsella, J. (1989). *Covering the Plague. AIDS and the American Media.* New Brunswick and London: Rutgers University Press.

Larsen, J. (2001, December 28). Iran's Birth Rate Plummeting at a Record Pace: Success Provides Models for Other Developing Countries. *Earth Policy Institute.* Retrieved from http://www.mnforsustain.org/iran_model_of_reducing_fertility.htm.

Mahdavi, P. (2008). *Passionate Uprisings. Iran's Sexual Revolution.* Stanford: Stanford University Press.

Montazeri, A. (2005). AIDS Knowledge and Attitudes in Iran: Results from a Population-based Survey in Tehran. *Patient Education and Counseling, 57,* 199–203.

Muir, J. (2002, April 24). Condoms Help Check Iran Birth Rate. *BBC News.* Retrieved from http://news.bbc.co.uk/2/hi/middle_east/1949068.stm.

Nemanipour, G., Shariat-Torbaghan, S., Yalda, A., et al. (2008). *Historical Perspective of Imam Khomeini Hospital Complex.* Tehran: Tehran University of Medical Sciences.

Plummer, K. (1988). Organizing AIDS. In P. Aggleton & H. Homans (Eds.), *Social Aspects of AIDS* (pp. 20–52). London: The Falmer Press.

Pocius, J. (2016). Of Bodies, Borders, and Barebacking: The Geocorpographies of HIV. In H. Randell-Moon & R. Tippet (Eds.), *Security, Race, Biopower: Essays on Technology and Corporeality* (pp. 21–41). London: Palgrave Macmillan.

Ramezani Tehrani, F., & Malek-Afzali, H. (2008, January–February). Knowledge, Attitudes and Practices Concerning HIV/AIDS Among Iranian at-risk Sub Populations. *La Revue de Santé de la Méditerranée orientale, 14*(1), 142–156.

Randell-Moon, H., & Tippet, R. (2016). Introduction. In H. Randell-Moon & R. Tippet (Eds.), *Security, Race, Biopower: Essays on Technology and Corporeality* (pp. v–xxvi). London: Palgrave Macmillan.

Rubin, G. (1984). Thinking Sex: Notes for a Radical Theory of the Politics of Sexuality. In C. Vance (Ed.), *Pleasure and Danger* (pp. 143–178). London: Routledge.

Sciolino, E. (2000). *Persian Mirrors. The Elusive Face of Iran.* New York: Simon and Schuster.

Stalker, K. (1998). Some Ethical and Methodological Issues in Research with People with Learning Difficulties. *Disability & Society, 13*(1), 5–19. https://doi.org/10.1080/09687599826885.

Takeyh, R. (2010). The Iran-Iraq War: A Reassessment. *The Middle East Journal, 64*(3), 365–383. https://doi.org/10.3751/64.3.12.

Tavoosi, A., Zaferani, A., Enzevaei, A., Tajik, P., & Ahmadinezhad, Z. (2004, May). Knowledge and Attitude Towards HIV/AIDS Among Iranian Students. *BMC Public Health, 4*(17). https://doi.org/10.1186/1471-2458-4-17.

Unaids. (2017a). UN AIDS DATA 2017. Retrieved from http://www.unaids.org/sites/default/files/media_asset/20170720_Data_book_2017_en.pdf.

Unaids. (2017b, May 12). Germany—ending AIDS by 2020. Retrieved from http://www.unaids.org/en/resources/presscentre/featurestories/2017/may/20170512_germany.

Vahdat, A., & Fattahi, M. (2017, November 29). Iran Challenges Taboos as HIV from Sex Rise. *The Seattle Times*. Retrieved from https://www.seattletimes.com/nation-world/iran-challenges-taboos-on-discussing-sex-as-hiv-rate-rises/.

Watney, S. (1988). AIDS "Moral Panic" Theory and Homophobia. In P. Aggleton & H. Homans (Eds.), *Social Aspects of AIDS*. London: Falmer Press.

CHAPTER 8

Gay/Queer Spaces in Tehran: Intimacy, Sociality, and Resistance

In this chapter, I provide empirical insights into how gay/queer Iranian men navigate their lives between different spaces—social, virtual, and physical—in order to accommodate their gay identity and sexual desires within the legal-social and Islamic context of modern Iran. By employing Foucauldian analytic frameworks that attend to questions of heterotopic spatiality, and in conjunction with Massey's notion of power geometries and how space is produced, I illuminate the complexity of queer Iranian men's spatio-temporal modes of sociality in relation to sexual practices and being gay/queer (see also Kjaran and Martino 2017). As discussed in Chap. 2, heterotopia describes spaces that are outside the traditionally normative or dominant institutional spaces of power (Foucault 1984). Heterotopic spaces are also temporal, which, in line with Massey, are

---

In this chapter, I employ the term "queer" along with the identity label "gay," as those spaces discussed here were frequented not only by those who identify as gay but also by bisexual men, men who have sex with men, lesbians, transgender, and gender-queers, and individuals who do not ascribe to any identity category. Sometimes the term "queer man" is used to indicate non-heterosexuality in general. Using queer is also aligned to my epistemological positioning, emphasizing instability of any identity category, as well as how being and acting in a queer way can transgress the dominant norms and discourses. In that respect, I use the verb "queering" with the meaning of transgressing or showing resistance to the dominant norms/discourses.

© The Author(s) 2019
J. I. Kjaran, *Gay Life Stories*,
https://doi.org/10.1007/978-3-030-12831-9_8

constantly in the making (being unmade and remade) and have the potential to transgress and disrupt the utopian ideal. Heterotopia can also be seen as a space where individuals feel secure and experience a supportive environment, where they can explore different identities. Moreover, this chapter draws attention to how spaces can be transformed, claimed, and even *queered* within the limits set by the dominant discourse on gender and sexuality. Although being on the margins of society and not fully visible within the public sphere, these heterotopic spaces offer opportunities for resistance, solidarity, and empowerment for gay-identifying Iranians. Within these spaces, the body becomes a site of resistance—both in terms of how they are embodied and occupied—but also through remaking (transforming) the space by resisting dominant religio-social norms/discourse. Putting the body in focus and how it can, through bodily transformation, act as a site of resistance to the dominant norms; I dedicate the first section of this chapter to examining the emerging tattoo subculture in Tehran. The subsequent sections focus on virtual and physical spaces, within the privacy of the home, as well as within the public sphere, and how gay/queer Iranian men navigate, claim, and use these spaces.

Tattoos in Tehran: Resisting the Official Aesthetics of the Body

Today is the day. I am going to get my first tattoo. I have been thinking about getting a tattoo for some time—but having it done in Tehran, in the Islamic Republic of Iran; I must be crazy. I feel excited but also a bit scared going to an underground tattoo parlor. All kinds of thoughts are going through my head. Will it be safe? Are the needles clean? Will it be painful? Do they have same skills as in the West? Will it be a disaster? Will I get into trouble? Part of me is saying: "Don't go Jón, just cancel the appointment." But I feel that I need to do this. I want to experience the underground tattoo scene in Tehran and the best way to do it is to have an embodied experience of getting "inked". I also decided this some months ago in one of the online chats I had with Arash, when he suggested I should do it during my fieldtrip in Tehran. I remember him saying that it would be good for you to get to know this part of the underground life in Tehran. He has also done a lot to prepare this, even designed my tattoo—an Iranian symbol. So, I will just need to place all my trust in Arash, who has made the appointment through a gay friend.

The excerpt is from my field notes, which I wrote some hours before I met Arash at the Imam Khomeini metro station. I saw him immediately at the southern entrance, smiling at me and joyfully asking: "Jón, are you ready for the tattoo? I am so excited about this." We take the metro to central Tehran, close to Laleh Park. We walk some minutes from the metro station in the unbearable August heat, mixed with pollution and fumes from the heavy traffic. Finally, we reach our destination—the underground tattoo parlor—located in a two-bedroom apartment. Hassan, who identifies as gay, runs it, and he lives there with his boyfriend. Before he started his work on me, he offered us some tea, and I took the opportunity to talk with him about the tattoo subculture in Iran. "It is increasing and today it is getting more popular to have a tattoo—especially amongst young middle class men." However, although getting a tattoo is not strictly illegal, from a religious perspective, it is considered to be immoral and is therefore denounced by the authorities. In fact, both society and authorities have often stigmatized people with tattoos, and some have even been arrested by the morality police or fined for showing their tattoos in public. In the official discourse, tattoos are seen as a sign of *Westoxification* (see Chap. 3), and often associated with criminality and anti-social behavior.[1] It has been reported that the Iranian police have sometimes publically displayed the tattoos of arrested men with the aim of connecting tattoos to criminal activities (Al Monitor). Thus, reaching a decision to get a tattoo involves being aware of the social stigma attached to it as well as the possible repercussions if discovered either by family members or the authorities.

Although getting a tattoo incurs social stigma and can lead to arrest and punishment for both genders, the repercussions are often harsher for women than for men. A young unmarried woman in an interview in *Al Monitor* draws attention to the gender dynamics involved in getting a tattoo: "My brothers would kill me if they find out" (Needles and Sins 2013, December 10). Sara, who has worked as a tattoo artist in Tehran for several years, said in an interview in the online magazine *The Observers* that many women "don't want to get tattoos before marriage because they're afraid their husbands might not like it or even think poorly of them."[2] In fact, it can be argued that the obsession in Iranian culture regarding women's purity—mostly in terms of virginity before marriage (Afary 2009, p. 25)—has been conflated with the female body in general; therefore, having a tattoo devalues women's desirability and impacts their marriage opportunities. In other words, girls who have tattoos are not seen as "respectable" and are depicted in the official discourse as "polluted" or "toxic"—and as being under the influence of a "morally degenerated" youth culture imported from the West—invoking again the official discourse of *Westoxification*.[3] Another aspect of the gender dynamics regarding tattoos in Iran, mentioned by Hassan, is that most of his colleagues are women. In fact, female tattoo artists outnumber men and are often highly sought after. Sara, for example, has acquired a good reputation for her quality work and can therefore choose her clients. However, being a tattoo artist in Iran can be a dangerous trade, as Sara revealed in an interview in *The Observers*: "About seven months ago, a policeman posed as a customer. However, when he saw I wore a scarf and a hijab, he changed his mind and said he would not report me. I was very lucky, and since then, I've become more careful in choosing my clients" (Working underground: The life of an Iranian tattoo artist 2013, July 15). Sara was saved by dressing modestly, in accordance with Islamic morality (wearing hijab and a scarf), and was not reported. Mohsen (not his real name), a popular tattoo artist in Tehran, was, however, not as lucky and was jailed for six months after being tortured in the Evin Prison. After he was released, a journalist asked him what had kept his spirit alive during the imprisonment: "I love being a tattoo artist—that's how" (DW. Made for minds). Thus, being a tattoo artist is a passion, a way of life, which was further confirmed by Hassan, who started the trade some years ago.

> I lie down on the bench with the left side of my body facing up. Hassan sterilizes the spot where he is going to place the tattoo. I feel the rush of cold moving over the spot but also a bit of numbness as he puts some anesthetic cream on it. He is very professional. I am comfortable, relaxed, and my previous doubts and fear are all gone. I am being taken good care of in this underground tattoo parlor. Then Hassan draws the outlines of the tattoo Arash and me had chosen some weeks ago. It is an Iranian symbol, written in Farsi, *hich*—which can mean different things, nothing and everything. It has its origins in Sufism and when written in a particular way it has a religious connotation. In my case we decide to skip the religious part of the symbol. I can hear that Hassan is preparing the machine—ink and needles are in place. He tells me that he will start now. I hear the sound from the machine; it's like a drilling sound, getting more intense as the machine moves closer to my body. Arash holds my hand—the tattoo work has begun.

"All done, you have a nice tattoo now," says Hassan after half an hour. Arash smiles at me, agreeing with Hassan. So does Mansur, a friend of Arash, who identifies as gay. He had just arrived and is going to drive me back to my place. He tells me that some weeks ago he had got his second tattoo from Hassan. I notice that he has some piercings in his left ear. While Hassan is finishing the work on me—covering the tattoo with a plastic film—I ask Mansur about what these tattoos mean for him:

> For me it is a freedom of being myself and deciding how my body looks. I cannot express myself openly—I mean being gay and all—so through my body art I find some ways. I have the *faravahar*[4] symbol on my shoulder— it's really nice and colorful, I love it. Hassan did a good job. My parents know that I have tattoos and are alright with it—but they don't know I am gay. Sometimes, when I wear a short t-shirt you can glimpse my tattoo, and I have noticed that sometimes people just look at me, like they are judging me. Also because I have piercings—that is not acceptable here in Iran.

Mansur draws attention to how he uses his body as a site of resistance— having both tattoos and piercings. Moreover, his modified body can be seen as a space of agency and personal empowerment, bearing in mind the limits set for gay/queer Iranians by the official religio-legal discourse. He feels that he can exercise control and choice over his own body through this kind of bodily modification. Peter Lentini has argued that in societies "in which people are under constant and increasing surveillance, individuals can thus exercise power over themselves by modifying their bodies" (Lentini 1999, p. 35). Thus, having tattoos or piercings can be seen as an act of political agency but also, as Victoria Pitts has argued, a "form of sexualized, embodied politics" (Pitts 2003, p. 87). It can, therefore, be argued that even though Mansur usually covers his tattoos when he is out in public, that by simply becoming tattooed, he is articulating a politics of dissent against dominant societal norms prescribing the aesthetics of the "proper" and "natural" body.

After my visit to Hassan's tattoo parlor, where I experienced the pain, stress, and the relief of having my first tattoo, I felt that I had somehow a deeper understanding of how the body can act as a site of resistance, and how some of my informants used bodily modification or clothes (see next section) to claim a space of agency. Moreover, it became clear to me that tattoo parlors such as the one run by Hassan can be understood as heterotopic spaces, as they open up spaces of possibility for individual subjects—gay and queers who resist the dominant discourse on the aesthetics of the body—where the tattooed subjects gain some personal empowerment.

Let's Party Until Dawn: Gay Intimacy and Sociality Within the Private Sphere

We don't have gay clubs or gay bars like you have in the West. In fact, we don't have any special place for gay people in Iran. But we have made some places for ourselves—for example at home or online. (Pouria)

In Chap. 2, I discussed the traditional distinction between the public and private spheres in Iran, particularly in relation to gender and sexuality. Traditional houses in Iran were divided into *andaruni*, the inner private part of the house, reserved for women and close family members, and *biruni*, the public space, mostly occupied by men (Arjmand 2017). This architectural division on the basis of gender symbolically represents the gender divide in society at large, as well as the division between the private and public in terms of confessions of the self. Gay Iranian men, in regards to their sexual identity, have internalized this strict division: Being "out" means negotiating your sexuality depending on the spatial relations, whether within the private space of friends and those you can trust, or out in the public. In this section, the focus will be on the private sphere, the private domain of the home, and how gay-identifying Iranian men make and remake that space for themselves, where they meet, flirt, and enjoy each other's company. Hence, gay and straight parties, as well as small gatherings in homes, are often held regularly in Iran, at least in Tehran (Mahdavi 2008). However, creating such spaces depends on the social (economic) class of the individual host, as it can be quite expensive to throw a party—cost of housing and also paying bribes to the morality police or *Basij* units.

During my fieldtrips to Tehran, I was invited to several "gay parties" in different parts of the city. I experienced how gay-identifying men "made a place for themselves," as Pouria speaks about in the beginning of this section. For example, I went twice to large parties in the northern part of Tehran, where both the guests and the host were clearly affluent and members of the upper middle class. I was also invited several times to smaller gatherings/parties in the southern and central part of the city, where both the host and guests were from the lower social (economic) background. This section will concentrate on two parties/gatherings— one in a rich neighborhood in the northern part of the city, and another one in the southern part. The following ethnographic vignettes, based on the field notes that I took during these two evenings/parties, provide an example of my impression of, and a glimpse into, these gatherings:

Rich man's world

Ramin identifies as gay and lives in a big penthouse apartment in the northern part of Tehran. It has several rooms, three bathrooms, and a large living room—I would say that the living room alone is almost 70 to 75 square meters. Large balconies, from where you have a good view over the city, surround the apartment. The apartment is well-furnished, handmade Persian carpets on the floor, and the walls are filled with both modern and more traditional paintings. The large living room is an ideal space for being transformed into a dance floor. This evening, Ramin will throw a big party for his gay friends. I help Ramin and Arash prepare for the party—moving chairs and tables, making space in the living room so the guests can dance, and putting glasses and snacks on some tables close to the living room. At 7pm the DJ arrives and starts to prepare the sound system. I feel that Ramin is getting a bit stressed, making phone-calls while ordering Arash and others around. "Everything needs to look good" he says. Around 8:30pm the first guests arrive. Gradually Ramin's big penthouse apartment is transformed into a "gay club". There is an open bar with all kinds of alcohol, the lights are turned down and the music gets louder—a mixture of Western and Iranian/Middle Eastern hits blast the air. The guests are dancing, some more intimately than others. The majority of the guests are in their 30s, but generally there is a mixture of all ages at the party, the oldest guest being 60 years old. All of them are dressed well, according to the latest fashion, and some wear shorts. I notice that some arrive in trousers but then change in an adjacent room into shorts and tank tops. After midnight, food is served. Then the music continues and everybody starts dancing again. Around 2am the music begins to slow down and some leave the party. Others sit on the balcony, smoke, drink, flirt and chat. I am never left alone or unattended—there is always someone asking me if I need something or if I am having a good time. Everybody is friendly towards me and most of the guests are willing to express their views on gay life in Iran. They know that I am a guest of Ramin, a foreigner, and here for a visit and doing research on gay life in Iran. (Fieldnotes, Tehran, August 3, 2015)

Taste of popcorn

It is shortly after 5pm. Arash and I stop in front of a small neighborhood mosque. Arash calls Farhod, and shortly afterwards he meets us in a side street opposite the mosque. We go with him some 800 meters to a small three-story apartment building. It is in rather good shape. We enter a door and go into a small courtyard. After that, we enter the house and walk down some stairs, entering the basement apartment. The apartment consists of one big living room, a small bedroom, kitchen and a bathroom. In the living room there are some couches, chairs and small tables. It is a rather open space, in fact ideal for small gay gatherings. I notice on the fridge in the kitchen that there is a magnet with the rainbow flag. Basir, Farhod's partner, greets us and offers us some tee. We talk for a while and after that we prepare the apartment for the evening. Saahand, a gay friend living with Farhod and Basir, joins us in the preparation. Soon, the guests arrive and it starts to be lively, the music of Madonna, Beyoncé and Rihanna fills the room (air) and some guests start to dance, moving their bodies in beat with the music. Farhod offers me some homemade wine, which reminds me of rather sweet rosé. I notice that some of the guests enter the bedroom right after they arrive, stay there for a while, before coming out into the spacious living room. Apparently, they have been changing clothes in there, putting on more colorful clothes or some other outfit. Thus, the bedroom is used as changing room. Mika, for example, enters the apartment as a full bearded man but then returns from the bedroom in a drag, looking like a full bearded woman. When I asked him about his appearance, he told me: "I define myself as gender-queer." "Just like Conchita Wurst from last year's Eurovision" I replied. Mika and some other guests nearby agree with my comments. Laughing and smiling, and tell me that they follow Eurovision and therefore know all about the bearded diva, Conchita Wurst. Another guest arrives who also changes clothes shortly afterwards, putting on more colorful trousers and a rather tight shirt. Farhod has also put on some more flashy clothes and wears his rainbow-flag bracelet. More guests arrive, a trans-woman and some more gay friends of Farhod and Basir. Most of the guests bring something with them, such as popcorn, cakes, snacks or some drinks. (Fieldnotes, Tehran, February 7, 2015)

As can be seen from these excerpts, during such parties, apartments' living rooms are transformed into queer/gay social spaces through the presence and embodiment of the guests. The bedroom or an adjacent room functions symbolically as a closet, both literally and metaphorically, into which the guests enter to change their clothes, and come out performing their gay/queer identity and embodiment more freely. Thus, the metamorphosis of the living room space can be understood as a sort of queer heterotopia, a space for the other to constitute themselves in a reality that is not readily available or legitimized outside of that space (Foucault 1984). It is a real space, made and remade by its inhabitants (guests), which exists within the real world, but it is strictly separate from the wider society. In other words, it is a space for the abjected gay/queer body to be reconstituted and reclaimed in its temporality, enabling one to forget or to escape momentarily the repressive and oppressive conditions in respect to the systematic denial and repudiation of sexual minorities, non-normative gender expression, and the social stigma attached to those who transgress the official norms with regards to gender and/or sexuality. These sentiments were expressed by Mika, who identifies as gender-queer: "Here [at the party in Farhod's and Basir's apartment], I can forget, I can have fun, just for a short time, I can be myself." Kia, who attended Ramin's party, made a similar statement, expressing how much he enjoyed coming to these kind of gatherings/parties: "I am Muslim and gay. I pray and fast during the Ramadan. But I go to gay parties, dance, drink alcohol and feel great—at least for short a time. Ramin's parties are the best." Later that evening, I saw how much fun Kia was having, going regularly to the open bar and dancing trance-like with the beat of the latest music hits.

Here, it needs to be emphasized that these queer/gay heterotopic private spaces in their very temporality are precariously unstable sites of queer/gay exposure and sociality. After the party is over, the guests go back into their real life, where they have to put on masks and hide their sexual identity. It is, therefore, in their temporality that such heterotopic spaces for gatherings and parties need to be understood. However, the freedom one has outside of these heterotopic spaces depends on one's social/economic class (position). One of the guests, aged 22 years and from a rich family, with whom I had talked to at Ramin's party, said: "I love the gay community in Tehran. It's no problem to be gay here—especially if you are rich." He spends three months a year in Western Europe where he can socialize freely with other gays and be himself. He can also throw parties whenever he feels like it or invite friends out for a "ride" in his BMW.

In fact, there is a distinction between Farhod's and Basir's party and those hosted by rich gay men such as Ramin, even though all of these gay parties can be understood as queer/gay heterotopic spaces offering sociality and comfortability for gay-identifying men. The latter are often more homogenous in terms of its guests, mostly being gay men who dress in accordance to the dominant gender norms—many being what some of my informants defined as "straight looking" (see Chap. 5). Moreover, in these parties, the host provides alcohol and snacks. It was somehow expected and a part of the image of being a good host—showing how well-off you are. However, in parties such as the one Farhod and Basir held, where the host and the guests are mostly from lower socio-economic backgrounds, the composition of the guests was usually more heterogeneous: gays, transgender individuals, and gender-queers. The guests dressed more defiantly, often against the dominant gender-norms, and in that sense often queered the dominant discourse on gender and sexuality. This space was also more welcoming and inclusive of diversity, and for me, the outsider, I felt that there was a stronger sense of community and reciprocity at those parties. As an example of that, everybody contributed to making the party a great experience—bringing food, drinks, or something else. Arash, who belongs to the upper middle class (in economic terms), mentioned this to me after the party:

> I have never felt as good as being there, I had such great fun, and everything is so easy and without any restriction. One of them had popcorn. One of them had cake. One of them had fruits (referring to the things the guests brought to the party) […] I've never seen that.

Arash had not previously witnessed such a community of care and intimacy during such gatherings, where everybody is somehow equal and made some kind of contribution. This he had not experienced in gay parties among the rich in the northern part of Tehran, where guests took it for granted they would be provided with drinks, music, and snacks. Another aspect of organizing and holding a party is to be aware of the risk involved, especially the possibility that the *Basij* units or the police will raid it. For those hosts with money, it is less a worry as they can afford to pay bribes to the authorities (the *Basij* units and police) and give out money to those who need to be kept silent. Ramin, and some of his guests I talked to at his party, mentioned this and added that they had no recollection of any parties held among their group of friends that had been raided so far. Farhod and Basir, on the other hand, told me that they had been at parties in the southern part of Tehran that had been raided by the police/*Basij* units. These accounts draw attention to how outside forces set certain limits on the creation of temporal queer/gay spaces, and how these forces distinguish between those who have money to pay bribes and those who do not. However, despite the risks involved, Farhod and Basir, and their friends, continue to go to gay gatherings as well as host them, as these spaces give them the opportunity to orient themselves as same-sex-desiring subjects, have fun, and be themselves.

PUBLIC SPACES: *CRUISING*[5] AND SOCIALIZING

We have our spaces—we make our spaces. We have cafés and restaurants. One café is on a top floor of a hotel in the northern part of Tehran—the owner is even gay. We meet there, talk and have a good time together. Then there is *Uni-street*—driving circle after circle, laughing and having a great time.[6]

In Tehran, according to many of the informants, there are a few sites where gay men can meet and gather in public. However, these sites change regularly due to the constant regulatory power of the government and, in line with Massey, are constantly unmade and remade by the members of the gay (queer) community with their presence, actions, and embodiment. Hence, these spaces are "always under construction" and imbued with a certain temporality (Massey 2009, p. 22). A coffee shop or a restaurant is temporally transformed into a gay/queer social space, often limited to particular days of the week, where gay/queer sociality can gain a certain degree of intelligibility. Ramtin, for example, gave an account, in Chap. 6, of how he found out during a bus ride that a particular restaurant was frequented by gays on Tuesday evenings. He began to attend those gatherings regularly and felt a degree of empowerment and emancipation, having the possibility to socialize with other gays, at least once a week. The restaurant became his space of agency. This also applies to straight young Iranians, who, since the 1990s, have claimed their space of agency in the expanding Tehran coffee shop scene, mostly in the northern part of the city. These coffee shops have, according to Shahram Khosravi, often been criticized by the authorities for being "places for immoral behavior" (Khosravi 2008, p. 147). Young people hang out at these "immoral" places where they "perform acts of defiance" against the official discourse on morality and "proper" behavior—interacting with the opposite sex, flirting, and having fun (Khosravi 2008, p. 147). Thus, as Khosravi has argued, these places of everyday resistance—coffee shops as well as shopping malls—enable young people of both genders to express "alternative ideas, opinions, and even moralities" (Khosravi 2008, p. 2). In other words, they carve out their own temporal space, set within the limits of the official religio-moral discourse.

However, being under strict surveillance from the authorities, restaurants, and coffee shops that do not follow the official regulations pertaining to spatial design, or have customers that repeatedly act and behave against "Islamic values," runs the risk of being closed down by the authorities (Khosravi 2008). For example, windows of cafés/restaurants should not be blocked from the view of the street in order to prevent any "improper" interactions between the opposite genders within these spaces. Shahryar, who identifies as gay and used to run a café in Mashad, frequented by gays, mentioned this when I met him for a chat at his former coffee shop. He told me that he had to ensure that nothing blocked the windows and that his guests behaved "correctly." "I was also required to have pictures of both Khomeini and Khameini on the wall. I usually just had them somewhere in the café where it was not too obvious. Or I tried to do something artistic or unusual." Shahryar is here referring to how he organized cans of *Illy/Lavazza* coffee around the framed pictures of the two supreme leaders. He was, on the one hand, following the official regulation that requires owners of public spaces to have these images on public display. On the other hand, he was also queering (resisting) those same rules/regulations by how he framed it within the space of his café. Thus, the temporality of space—materialized in the coffee shop or a particular restaurant—for gay sociality and enactment of same-sex desire, speaks phenomenologically to what Ahmed refers to as "the contingency of bodies coming into contact with other bodies" (Ahmed 2006, p. 565; Kjaran and Martino 2017). The "contingency of bodies" is then set within the limits of the official regulations regarding the public spaces and Islamic values that should be followed therein.

Contact with other gay/queer bodies is also established at *Uni-street* by "driving circle after circle," as mentioned by one of my informers in the beginning of this section. In the following ethnographic vignette, I give account of my impression when I joined some of my informants and friends for *car cruising* along *Uni-street*.

Car cruising

Arash picks us up at Farhod's and Basir's apartment. He has borrowed his father's car. I sit in the backseat with Basir, Farhod is in the front passenger seat. We are heading for Uni-street, which is a well-known spot for gay cruising in Tehran. The cruising is mostly done in cars by driving first around 850 meters down the Uni-street, which has two lanes, then taking a U-turn at the traffic lights at the end of the street, close to College bridge, and then driving back, turning around again and driving back down the street. This is often done circle after circle. We are there at around 10pm and already there are some four other cars driving up and down the street. They are all full of guys, presumably gay, participating in the same "cruising" game. The traffic light is red, a car stops right beside the car we are in. Four guys occupy it, loud music is being played, the windows are pulled down—flirting starts and some words are exchanged. Then the traffic light is green and Arash takes the U-turn and drives again down Uni-street. This we do circle after circle—other cars join us. Everybody is having fun. We talk about the guys in the other cars—whether they are cute or sexy. Basir blows kisses to some guys in other cars when we drive past them. I am sitting with him in the backseat and he says to me: "This is so much fun. We don't have gay clubs or bars out in the public where we can meet other gays and flirt. So this is what we do and can do—this is our way of cruising and flirting in public." All of them are having a wonderful time and we "car cruise" along Uni-street for more than an hour. "You are cute" Arash screamed to someone in another car. Arash asks Basir if he has seen that guy on *Hornet* or *Grindr* (online dating applications). During our time there, we only saw the police approaching once and when that happened we drove away from Uni-street to a side street close by. After that, we returned again to the street and drove a couple more circles. (Fieldnotes, Tehran, August 2, 2015)

The official name of *Uni-street* is Engelab-e Islami street (Islamic Revolution Street), but most of my informants simply referred to the street as *Uni-street*, perhaps finding the official name too long or as a sign of defiance to the official revolutionary rhetoric. Part of the Tehran University is situated along the street, from which the street draws its colloquial name. As can be seen from my ethnographic vignette, *car cruising* is great fun. The car, being in-between the private and public space, intertwining these two spheres, functions as a space of agency for its occupants. Protected by the privacy of the car but at the same time driving in public, creates a temporal heterotopic space for gay sociality, interactions, and bodily (sexual) orientations. Usually the aim of *car cruising* is not to find a sex date but more to have fun and flirt with other gays/guys in public. In that sense, the car itself becomes an extension of the body into a gay/queer temporal space, in which you can have fun and feel alive for a moment despite the restrictions and limits set by the official religio-legal discourse on same-sex desire and livability. However, as in the case of the coffee shops, the panoptic surveillance of the state can at any moment disrupt the activities of *car cruising* and render those involved in trouble with the authorities. My fellow "car cruisers" had heard stories of the police stopping cars along *Uni-street*, searching and checking for something "illegal," or if its occupants are breaching the Islamic moral order. That is why Arash turned away from *Uni-street* when we spotted a police patrol car. It also needs to be noted that *car cruising* is only available to those gay-identifying men who either own a car or have access to one. Given the fact that owning and buying a car in Tehran can be rather costly, the temporal space of *car cruising* draws attention to the intersection of sexuality and social (economic) position in terms of gay livability, as well as access to particular gay/queer spaces, and how these spaces are navigated and experienced. Those who do not have the financial means and come from lower social backgrounds have to find other ways to access the space of *car cruising*—for example, by knowing someone who has a car—or limit their public *cruising* activities to other spaces, which are often rendered as improper, dangerous, or morally corrupt by some members of the Iranian gay/queer community.

Close to *Uni-street* are some other "cruising" spots for same-sex-desiring men. *College Street*, so called because the American College used to be there before the Islamic Revolution in 1979, is, according to my informants, famous for its rent-boys, picked up along that street by their patrons. The same applies to Daneshju Park, which is known to be frequented by rent-boys and transsexuals searching for customers. Arash had strong opinions about this park: "I never go to this place because it's not a good place ... people come from other cities ... *loose* people go to this park ... you go there only if you want sex." He seemed to associate this park with a sort of abjected status, given its reputation as a space purely for buying and/or meeting simply for the purpose of having anonymous sex. What Arash is speaking to here are hierarchies and exclusions among gay Iranian men: those "good" and "respectable" queers/gays, who meet in coffee shops or have fun together while doing *car cruising* along *Uni-street,* and the "bad" queers/gays—from the lower classes or from places outside Tehran—who go to Daneshju Park *cruising,* looking for anonymous sex. In fact, those I spoke to about Daneshju Park had opinions similar to Arash, and mentioned that everybody knew about it—what sorts of people frequented it, and the activities taking place there—even the police. Thus, during my second fieldtrip in Tehran, I decided to explore this "open secret" and stay there for couple of hours.

The park has many paths and small corners, ideal for privacy and some intimacy. In the middle of the park is a fountain, where there is a sculpture of a boy urinating and some sculptural formations, which are interpreted by many Iranian gays I spoke to as resembling the letters G.A.Y. (see Fig. 8.1). Within the park, the *cruising* practices are conducted in the open, but require knowledge of a certain inside language and "protocols" or codes of conduct.

Fig. 8.1 "G.A.Y" water fountain in Daneshju Park

Arash explained to me: "You see it's easy. If, for example, you see some-one you fancy, you go up to him and sit beside him on the bench. Then you start talking to him, asking him some questions and so on. If you are attracted to one another, you might choose to go to some other place for sex which is more private." Thus, the main objective behind "bench love" is to prepare for further encounters, usually of a sexual nature. The public toilets in Daneshju Park are also an important site in creating gay/queer relationality. They are often used to convey information, such as phone numbers for sex-dates or "services" on offer with regards to sex. One of my informants, born in 1974, recalled that when he was younger, he used to put messages on paper or write on the wall in some public toilets, espe-cially in this park. After the Internet became more available in Iran at the turn of the last century, he claimed that he moved his cruising activities primarily to cyberspace. According to Arash: "Boys come from other cities to Tehran … and put their number there, for fun or to earn money." For example, those looking for sex with other men write their phone numbers on the toilet wall and also indicate what kind of "activity" they have in mind or the "service" this person is willing to offer. The word *kooni* (ass—bottom—insertee in penetrative anal sex) was often written on the toilet walls along with a phone number. Arash informed me that it is a word

Fig. 8.2   The word mikonam is written here on a toilet wall in Daneshju Park

used by many rent-boys when offering their "services." In another instance, the word *mikonam* (fucker—top—inserter in penetrative anal sex) was written on the wall (see Fig. 8.2).

A park such as Daneshju Park functions therefore as a form of heterotopia—public contradictory sites of recognizability for enacting gay/queer sexual relations and orientations, which are at once dangerous spaces of abjection and stigmatization, as well as possibilities for pursuing sexual pleasure under repressive Islamic social conditions that constitute homosexuality as a sickness and a criminal offense (Kjaran and Martino 2017).

Iranian non-heterosexual men, who are searching for more intimate relations in terms of sex, commonly use the virtual space of dating applications, such as *Manjam, Hornet,* or *Grindr.* These applications are not blocked by the authorities, and are open for everybody to explore the online gay scene, *cruising* virtually and picking up men. Pouria gives an impression of how he first learned about these applications and discovered a whole community out there:

I started to visit Manjam around nine years ago and until that time I did not know the huge number of gay people in Iran. Afterwards, I started dating different guys and at the same time I gained more information about gay life in Iran. It helped me a lot. Before I started to cruise online, I thought I was the only gay in Iran. I thought gays only existed in the movies or in some other countries. So through these applications I found some kind of self-confidence. Sometimes I even searched for all the people in Iran that were listed as gay on these applications and I discovered something like one hundred thousand people on Manjam at that time. It made me so happy, although I knew that many of these profiles were fake ones.

Pouria refers to dating applications such as *Manjam* as a virtual space for constructing a gay/queer community, which helped him to come to terms with his sexuality. By entering that space for the first time, he felt that he was not alone any more. In that respect, online dating applications created for him a particular space of agency where he could reflect on himself through others. This space also gave him the opportunity to have sex, and also enabled him to relate to and interact with other gay-identifying men. Thus, these virtual spaces, which most queer Iranian men have access to, speak to the mirroring effects of heterotopias: Physically I am absent from that space, but from its standpoint, I discover my absence and see myself over there, on the other side of the computer screen (mirror), in this unreal virtual space. By entering that space, I direct my "eye toward myself" (Foucault 1984, p. 4) and become reconstituted within that particular space, which is simultaneously denied in other sites constrained by power geometries within the broader society.

Virtual spaces are partly private—profile and online chats—but also public, meaning that you are on public display within that space, and can be seen both by the authorities and other users. As a matter of fact, these online dating applications can be compared to the Benthamian notion of the *panopticon*: You never know who is directing their *gaze* on you, watching you and checking you out, as you traverse the public/private divide by entering the space of online dating applications. Most of my informants were aware that these virtual heterotopic spaces are subject to surveillance by the state authorities. They, hence, corroborate the many accounts by queer men interviewed by Human Rights Watch (2010) and other sources, which document accounts of fear about such exchanges with other queer men online, related to knowledge of entrapment and surveillance at the hands of the authorities (Sreberny-Mohammadi and Mohammadi 1994/2012, pp. 61–63; Sreberny and Khiabany 2010). Therefore, some of them took great precautions when *cruising* online. One way to protect oneself and reduce the risk of being "spotted" is not to have a profile picture attached to the account, or to use a VPN (Virtual Private Network) when *cruising* online. However, despite the specter of state surveillance, most queer

Iranians I met and talked to during my fieldtrips to Iran had an account for different dating applications, and were frequently online, which points to the specificity of the conditions governing gay Iranian men's desire and their need to carve out a private/public space for intimacy and *cruising*.

* * *

In this chapter, it has been argued that Daneshju Park, coffee shops, and car *cruising* along *Uni-street* function as temporal heterotopic spaces for enacting the livability of gay/queer Iranian men. These are spaces of legitimacy and reclamation in response to geometries and geographies of power and subjection that render embodied gay/queer sociality as abjected and outside of the norm. In fact, this is about creating a space for the gay/queer gaze to be enacted in the form of material embodiments realized in spaces that afford a reconstitution of the self on the other side of the glass. In other words, within the heterotopic space(s), sexualities can be constructed, practiced, and performed, that is, sexualities that both transgress and contest the heterosexual discourse (Steyaert 2010). Heterotopic spaces, as discussed in this chapter, can therefore be seen both as spaces where individuals feel secure and experience a supportive environment and as sites of defiance and resistance. Private parties and gatherings are a good example of gay sociality and support, whereas coffee shops function both as a space of relationality and community building, but also offer a venue for expressing alternative ideas and showing defiance against the official religio-legal-moral discourse on how to act, dress, and behave. This also applies to tattoo parlors, which can be seen as sites of transgression and resistance, whereby having a tattoo defies the official discourse on bodily aesthetics. Thus, in short, these spaces created by gay/queer-identifying individuals through their embodiment, acts, and behavior, albeit in their temporality, give them an opportunity to follow "different lines of connection, association, and even exchange …which might not have otherwise been reachable within the body horizon of the social" (Ahmed 2006, p. 564).

Notes

1. Even high-ranking Iranians, such as the Iranian football player Ashkan Dejagah, who played with the Iranian national team at the FIFA World Cup in 2014 and again in 2018, have been accused of being "westernized" and thus reprimanded by the authorities because they have tattoos. Hence, when playing for Iran, Dejagah usually wears long sleeves to cover his body art (see Radka 2014).

2. Working underground: The life of an Iranian tattoo artist 2013, July 15.
3. These negative attitudes toward tattooed women have also circulated to a certain extent in the West, although they have in recent years diminished (see here Swami and Furnham 2007).
4. Faravahar is an old Persian symbol and was the Imperial Coat of Arms before the Islamic Revolution. It was also the symbol of the state religion of the Persian Empire—Zoroastrianism.
5. *Cruising*, gay slang, refers to walking or driving in a particular locality in search for sex. This term can also be used for activities for finding a sexual partner online.
6. Chat with an informant at a party during my second fieldtrip in August 2015.

References

Afary, J. (2009). *Sexual Politics in Modern Iran*. Cambridge: Cambridge University Press.

Ahmed, S. (2006). Orientations: Toward a Queer Phenomenology. *GLQ: A Journal of Lesbian and Gay Studies, 12*(4), 543–574.

Arjmand, R. (2017). *Public Urban Space, Gender and Segregation. Women-only Urban Parks in Iran*. London and New York: Routledge.

Foucault, M. (1984). Of Other Spaces, Heterotopias. *Architecture, Mouvement, Continuité, 5*, 1–9.

Human Rights Watch. (2010). We Are a Buried Generation. Discrimination and Violence Against Sexual Minorities in Iran. Retrieved from https://www.hrw.org/sites/default/files/reports/iran1210webwcover_0.pdf.

Khosravi, S. (2008). *Young and Defiant in Tehran*. Philadelphia: University of Pennsylvania Press.

Kjaran, J. I., & Martino, W. (2017). In Search of Queer Spaces in Tehran: Heterotopias, Power Geometries and Bodily Orientations in Queer Iranian's Men Lives. *Sexualities*. https://doi.org/10.1177/1363460717713383. Published online.

Lentini, P. (1999). The Cultural Politics of Tattooing. *Arena Journal, 13*, 31–50.

Mahdavi, P. (2008). *Passionate Uprisings. Iran's Sexual Revolution*. Stanford: Stanford University Press.

Massey, D. (2009). Concepts of Space and Power in Theory and Political Practice. *Documents D'Anàlisi Geogràfica, 55*, 15–26.

Needles and Sins. (2013, December 10). Tattoos in Iran Today. Retrieved from http://www.needlesandsins.com/2013/12/tattoos-in-iran-today.html.

Pitts, V. (2003). *In the Flesh. The Cultural Politics of Body Modification*. New York: Palgrave Macmillan.

Radka, R. (2014, June 4). World Cup 2014: Iran—The Secrets Behind the Players. *The Guardian*. Retrieved from https://www.theguardian.com/football/2014/jun/04/world-cup-2014-iran-secrets-players.

Sreberny, A., & Khiabany, G. (2010). *Blogistan. The Internet and Politics in Iran.* London: I. B. Tauris.

Sreberny-Mohammadi, A., & Mohammadi, A. (1994/2012). *Small Media, Big Revolution. Communication, Culture, and the Iranian Revolution* (pp. 61–63). Minneapolis: University of Minnesota Press.

Steyaert, C. (2010, December). Queering Space: Heterotopic Life in Derek Jarman's Garden. *Gender, Work & Organization, 17*(1), 45–68. https://doi.org/10.1111/j.1468-0432.2008.00404.x.

Swami, V., & Furnham, A. (2007, December). Unattractive, Promiscuous and Heavy Drinkers: Perceptions of Women with Tattoos. *Body Image, 4*(4), 343–352. https://doi.org/10.1016/j.bodyim.2007.06.005.

Working Underground: The Life of an Iranian Tattoo Artist. (2013, July 15). *The Observers.* Retrieved from http://observers.france24.com/en/20130715-needles-hijabs-iranian-tattoo-artist.

CHAPTER 9

Conclusion: Gay Livability
in a Queer Dystopia

The image of the global north as a "utopia" in terms of gender equality, recognition, livability, and the legal rights of its LGBTQ population has in the past decades been portrayed in the Western (pink) media discourse, which has cited reports from international organizations, such as the OECD (Organisation for Economic Cooperation and Development), World Economic Forum, and ILGA (International Lesbian, Gay, Bisexual, Trans, and Intersex Association) (see e.g., ILGA 2017).[1] As a matter of fact, the global north is often depicted against the "uncivilized" and dystopic societies of the global south, particularly the Middle East, with regards to the sexual/civil rights of gays and lesbians. As discussed in Chap. 1, this kind of discourse, which presents some societies as tolerant and open, while others are labeled as homophobic and barbaric, draws on the binary notion of utopic/dystopic thought. Moreover, as Jasbir Puar has argued, this "homonationalist" rhetoric has contributed to a racist, anti-Arab, and Islamophobic policies, which have not improved the situation of the respective LGBTQ population in the global south. On the contrary, international criticism and sanctions directed at the Islamic Republic of Iran for its mistreatment of sexual minorities has in some cases increased repression. Moreover, as I argued in Chap. 4, the discourses (re)produced by Western (pink) media on same-sex desires have mostly been framed around victimization and persecution of gays within Iran, not taking into account the embodied experiences of gay-identifying men inside of Iran, who themselves are a heterogeneous group, experiencing state homophobia and persecutions differently, depending on their social

© The Author(s) 2019
J. I. Kjaran, *Gay Life Stories*,
https://doi.org/10.1007/978-3-030-12831-9_9

position and geographical location. In other words, the pink/gay press in the West has not incorporated a more nuanced analysis and reporting on the situation of gays and lesbians in homophobic states such as the Islamic Republic of Iran, rendering the gay subject within Iran solely as a victim and in constant danger of being killed or persecuted by a repressive/oppressive Islamic regime.

Not denying the fact that gays, as well as men who have sex with men, are persecuted, and even executed in post-revolutionary Iran, the reality and the embodied experiences of gay-identifying Iranian men are often more complicated and multifaced. The picture of gay life in Iran is therefore often at odds with the one painted in the global north. Although not being a "gay paradise" in terms of livability and sexual rights, Iranian gays try to find ways of accommodating their desires within those limits set by the legal-social and historical context of today's Islamic Republic of Iran. They do not try to imitate the West in terms of identity politics or practices, as Joseph Massad has argued with regards to gay Arabs in the Middle East (Massad 2007). Neither do they perceive Iran as a "grand prison" where they constantly need to fear for their lives. In Chap. 5, I therefore focused on the practices of the self and how my informants/participants worked on their self, which entailed both knowing and caring for the self. The "knowing" aspect of the self focused on practices of coming to terms with your sexuality and adopting a gay identity—neither imitating nor importing Western gay identity labels, but rather acculturating (adjusting) them to the Iranian context. As a part of knowing and caring of the self, most of my informants tried to claim a liminal space for their feelings and identity, in which they could be themselves. These liminal spaces were both made and remade, depending on time, place, circumstances, and the occasion. Thus, in order to make their life meaningful, to have sex, to go on a date, or to spend intimate time with their boyfriends, different strategies were employed, within the limits of their own subjugation. They, therefore, all tried to transform the self in a Foucauldian sense within the liminal space of their gay existence—whether avoiding the marriage imperative, finding a place for sex, or just establishing some connection to the underground gay community.

All of my informants told me that they had to put on "straight masks" in public and when interacting with family members. The mask, which for many symbolized oppression and made them depressed, could only be taken down within particular spaces. These heterotopic queer spaces—outside the traditional, normative, or dominant institutional spaces of power—were made and remade by the members of the underground gay/queer community in Tehran. As I discussed in Chap. 8, Daneshju Park, coffee shops, and car *cruising* along *Uni-street* function as temporal heterotopic spaces for enacting the livability of gay/queer Iranian men. These are spaces of legitimacy and reclamation in response to geometries and geographies of power and subjection that render embodied gay/queer sociality as abjected and outside of the norm. In fact, this is about creating a space for the gay/queer gaze to be enacted in the form of material embodiments realized in spaces that afford a reconstitution of the self. In other words, within the heterotopic space(s), sexualities can be constructed, practiced, and performed—that is, sexualities that both transgress and contest the heterosexual discourse (Steyaert 2010). Heterotopic spaces, made and remade by queer/gay Iranian men, can therefore be seen both as spaces where individuals feel secure and experience a supportive environment and as sites of defiance and resistance. Private parties and gatherings are a good example of gay sociality and support, whereas coffee shops function both as a space of relationality and community building, and also offer a venue for expressing alternative ideas and showing defiance against the official religio-legal-moral discourse on how to act, dress, and behave. This also applies to tattoo parlors, which can be seen as sites of transgression and resistance, whereby having a tattoo defies the official discourse on bodily aesthetics. Thus, in short, these spaces created by gay/queer-identifying individuals through their embodiment, acts, and behavior, albeit temporarily, give them an opportunity to follow "different lines of connection, association, and even exchange …which might not have otherwise been reachable within the body horizon of the social" (Ahmed 2006, p. 564).

Iranian gay/queer men have not only created heterotopic spaces for sociality and relationality, but some of them have also been active in transforming the discourse on same-sex desire within the limits set by the hegemonic religious-political discourse. As discussed in Chap. 6, queer activists within Iran introduced and created the identity category *hamjins-gara'i*, a positive word for expressing same-sex desires. It has opened up new possibilities for Iranian gays to express their feelings and identity in a positive way, and in their own language without having to employ the Western gay identity label. Moreover, it has influenced the official discourse and terminology in terms of sexual categories, despite the limits to public debate in the Islamic Republic given the official medico-religious-legal disavowal of homosexuality and criminalization of same-sex relations.

As in the West, the queer/gay community in Iran has been affected by the HIV/AIDS epidemic. In Chap. 7, the main focus was on how *biopower* operates at different levels in terms of HIV/AIDS, sexuality, and gender. At the societal level and within the official statistics, HIV/AIDS is mostly understood to affect those on the margins of society, for example, IV drug addicts. In fact, homosexuality or non-heterosexuality is rarely or only vaguely mentioned in research papers as a mode of HIV/AIDS transmission in Iran. These groups are silenced and not mentioned as a possible target group in terms of HIV/AIDS infections, which is in line with the official discourse on disavowal of homosexuality and the criminalization of same-sex sexual acts. At the institutional level, the operation of an HIV-center in Tehran was described and analyzed. It was argued that the center operates mostly for those on the margins of Iranian society, a site for abjected bodies, which are regulated within its isolated space. In that sense, the HIV-center draws attention to how subjects are in general constructed through religio-cultural discourses and practices of *biopower*, especially in terms of sexuality and other practices, which are assumed to be outside of what is perceived intelligible within post-revolutionary Iranian society. This was also felt at the individual level in terms of being tested for HIV/AIDS. The process of testing draws attention to the various power dynamics involved. In that sense, the nature of testing and indeed giving a testimony, meaning telling the truth or giving evidence about yourself, relates to confessing about your inner self. Thus, taking a test, in this case an HIV-test, means revealing some truth about yourself, with regards to not only biometrics in the form of a small blood sample but also giving information about your inner self, related to your sexuality and/or past sexual practices. The chapter also addressed livability in terms of being HIV-positive and gay. It gives an account of how being gay and seropositive was experienced by Amir and Hassan. In their case, different modalities of power had implications for their life and full civic participatory action. They both experienced prejudices and homophobia, especially Amir, who felt that he was not perceived as a "real person," neither by the medical authorities nor society in general. Instead he was stigmatized as a sick person in a double sense, infected by not only HIV but also the "gaydisease." He is therefore seen as something "toxic," and within the official discourse, he is rendered as an abject.

Now, coming back to the question I put forth in Chap. 1, and which has in fact navigated the research since I started the project in 2014: "How are the terms of recognizability, enactment and livability of same-sex desire, in the Iranian context, understood and negotiated by gay Iranian men under historically specific conditions of disavowal and criminalization of homosexuality?" (Martino and Kjaran 2019). In Chap. 3, it was argued that in terms of discourses on sexuality and same-sex desire, there are both discontinuities and continuities between the past and the present, between the period of the Shah and post-revolutionary Iran. In that respect, some discursive themes of the past continue in the present. They are in many ways reproduced by the contemporary Islamic regime, which has replaced the modernist/secular logic of the Shah period with religious arguments/ rhetoric in its disavowal and regulation of sexual minorities. Thus, the current social/historical conditions under which gay-identifying men live in the Islamic Republic of Iran are influenced by the official discourse on homosexuality as well as regulations/laws pertaining to same-sex sexual acts. As I have argued throughout the book, the societal/official discourse on homosexuality depicts gays either as "sick" (mentally ill)—in need of being helped/cured—or morally corrupt. In terms of moral corruption, the term *Westoxification* is often used in the official discourse, referring to the negative influences of the West on young people and those who do not comply with the official moral discourse (norms) on sexuality, gender performances, or the aesthetics of the body. These "Weststruck" individuals, including gay-identifying men, are seen as "toxic" and "unauthentic." As already mentioned, outside of Iran, gay-identifying Iranian men are mostly positioned as victims in need of being liberated and saved. Thus, there are conflicting discourses in and outside of Iran that position, and constitute, the gay Iranian subject in different ways.

In terms of recognizability, gays (homosexuals) are not acknowledged as a "category of a person," neither by society nor by authorities (Martino and Kjaran 2019). Thus, in line with Ahmadinejad's speech in New York in 2007, these groups do not officially exist in contemporary Iran. In that sense, the logic of the "epistemology of the closet" does not apply to Iranian gays or lesbians. They do not "come out" in the Western sense of the "closet," as they already know that they cannot seek any recognition or acceptance, neither from the society nor from their family members. They, therefore, live a masked existence, keeping their same-sex desires discreet and pursuing their "other life" in secret. In fact, this resonates with premodern times in Iran, when homosexuality and same-sex desires were tolerated as long as they were pursued in secret and discreetly, otherwise there would be repercussions. Today, the Iranian penal code criminalizes male same-sex sexual practices (mostly focusing on anal intercourse). In legal texts, these sexual crimes are defined as *lavat* (sodomy) for which execution may be administered. However, as mentioned by my informants, it is often difficult to prove that a person has been engaged in *lavat*, as normally four adult Muslim men need to confirm that they witnessed the actual penetration (Afary 2009). Moreover, they had rarely heard about gays being killed by the authorities in large cities such as Tehran. Thus, the fear of being arrested and killed for being gay (a common discursive theme in the Western media) was not the main concern of my informants. They were more concerned about pressure from the family to get married (marriage imperative), having to serve in the military, or if someone would find out about their secret (see Chap. 5). Many of them mentioned that because homosexuality is not recognized in Iranian society, and criminalized by the authorities, they always felt insecure and did not have any rights whatsoever. For example, if they got attacked or mistreated, they could not report it to the police. Some of my informants had experienced being raped and/ or sexually harassed. Others had heard stories of gays being blackmailed by their ex-lovers. Additionally, the psychological pressure most of my informants endured, as of living a masked existence, left some of them feeling depressed and continuously stressed.

Coming from the global north, which, as already mentioned, has often been depicted as "queer utopia," it was hard for me to see how life as a gay-identifying individual could be possible under these conditions. However, when addressing interpretive questions of quality of life and livability for gay-identifying men in a transnational context such as Iran, it is necessary to go beyond the binary thought of utopia/dystopia, and adopt, as Nancy Fraser has argued, a "wide-ranging, open-ended mode of reasoning" (Fraser 2009, p. 41). Thus, during my fieldwork, I tried to understand the specificity of sexuality governance in Iran and how it influenced the lives of my informants. In other words, how did my gay friends and informants make a life for themselves as gay subjects? I have summarized earlier in this chapter, some of the strategies they have used to survive and pursue their lives within the limits set by the legal-religious discourse of the Islamic Republic of Iran. I have also emphasized throughout the book that none of my informants perceived themselves as a victim.[2] Rather, they positioned themselves as active agents in taking care of the self. They also agreed that it was possible, within the limits set by the official discourse and regulations on same-sex desire, to live a "gay life" in Iran. But how livable is that life in terms of quality, and the pursuit of happiness?

There is no one answer to that question, as it can be individually based on how you define quality of life. Moreover, it is determined by different factors, such as age, health, and economic/social position. For example, those of my informants who came from wealthy families or were themselves rich, had generally more freedom to pursue their life, and seemed to be more satisfied with their lives. They could often go abroad, had the means to pay bribes and throw parties, and some of them even had their own apartment to meet friends and lovers. One of my informants, whose father owns several factories, told me: "I love the gay community in Tehran. It's no problem to be gay here—especially if you are rich." However, being rich does not relieve them of the pressure from their families in terms of marriage or finding them a future wife. Nor were they able to take off the "straight mask" when in Iran. Thus, for all of my informants, and friends, living a masked existence became stressful and caused them some inner conflict. However, to make their lives bearable, they created communities, both within the private and public sphere, where they gained support from each other and found ways to feel happy. There, they could take off the mask, at least temporarily, find hope, as well as transcend time and space by moving into the "garden of mystic lovers" which Rumi speaks of in one of his poems (Rumi: The Book of Love. Poems of Ecstasy and Longing).

NOTES

1. The World Economic Forum has also published a list of the ten gay-friendliest countries. See World Economic Forum, July 8, 2015.
2. It needs to be emphasized that the voices and embodied experience of my informants presented in this book provide only some insight into the livability of gay-identifying men in Iran. Thus, I do not claim to be giving a representative account of being gay in Iran.

REFERENCES

Afary, J. (2009). *Sexual Politics in Modern Iran*. Cambridge: Cambridge University Press.

Ahmed, S. (2006). Orientations: Toward a Queer Phenomenology. *GLQ: A Journal of Lesbian and Gay Studies, 12*(4), 543–574.

Fraser, N. (2009). *Scales of Justice: Reimagining Political Space in a Globalizing World*. New York: Columbia University Press.

ILGA. (2017). Sexual Orientations in the World—Overview. Retrieved from https://ilga.org/maps-sexual-orientation-laws.

Martino, W., & Kjaran, J. I. (2019). The Politics of Recognizability: Giving an Account of Iranian Gay Men's Lives Under Repressive Conditions of Sexuality Governance. *International Journal of Middle East Studies, 51* (1), 21–41.

Massad, J. (2007). *Desiring Arabs.* Chicago: The University of Chicago Press.

Rumi: The Book of Love. Poems of Ecstasy and Longing (transl. by Barks, C.). (2002). Harper-Collins e-books. Retrieved from http://sino.mk/wp-content/uploads/2015/02/Banks-Coleman-Rumi-Book-Love.pdf.

Steyaert, C. (2010, December). Queering Space: Heterotopic Life in Derek Jarman's Garden. *Gender, Work & Organization, 17*(1), 45–68. https://doi.org/10.1111/j.1468-0432.2008.00404.x.

Epilogue

Jón I don't see any good future now for gays in Iran. I had [a] lot of hope. But now. I am not so sure. It's not about the government or politics. They do not kill us here. It is about people and society in general. They do not accept gays here—so much pressure from society, friends, and family. I have sometimes thought about death because wearing a mask and living your life in secret can be so hard. I want to have a life—not a better life but just a life. Because I don't have a life here as a gay man. I am applying for [a] visa to Europe and I want [to] apply for refuge in the Netherlands. That is my plan now. [Excerpt from a WhatsApp chat with Arash, July 2018]

More than four years have passed since I first visited Iran. In the meantime, much has changed on the political world stage, as well as for some of my informants/friends inside of Iran. When I started my fieldwork in 2014, I could sense optimism in the air following the 2013 presidential election of reformist Hassan Rouhani, who ran on the political platform of improving Iran's relationship with the West. Finally, after eight years of Mahmoud Ahmadinejad's presidency, the Iranian youth were feeling hopeful again. In line with his promises, Rouhani began nuclear negotiation with the West, and in 2015 the Islamic Republic of Iran agreed to limit its sensitive nuclear activities and allow international inspectors to monitor its program in exchange for ending economic sanctions, and freeing up tens of billions of dollars in oil revenue and frozen assets. The Iranian

© The Author(s) 2019
J. I. Kjaran, *Gay Life Stories*,
https://doi.org/10.1007/978-3-030-12831-9

public felt the effects of the agreement quickly, as inflation went down and the Iranian rial appreciated slightly. Thus, in 2015, I could sense that people were generally more relaxed and optimistic about the future. Arash, my key informant and a good friend, said to me back in 2014/2015 that things would now get better for gays. He was generally optimistic about the future even though he had, in the past, endured pressure and harshness from his family for being gay. In that sense, better relations with the West and an improved economic situation were somehow increasing the hope of young Iranians that the authorities would initiate further reforms that would increase their personal freedom. This did not happen, although you could sense that the authorities were somehow more relaxed regarding dress code and style, and the presence of the morality police on the streets of Tehran was not as obvious as before.

In 2018, three years later, Arash had changed his tone. He is now more pessimistic about his future in Iran as can be seen from the quote above. The war in Syria is still being waged, and Iran's involvement has increased with each day and month, running the risk of open conflict with Israel, its archenemy in the region. After Donald Trump came to power, Iran has been put on a list of countries whose citizens cannot enter the US. The Trump administration's latest action against Iran and its citizen was to terminate US participation in the nuclear agreement signed in April 2015 and reinstate economic sanctions. Thus, today the economic situation in Iran is getting worse every day, fuelling inflation and depreciation of the rial. Hand in hand with difficulties abroad, the authorities have become more repressive and less tolerant toward any criticism. Protests that broke out at the end of year in 2017 were rapidly quelled, and recently the social and communication application Telegram has been blocked, a medium considered to be "secure" and used by many of my informants. Many of them have switched to less "secure" applications such as WhatsApp.

All in all, the current situation in the Islamic Republic of Iran has changed the tide of optimism into deep pessimism, at least among young Iranians who expected reform and change for the better when Rouhani became president. For some gay-identifying men, the picture is even darker, as expressed by Arash. For him, the only way to pursue life as a gay-identifying man is outside of Iran. He emphasizes that he is neither worried about being killed by the authorities nor does he perceive them as an obstacle to his well-being. It is more family and society in general that force him to live in secret and put on a "straight mask" on a daily basis.

Arash is, therefore, waiting for his turn to leave Iran, hoping that he will be granted asylum in the Netherlands, which for him is a "gay paradise"— a place where gays are recognized by friends and family, included in the nation-state, and can enjoy their life in the open. Morteza and Nima have already left Iran, and are now living and studying in the West. Other informants and friends are still living in Iran, navigating between a masked existence and finding ways to enjoy life by being themselves. I dedicate this book and my research to them.

Helsinki, August 3, 2018

Appendix: Overview of the Key Gay-identifying (Queer) Informants/ Participants

	Name/pseudonym	Age	Location	Socio-economic status[a]	Educational status
1	Afshin	20s	Tehran	Low	In university
2	Ali Reza	20s	Tehran	Middle	In university
3	Amir	20s	Tehran	Low	High school degree
4	Arash	20s	Tehran	Middle	In university
5	Ardalan	30s	Tehran	Low	High school degree
6	Arman	20s	Tehran	Middle	In university
7	Armin	40s	Tehran	Middle	University degree
8	Arsham	40s	Toronto	Middle	University degree
9	Arslan	20s	Tehran	Low	In university
10	Basir	20s	Tehran	Low	High school degree
11	Farhod	20s	Tehran	Low	High school degree
12	Hassan	30s	Tehran	Low	High school degree
13	Hassan (tattoo artist)	30s	Tehran	Middle	High school degree
14	Kasra	20s	Tehran	Middle	High school degree
15	Kia	20s	Tehran	Middle	University degree
16	Mansur	20s	Tehran	Middle	High school degree
17	Mehrdad	30s	Tehran	Low	High school degree
18	Mika	20s	Tehran	Low	University degree
19	Morteza	20s	Tehran	Middle	In university
20	Muhammad	50s	Tehran	High	University degree

(*continued*)

© The Author(s) 2019
J. I. Kjaran, *Gay Life Stories*,
https://doi.org/10.1007/978-3-030-12831-9

(continued)

	Name/pseudonym	Age	Location	Socio-economic status[a]	Educational status
21	Nima	30s	Tehran/ Toronto	Middle	University degree
22	Pouria	30s	Tehran	High	University degree
23	Ramtin	20s	Tehran/ Istanbul	Low	High school degree
24	Saaed	20s	Tehran	Low	High school degree
25	Sharyar	30s	Mashad	Middle	High school degree

[a]I apply the APA (American Psychological Association, 2018) definition of socio-economic status, which is often measured as a combination of income, education, and occupation. Here I break it into three levels: high, middle, and low to describe the three categories of which my informants or their families fall into. For example, if an informant came from an educated and a wealthy family, lived in the northern part of Tehran and attended university, he was placed in the "high" category

BIBLIOGRAPHY

A Timeline of HIV/AIDS. (n.d.). *Aids.gov*. Retrieved from https://www.hiv.gov/sites/default/files/aidsgov-timeline.pdf.

Abrahamian, E. (1993). *Khomeinism. Essays on the Islamic Republic*. California: University of California Press.

Abrahamian, E. (2012). *A History of Modern Iran*. Cambridge: Cambridge University Press.

Abu-Lughod, L. (2013). *Do Muslim Women Need Saving?* Boston: Harvard University Press.

Abu-Raddad, L. J., Akala, F. A., Semini, I., Riedner, G., Wilson, D., & Tawil, O. (2010). *Characterizing the HIV/AIDS. Epidemic in the Middle East and North Africa. Time for Strategic Action*. Washington: The International Bank for Reconstruction and Development/The World Bank.

Afary, J. (2009). *Sexual Politics in Modern Iran*. Cambridge: Cambridge University Press.

Afary, J., & Anderson, K. (2005). *Foucault and the Iranian Revolution. Gender and the Seductions of Islamism*. Chicago: Chicago University Press.

Ahmed, S. (2002). This Other and Other Others. *Economy and Society, 31*(4), 558–572. https://doi.org/10.1080/03085140022000020689.

Ahmed, S. (2006a). Orientations: Toward a Queer Phenomenology. *GLQ: A Journal of Lesbian and Gay Studies, 12*(4), 543–574.

Ahmed, S. (2006b). *Queer Phenomenology. Orientation, Objects, Others*. Durham and London: Duke University Press.

© The Author(s) 2019
J. I. Kjaran, *Gay Life Stories*,
https://doi.org/10.1007/978-3-030-12831-9

Al Monitor. The Pulse of the Middle East. Tattoos in Iran (no author). Retrieved from https://www.al-monitor.com/pulse/galleries/tattoos-in-iran.html.

Al-e Ahmad, J. (1984). *Occidentosis: A Plague from the West* (R. Campbell, Trans.). Berkeley: Mizan Press Berkeley.

Algar, H. (1984). Introduction. In *Occidentosis: A Plague from the West* (J. Al Ahmad, Ed. and R. Campbell, Trans.). Berkeley: Mizan Press Berkeley.

Alimardani, M. (2018, January 1). What Telegram Owes Iranians. Never in History Has a Protest Movement Depended So Much on One Technological Platform. Will the Company Uses Its Power Wisely? *Politico Magazine.* Retrieved from https://www.politico.com/magazine/story/2018/01/01/irans-telegram-revolution-216206.

Allan, J. (1999). *Actively Seeking Inclusion: Pupils with Special Needs in Mainstream Schools.* London: Falmer.

Allan, J. (2008). *Rethinking Inclusion: The Philosophers of Difference in Practice.* Dordrecht: Springer.

Altman, L. (1981, July 3). Rare Cancer Seen in 41 Homosexuals. *The New York Times.* Retrieved from http://www.nytimes.com/1981/07/03/us/rare-cancer-seen-in-41-homosexuals.html.

Amanat, A. (2017). *Iran. A Modern History.* New Haven: Yale University Press.

American Psychological Association. (2018). Socioeconomic status. Retrieved from http://www.apa.org/topics/socioeconomic-status/.

Amnesty International. (2016, August, 2). Iran: Hanging of Teenager Shows Authorities' Brazen Disregard for International Law. Retrieved from https://www.amnesty.org/en/latest/news/2016/08/iran-hanging-of-teenager-shows-brazen-disregard-for-international-law/.

Amnesty International. (2017, April 11). *The Death penalty in 2016: Facts and Figures.* Retrieved from https://www.amnesty.org/en/latest/-news/2017/04/death-penalty-2016-facts-and-figures/.

An Interview with Khomeini. (1979, October 7). *The New York Times.* Retrieved from https://www.nytimes.com/1979/10/07/archives/an-interview-with-khomeini.html.

Arjmand, R. (2017). *Public Urban Space, Gender and Segregation. Women-only Urban Parks in Iran.* London and New York: Routledge.

Armstrong, E., & Crage, S. M. (2006, October 1). Movements and Memory: The Making of the Stonewall Myth. *American Sociological Review, 71*(5), 724–751. https://doi.org/10.1177/000312240607100502.

Axworthy, M. (2013). *Revolutionary Iran. A History of the Islamic Republic.* London: Allen Lane / Penguin.

Bakhtavar, S. (2009). *Iran. The Green Movement.* Irving, Texas: Parsa Enterprises.

Ball, K. (2005). Organization, Surveillance and the Body: Towards a Politics of Resistance. *Organization, 12*(1), 89–108. https://doi.org/10.1177/135050840504857.

Basaran, O. (2014, March 10). "You Are Like a Virus": Dangerous Bodies and Military Medical Authority in Turkey. *Gender and Society, 28*(4), 562–582. https://doi.org/10.1177/0891243214526467.

Bashi, G. (2010). Feminist Waves in the Iranian Green Tsunami? In N. Hashemi & D. Postel (Eds.), *The People Reloaded: The Green Movement and the Struggle for Iran's Future* (pp. 37–41). New York: Melville House.

Beachy, R. (2015). *Gay Berlin: Birthplace of a Modern Identity*. New York: Vintage Press.

Beeman, W. O. (2005). *The Great Satan Vs. the Mad Mullahs. How the United States and Iran Demonize Each Other*. Chicago: University of Chicago Press.

Besley, T. (2005). Foucault, Truth Telling and Technologies of the Self in Schools. *Journal of educational enquiry, 6*(1), 76–89.

Blasius, M. (2013). Theorizing the Politics of (Homo)sexualities Across Cultures. In L. M. Weiss & M. Boisa (Eds.), *Global Homophobia I* (pp. 218–245). Chicago: University of Illinois Press.

Brown, G. (2015). Queer movement. In D. Paternotte & M. Tremblay (Eds.), *The Ashgate Research Companion to Lesbian and Gay Activism* (pp. 73–84). London: Routledge.

Brown, H., & Thompson, D. (1997). The Ethics of Research with Men Who Have Learning Disabilities and Abusive Sexual Behavior: A Minefield in a Vacuum. *Disability & Society, 12*(5), 695–707.

Bucar, E. M., & Shirazi, F. (2012). The 'Invention' of Lesbian Acts in Iran: Interpretive Moves, Hidden Assumptions, and Emerging Categories of Sexuality. *Journal of Lesbian Studies, 16*(4), 416–434. https://doi.org/10.1080/10894160.2012.681263.

Butler, J. (1990). *Gender Trouble. Feminism and the Subversion of Identity*. New York: Routledge.

Butler, J. (1991). Imitation and Gender Insubordination. In D. Fuss (Ed.), *Inside/Out: Lesbian Theories, Gay Theories* (pp. 13–31). London: Routledge.

Butler, J. (1993). *Bodies that Matter. On the Discursive Limits of Sex*. New York: Routledge.

Butler, J. (2005). *Giving an Account of Oneself*. New York: Fordham University Press.

Caliskan, M., & Dikmen, Y. (2015, June 28). Turkish Police Use of Water Cannon to Disperse Gay Pride Parade. *Reuters*. Retrieved from https://www.reuters.com/article/us-turkey-rights-pride/turkish-police-use-water-cannon-to-disperse-gay-pride-parade-idUSKCN0P80OQ20150628.

Callis, A. S. (2009, November 25). Playing with Butler and Foucault: Bisexuality and Queer Theory. *Journal of Bisexuality, 9*(3–4), 213–233. https://doi.org/10.1080/15299710903316513.

Casey, C. (1995). *Work, Self and Society: After Industrialism*. London: Sage.

Coffey, A. (1999). *The Ethnographic Self. Fieldwork and the Representation of Identity*. London: Sage Publications.

Connell, R. (2008). A Thousand Miles from Kind: Men, Masculinities and Modern Institutions. *The Journal of Men's Studies, 16*(3), 237–252.

Country of Origin Information Portal. Ministry of Internally Displaced Persons from the Occupied Territories, Accommodation and Refugees of Georgia. (2017, November 9). Iran. Exemption from the Compulsory Military Service. Retrieved from http://coi-mra.gov.ge/en/2017/11/09/iran-exemption-from-the-compulsory-military-service-november-2017/#_ftnref10.

D'Emilio, J. (1992a). After Stonewall. In J. D'Emilio (Ed.), *Making Trouble: Essays on Gay History Politics, and the University* (pp. 234–274). New York: Routledge.

D'Emilio, J. (1992b). *Making Trouble: Essays on Gay History, Politics, and the University*. New York and London: Routledge.

D'Emilio, J. (2002). *The World Turned: Essays on Gay History, Politics, and Culture*. Durham, NC: Duke University Press.

Dabashi, H. (2011a). *The Green Movement in Iran*. Edited with an Introduction by Navid Nikzadfar. New Brunswick, NJ: Transaction.

Dabashi, H. (2011b). *Shi'ism: A Religion of Protest*. Cambridge, MA: Harvard University Press.

Dave, N. N. (2011, April 15). Activism as Ethical Practice: Queer Politics in Contemporary India. *Cultural Dynamics, 23*(1), 3–20. https://doi.org/10.1177/0921374011403351.

Day of Fighting against Homophobia and Transphobia in Iran. (2012, June). Retrieved from http://hamjensgera.com/article/33.

Dean, T. (2009). *Unlimited Intimacy. Reflections on the Subculture of Barebacking*. Chicago: University of Chicago Press.

Dehghan, S. K. (2017, December 31). Iran Correspondent. Rouhani Acknowledges Iranian Discontent as Protests Continue. *The Guardian*. Retrieved from https://www.theguardian.com/world/2017/dec/31/protesters-who-spread-fear-and-violence-will-be-confronted-says-iran.

DePalma, R., & Atkinson, E. (2009). *Interrogating Heteronormativity in Primary-Schools: Project*. London: Trentham Books.

Duffy, N. (2014, August 20). Iranian Lesbian Couple Marry in Stockholm. *Pink News*. Retrieved from https://www.pinknews.co.uk/2014/08/20/iranian-lesbian-couple-marry-in-stockholm/.

Duffy, N. (2015, April 28). Gay Iranian: Lib Dem Simon Hughes 'Saved My Life' and Helped Me Escape the Death Penalty. *PinkNews*. Retrieved from https://www.pinknews.co.uk/2015/04/28/gay-iranian-lib-dem-simon-hughes-saved-my-life-and-helped-me-escape-the-death-penalty/.

Duggan, L. (2002). The New Homonormativity. The Sexual Politics of Neoliberalism. In R. Castronovo & D. D. Nelson (Eds.), *Materializing Democracy: Toward a Revitalized Cultural Politics* (p. 179). Durham and London: Duke University Press.

DW. Made for Minds. Passion for Tattoos Leads to Lashings in Iran. (2014, January 22). Retrieved from https://www.dw.com/en/passion-for-tattoos-leads-to-lashings-in-iran/a-17367681.

Fader, L. (2014, April 24). Newsweek Rewind: 30 Years Ago, Scientists Discovered the Cause of AIDS. *Newsweek.* Retrieved from http://www.newsweek.com/newsweek-rewind-30-years-ago-scientists-discovered-cause-hiv-248566.

Fallahzadeh, H., Morowatisharifabad, M., & Ehrampoosh, M. H. (2009, April). HIV/AIDS Epidemic Features and Trends in Iran, 1986–2006. *AIDS and Behavior, 13*(2), 297–302. https://doi.org/10.1007/s10461-008-9452-7.

Fanon, F. (2008). *Black Skin, White Masks* (C. L. Markmann, Trans.). London: Pluto Press.

Fernando, M. L. (2010). Reconfiguring Freedom: Muslim Piety and the Limits of Secular Law and Public Discourse in France. *American Ethnologist, 37*(1), 19–35.

Fleming, P., & Sewell, G. (2002, November 1). Looking for the Good Soldier, Svejk: Alternative Modalities of Resistance in the Contemporary Workplace. *Sociology, 36*(4), 857–873. https://doi.org/10.1177/003803850203600404.

Fleming, P., & Spicer, A. (2003, February 1). Working at a Cynical Distance: Implications for Power, Subjectivity and Resistance. *Organization, 10*(1), 157–179. https://doi.org/10.1177/1350508403010001376.

Forbes, S. (2016–2017). The Reconstruction of Homosexuality and Its Consequences in Contemporary Iran. *The SOAS Journal of Postgraduate Research,* 10, 25–47. Retrieved from http://eprints.soas.ac.uk/24678/1/07_SForbes_Reconstruction_Homosexuality.pdf.

Fornet-Betancourt, R., Becker, H., Gomez-Muller, A., & Gauthier, J. D. (1987). The Ethic of Care for the Self as a Practice of Freedom: An Interview with Michel Foucault on January 20, 1984. *Philosophy Social Criticism, 12,* 112–131.

Foucault, M. (1978). *History of Sexuality. Volume I: An Introduction.* New York: Random House.

Foucault, M. (1980). *Power/knowledge: Selected Interviews and Other Writings, 1972–1977* (C. Gordon, Ed. and C. Gordon, L. Marshall, J. Mepham, & K. Soper, Trans.). New York, NY: Pantheon Books.

Foucault, M. (1982). Afterword: The Subject and Power. In H. L. Dreyfus & P. Rabinow (Eds.), *Michel Foucault: Beyond Structuralism and Hermeneutics* (pp. 208–226). Chicago, IL: University of Chicago Press.

Foucault, M. (1984a). Of Other Spaces, Heterotopias. *Architecture, Mouvement, Continuité, 5,* 1–9.

Foucault, M. (1984b). Nietzsche, Genealogy, History. In P. Rabinow (Ed.), *The Foucault Reader* (pp. 76–100). New York: Pantheon.

Foucault, M. (1988a). *The Care of the Self: The History of Sexuality.* New York: Vintage.

Foucault, M. (1988b). Technologies of the Self. In L. Martin, H. Gutman, & P. Hutton (Eds.), *Technologies of the self: A seminar with Michel Foucault* (pp. 16–49). Amherst: University of Massachusetts Press.

Foucault, M. (1990). *The History of Sexuality: Vol. 1. An Introduction* (R. Hurley, Trans.). New York, NY: Vintage Books.

Foucault, M. (1991). *Discipline and Punish. The Birth of the Prison.* London: Penguin.

Foucault, M. (1994). *The Birth of the Clinic: An Archaeology of Medical Perception.* New York: Vintage Books.

Foucault, M. (1998). *The History of Sexuality: The Will to Knowledge.* London: Penguin.

Foucault, M. (2002). *The Archeology of Knowledge* (A. Sheridan, Trans.). London: Routledge.

Foucault, M. (2005). *Hermeneutics of the Subject: Lectures at the College de France: 1981–1982* (F. Gros, Ed. and G. Burchell, Trans.). New York, NY: Palgrave Macmillan.

Foucault, M., & Miskowiec, J. (1986). Of Other Spaces. *Diacritics, 16,* 22–27.

Fraser, N. (2009). *Scales of Justice: Reimagining Political Space in a Globalizing World.* New York: Columbia University Press.

Frydlewicz, R. (1983, April 11). Newsweek Cover Story Explains AIDS to the General Public. Retrieved from http://thestarryeye.typepad.com/gay/2012/04/newsweek-explains-aids-to-the-general-public-april-11-1983-.html.

Gardell, J., & Greider, R. S. W. (2007). *And the Band Played on: Politics, People, and the AIDS Epidemic.* New York: St. Martin's Griffin.

Gay European Tourism Association (GETA). (n.d.). GETA ist hier, um Ihnen zu helfen. Retrieved from http://www.geta-europe.org/.

Gokah, T. (2006). The Naïve Researcher: Doing Social Research in Africa. *International Journal of Social Research Methodology, 9*(1), 61–73. https://doi.org/10.1080/13645570500436163.

Goldstein, J. S. (2003). War and Gender. In C. R. Ember & M. Ember (Eds.), *Encyclopedia of Sex and Gender. Men and Women in the World's Cultures* (pp. 107–116). New York: Kluwer Academic/Plenum Publishers.

Gramsci, A. (1995). *Selections from the Prison Notebooks of Antonio Gramsci.* New York: International Publishers.

Gregg, G. S. (2005). *The Middle East. A Cultural Psychology.* Oxford: Oxford University Press.

Grindley, L. (2016, August 5). Teen Executed for Gay Sex in Iran Is Latest in Long Trend. *Advocate.* Retrieved from https://www.advocate.com/world/2016/8/05/teen-executed-gay-sex-iran-latest-long-trend.

Haghdoost, A. A., Mostafavi, E., Mirzazadeh, A., Navadeh, S., Feizzadeh, A., et al. (2011, January). Modelling of HIV/AIDS in Iran up to 2014. *Journal of AIDS and HIV Research, 3*(12), 231–239. https://doi.org/10.5897/jahr11.030.

Hashemi, N., & Postel, D. (Eds.). (2010). *The People Reloaded: The Green Movement and the Struggle for Iran's Future.* New York: Melville House.

Hearn, J. (2015). *Men of the World. Genders, Globalization, Transnational Times.* London: Sage.

Hillmann, M. C. (1988). Introduction. In J. Al-e-Ahmad (Ed.), *By the Pen* (pp. ix–xxiv). Austin, TX: University of Texas.

Homosexuality iii. In Persian Literature. (2012, March 23). In *Encyclopædia Iranica.* Retrieved from http://www.iranicaonline.org/articles/homosexuality-iii.

Human Rights & Democracy for Iran. A Project of the Abdorrahman Boroumand Center. (n.d.). *Hassan Afshar.* Retrieved from https://www.iranrights.org/memorial/story/-7843/hassan-afshar.

Human Rights Watch. (2005, July 26). *Iran: End Juvenile Executions.* Retrieved from https://www.hrw.org/news/2005/07/26/iran-end-juvenile-executions.

Human Rights Watch. (2008a). *We Need a Law for Liberation. Gender, Sexuality, and Human Rights in a Changing Turkey.* Retrieved from https://www.hrw.org/sites/default/files/reports/turkey0508webwcover.pdf.

Human Rights Watch. (2008b, September 17). *UN: Hold Ahmadinejad Accountable for Iran Rights Crisis. Executions Increase Almost 300 Percent, Persecution of Rights Defenders Intensifies.* Retrieved from https://www.hrw.org/news/2008/09/17/un-hold-ahmadinejad-accountable-iran-rights-crisis

Human Rights Watch. (2010). *We Are a Buried Generation. Discrimination and Violence Against Sexual Minorities in Iran.* Retrieved from https://www.hrw.org/sites/default/files/reports/iran1210webwcover_0.pdf.

IGLHRC. (2015). Lesbian, Gay, Bisexual and Transgender Rights in Iran. Analysis from Religious, Social, Legal and Cultural Perspectives. Retrieved from http://iran.outrightinternational.org/wp-content/uploads/LGBTRightsInIran_EN.pdf.

ILGA. (2017). Sexual Orientations in the World—Overview. Retrieved from https://ilga.org/maps-sexual-orientation-laws.

Ingrey, J. C. (2013). *The Public School Washroom as Heterotopia: Gendered Spatiality and Subjectification.* Electronic Thesis and Dissertation Repository. Paper 1768. Ontario: University of Western.

IPPF. (n.d.). *Family Health Association of Iran.* Retrieved from https://www.ippf.org/about-us/member-associations/iran.

Iran Bans the Teaching of English in Primary Schools, Official Says. (2018, January 7). *Guardian.* Retrieved from https://www.theguardian.com/world/2018/jan/07/iran-bans-teaching-english-primary-schools-official-says.

Iranian AIDS Research Center (IRCHA). Retrieved from http://ircha.tums.ac.ir/index.jsp?fkeyid=&siteid=95&pageid=5319#.

IRQR. (n.d.). Iranian Railroad for Queer Refugees. Retrieved from http://irqr.ca/2016/.

Jackson, A. Y. (2013, March 1). Making Matter Making Us: Thinking with Grosz to Find Freedom in New Feminist Materialisms. *Gender and Education, 25*(6), 769–775. https://doi.org/10.1080/09540253.2013.832014.

Jafari, M. (2015, July 25). Islamic Jurisprudence-Inspired Legal Approaches towards Male Homosexuals. In *Lesbian, Gay Bisexual and Transgender Rights in Iran: Analysis from Religious, Social, Legal and Cultural Perspectives* (pp. 19–25). International Gay and Lesbian Human Rights Commission. Retrieved from http://iran.outrightinternational.org/wp-content/uploads/LGBTRightsInIran_EN.pdf.

Johnson, P. (2006). Unravelling Foucault's Different Spaces. *History of Human Sciences, 19*(4), 75–90. https://doi.org/10.1177/0952695106069669.

Karimi, A. (2017, January 19). Hamjensgara Belongs to Family; Exclusion and Inclusion of Male Homosexuality in Relation to Family Structure in Iran. *Identities. Global Studies in Culture and Power, 25*(4), 456–474. https://doi.org/10.1080/1070289X.2017.1286921.

Karsh, E. (2009). *The Iran-Iraq War.* New York: The Rosen Publishing Group.

Kayhan Bad Company (homepage). (2015). Retrieved from http://kbdco.com/.

Keddie, N. R. (2006). *Modern Iran: Roots and Results of Revolution.* Boston: Yale University Press.

Khosravi, S. (2008). *Young and Defiant in Tehran.* Philadelphia: University of Pennsylvania Press.

Kierkegaard, S. (1989). *The Sickness Unto Death* (A. Hannay, Trans.). London: Penguin.

Kinsella, J. (1989). *Covering the Plague. AIDS and the American Media.* New Brunswick and London: Rutgers University Press.

Kjaran, J. I., & Martino, W. (2017). In Search of Queer Spaces in Tehran: Heterotopias, Power Geometries and Bodily Orientations in Queer Iranian's Men Lives. *Sexualities.* https://doi.org/10.1177/1363460717713383. Published online.

Knights, D., & McCabe, D. (2000, August 1). 'Ain't Misbehavin'? Opportunities for Resistance Under New Forms of 'Quality' Management. *Sociology, 34*(3), 421–436. https://doi.org/10.1177/S0038038500000274.

Korycki, K., & Nasirzadeh, A. (2014, January 1). Desire Recast: The Production of Gay Identity in Iran. *Journal of Gender Studies, 25*(1), 50–65. https://doi.org/10.1080/09589236.2014.889599.

Kozinets, R. V. (2010). *Netnography: Doing Ethnographic Research Online.* London: Sage.

Krash, E. (2009). *The Iran-Iraq War.* New York: The Rosen Publishing Group.

Kuhn, B. (2011). *Gay Power! The Stonewall Riots and the Gay Rights Movement 1969.* Minneapolis: Twenty-First Century Books.

Kunda, G. (1992). *Engineering Culture: Control and Commitment in a High-tech Corporation.* Philadelphia: Temple University Press.

Ladinsky, D. (2003). *The Subject Tonight Is Love. 60 Wild and Sweet Poems of Hafiz.* New York: Penguin.

Larsen, J. (2001, December 28). Iran's Birth Rate Plummeting at a Record Pace: Success Provides Models for Other Developing Countries. *Earth Policy Institute.* Retrieved from http://www.mnforsustain.org/iran_model_of_reducing_fertility.htm.

Lee, R. (1995). *Dangerous Fieldwork.* London: Sage Publications.

Lehtonen, J. (2015). Going to the 'Men's School'? Non-heterosexual and Trans Youth Choosing Military Service in Finland. *NORMA: International Journal for Masculinity Studies, 10*(2), 117–135. https://doi.org/10.1080/18902138.2015.1050861.

Lentini, P. (1999). The Cultural Politics of Tattooing. *Arena Journal, 13,* 31–50.

Livia, A., & Hall, K. (1997). "It's a Girl!": Bringing Performativity Back to Linguistics. In A. Livia & K. Hall (Eds.), *Queerly Phrased: Language, Gender and Sexuality* (pp. 3–18). Oxford: Oxford University Press.

Long, S. (2009). Unbearable Witness: How Western Activists (Mis)recognize Sexuality in Iran. *Contemporary Politics, 15*(1), 119–136. https://doi.org/10.1080/13569770802698054.

Lynch, R. (2011). Foucault's Theory of Power. In D. Taylor (Ed.), *Michel Foucault. Key Concepts* (pp. 13–27). Durham: Acumen.

Mahdavi, P. (2007). Passionate Uprisings: Young People, Sexuality, and Politics in Post-Revolutionary Iran. *Culture, Health, and Sexuality. An International Journal for Research, Intervention, and Care, 9*(5), 445–457. https://doi.org/10.1080/13691050601170378.

Mahdavi, P. (2008). *Passionate Uprisings. Iran's Sexual Revolution.* Stanford: Stanford University Press.

Manchanda, N. (2014). Queering the Pashtun: Afghan Sexuality in the Homo-nationalist Imaginary. *Third World Quarterly, 36*(1), 130–146. https://doi.org/10.1080/01436597.2014.974378.

Martino, W., & Kjaran, J. I. (2019). The Politics of Recognizability: Giving an Account of Iranian Gay Men's Lives Under Repressive Conditions of Sexuality Governance. *International Journal of Middle East Studies, 51*(1), 21–41.

Mason, J. D. (2014, July 9). Why LGBT People Around the World Need Israel. *Advocate.* Retrieved from https://www.advocate.com/commentary/2014/07/09/op-ed-why-lgbt-people-around-world-need-israel.

Massaad, J. (2007). *Desiring Arabs.* Chicago: The University of Chicago Press.

Massey, D. (2009). Concepts of Space and Power in Theory and Political Practice. *Documents D'Anàlisi Geogràfica, 55,* 15–26.

Mathiesen, T. (1989). *Makt og medier. En innføring i mediasosiologi.* Oslo: Pax.

McAlister, M. (2005). *Epic Encounters. Culture, Media, and U.S. Interests in the Middle East Since 1945.* Berkeley: University of California Press.

McDonald, J. (2015, May 29). Iran Set To Strengthen Trans Legal Protections. *Out*. Retrieved from https://www.out.com/news-opinion/2015/5/29/iran-set-strengthen-trans-legal-protections.

Mendieta, E. (2011). The Practice of Freedom. In D. Taylor (Ed.), *Michel Foucault. Key Concepts* (pp. 111–127). Durham: Acumen.

Merabet, S. (2014). *Queer Beirut*. Austin, Texas: University of Texas Press.

Milani, A. (2011). *The Shah*. London: Macmillan.

Miller, T. (2013). Messy Ethics. Negotiating the Terrain between Ethics Approval and Ethical Practice. In J. MacClancy & A. Fuentes (Eds.), *Ethics in the Field. Contemporary Challenges* (pp. 140–155). New York: Berghahn.

Mirsepassi-Ashtiani, A. (1994). The Crisis of Secular Politics and the Rise of Political Islam in Iran. *Social Text, 38*, 51–84. https://doi.org/10.2307/466504.

Mir-Hosseini, Z., & Hamzic, V. (2010). *Control and Sexuality: The Revival of Zina Laws in Muslim Contexts*. London: Women Living Under Muslim Laws.

Moinipour, S. (2017). Refugees Against Refugees: The Iranian Migrants' Perception of the Human Rights of Afghans in Iran. *The International Journal of Human Rights, 21*(7), 823–837.

Monette, P. (1988). *Borrowed Time: An AIDS Memoir*. San Diego: Harcourt Brace Jovanovich.

Montazeri, A. (2005). AIDS Knowledge and Attitudes in Iran: Results from a Population-based Survey in Tehran. *Patient Education and Counseling, 57*, 199–203.

Muir, J. (2002, April 24). Condoms Help Check Iran Birth Rate. *BBC News*. Retrieved from http://news.bbc.co.uk/2/hi/middle_east/1949068.stm.

Najarian-Najafi, Z. G. (2017, July 13). The Ayatollah in the Moon: On Class Power and Dynamics in Islamist Iran. Retrieved from https://medium.com/@zacharygeorgenajariannajafi/the-ayatollah-in-the-moon-on-class-power-and-dynamics-in-islamist-iran-c248fc5cbe06.

Najmabadi, A. (2005). *Women with Mustaches and Men Without Beards: Gender and Sexual Anxieties of Iranian Modernity*. Berkeley: University of California Press.

Najmabadi, A. (2013, May). Genus of Sex or the Sexing of Jins. *International Journal of Middle Eastern Studies, 45*(2), 211–231. https://doi.org/10.1017/S0020743813000044.

Najmabadi, A. (2014). *Professing Selves: Transsexuality and Same-Sex Desire in Contemporary Iran*. Durham, NC: Duke University Press.

Naughty But Nice Rob. (2013, January 13). Reza Farahan, 'Shahs of Sunset' Star: Ryan Seacrest 'Is Helping the Peace Process'. *HuffPost*. Retrieved from https://www.huffingtonpost.com/2013/01/07/reza-farahan-shahs-of-sunset-ryan-seacrest_n_2427564.html.

Needles and Sins. (2013, December 10). Tattoos in Iran Today. Retrieved from http://www.needlesandsins.com/2013/12/tattoos-in-iran-today.html.

Nemanipour, G., Shariat-Torbaghan, S., Yalda, A., et al. (2008). *Historical Perspective of Imam Khomeini Hospital Complex*. Tehran: Tehran University of Medical Sciences.

Ojakangas, M. (2005). Impossible Dialogue on Bio-Power. Agamben and Foucault. *Foucault Studies, 2*, 5–28. https://doi.org/10.22439/fs.v0i2.856.

OutRight Action International. (2016, July 28). Human Rights Report: Being Transgender in Iran. Retrieved from http://www.refworld.org/docid/58c2b6e44.html.

Panisch, A. (2015, April 10). What's It Like to Be Gay or Trans in Iran? *Out*. Retrieved from https://www.out.com/news-opinion/2015/4/10/vice-investigates-transexual-life-iran.

Parsi, A. (2015, January 14). Iranian Queers and Laws. Fighting for Freedom of Expression. *Harvard International Review*. Retrieved from http://hir.harvard.edu/article/?a=9885.

Pitts, V. (2003). *In the Flesh. The Cultural Politics of Body Modification*. New York: Palgrave Macmillan.

Plummer, K. (1988). Organizing AIDS. In P. Aggleton & H. Homans (Eds.), *Social Aspects of AIDS* (pp. 20–52). London: The Falmer Press.

Pocius, J. (2016). Of Bodies, Borders, and Barebacking: The Geocorpographies of HIV. In H. Randell-Moon & R. Tippet (Eds.), *Security, Race, Biopower: Essays on Technology and Corporeality* (pp. 21–41). London: Palgrave Macmillan.

Posner, G. (1996). *Citizen Perot: Escape from Iran*. New York: Random House.

President Misquoted Over Gays in Iran: Aide. (2007, October 10). *Reuters*. Retrieved from https://www.reuters.com/article/us-iran-gays/president-misquoted-over-gays-in-iran-aide-idUSBLA05294620071010.

Puar, J. K. (2007). *Terrorist Assemblages: Homonationalism in Queer Times*. Durham, NC: Duke University Press.

Puar, J. K. (2010, July 1). Israel's Gay Propaganda War. *The Guardian*. Retrieved from https://www.theguardian.com/commentisfree/2010/jul/01/israels-gay-propaganda-war.

Queer Nation NY. (2016). *Queer Nation NY History*. Retrieved from http://queernationny.org/history.

Rabinow, P., & Rose, N. (2006). Biopower Today. *BioSocieties, 1*, 195–217. https://doi.org/10.1017/S1745855206040014014.

Radka, R. (2014, June 4). World Cup 2014: Iran—The Secrets Behind the Players. *The Guardian*. Retrieved from https://www.theguardian.com/football/2014/jun/04/world-cup-2014-iran-secrets-players.

Ramezani Tehrani, F., & Malek-Afzali, H. (2008, January–February). Knowledge, Attitudes and Practices Concerning HIV/AIDS Among Iranian at-risk Sub Populations. *La Revue de Santé de la Méditerranée orientale, 14*(1), 142–156.

Randell-Moon, H., & Tippet, R. (2016). Introduction. In H. Randell-Moon & R. Tippet (Eds.), *Security, Race, Biopower: Essays on Technology and Corporeality* (pp. v–xxvi). London: Palgrave Macmillan.

Rastegar, M. (2013). Emotional Attachments and Secular Imaginings: Western LGBTQ Activism on Iran. *GLQ: A Journal of Lesbian and Gay Studies, 19*(1), 1–29. https://doi.org/10.1215/10642684-1729527.

Reaching Out Winnipeg. (2013, August 13). *Gay Men in Iran's Military Can Seek Exemption.* Retrieved from https://reachingoutwinnipeg.com/2013/08/13/gay-men-in-irans-military-can-seek-exemption/.

Ritchie, J. (2010, October 1). How Do You Say "Come Out of the Closet" in Arabic? Queer Activism and the Politics of Visibility in Israel-Palestine. *GLQ: The Journal of Lesbian and Gay Studies, 16*(4), 554–575. https://doi.org/10.1215/10642684-2010-004.

Robertson, B. (2012). *Reverberations of Dissent: Identity and Expression in Iran's Illegal Music Scene.* New York: Bloomsbury Academics.

Rubin, G. (1984). Thinking Sex: Notes for a Radical Theory of the Politics of Sexuality. In C. Vance (Ed.), *Pleasure and Danger* (pp. 143–178). London: Routledge.

Rumi: The Book of Love. Poems of Ecstasy and Longing (transl. by Barks, C.). (2003). San Francisco: Harper-Collins.

Sade-Beck, L. (2004). Internet Ethnography: Online and Offline. *International Journal of Qualitative Research, 3*(2), 45–51.

Samimi, M. (2014, October 11). *Stigma Complicates Treatment of Iranian Women's Mental Illness.* Retrieved from https://www.huffingtonpost.com/mehrnaz-samimi/stigma-complicates-treatm_b_5670304.html.

Scheper-Hughes, N. (2004, March). Parts Unknown: Undercover Ethnography of the Organs-trafficking Underworld. *Ethnography, 5*(1), 29–73. https://doi.org/10.1177/1466138104041588.

Schulman, S. (2012). *Israel/Palestine and the Queer International.* Durham/London: Duke University Press.

Schut, M., & van Baarle, E. (2017, January). Dancing Boys and the Moral Dilemmas of Military Missions: The Practice of Bacha Bazi in Afghanistan. In A. B. Bah (Ed.), *International Security and Peace Building. Africa, the Middle East, and Europe.* Bloomington and Indianapolis: Indiana University Press.

Sciolino, E. (2000). *Persian Mirrors. The Elusive Face of Iran.* New York: Simon and Schuster.

Sedgwick, E. K. (1993). Epistemology of the Closet. In H. Abelove, M. A. Barale, & D. M. Halperin (Eds.), *The Lesbian and Gay Studies Reader* (pp. 45–62). New York: Routledge.

Semati, M. (2017). Sounds like Iran: On Popular Music of Iran. *Popular Communication. The International Journal of Media and Culture, 15*(3), 155–162.

Shakhsari, S. (2012). From Homoerotics of Exile to Homopolitics of Diaspora. *Journal of Middle East Women's Studies, 8*(3), 14–40. https://doi.org/10.2979/jmiddeastwomstud.8.3.14.

Sharafedin, B. (2013, January 24). Iran's Evin Prison: Jail or 'Hotel'? *BBC News*. Retrieved from https://www.bbc.com/news/world-middle-east-21159392.

Shariati, A. (1979). *On the Sociology of Islam*. Berkeley: Mizan Press.

Sharp, J. P., Routledge, P., Philo, C., & Paddison, R. (2000). Entanglements of Power. Geographies of Domination / Resistance. In J. P. Sharp, P. Routledge, C. Philo, & R. Paddison (Eds.), *Entanglements of Power. Geographies of Domination / Resistance* (pp. 1–43). London: Routledge.

Shiravand, S. (2015). *Sovereignty Without Nationalism, Islam Without God. A Critical Study of the Works of Jalal Al-e Ahmad*. Unpublished doctoral thesis, p. 117. University of Alberta, Department of Sociology, Edmonton.

Sinclair-Webb, E. (2000). "Our Bülent Is Now a Commando": Military Service and Manhood in Turkey. In M. Ghoussoub & E. Sinclair-Webb (Eds.), *Imagined Masculinities: Male Identity and Culture in the Modern Middle East* (pp. 65–92). London: Saqi Books.

Singerman, D. (2007, September). The Economic Imperatives of Marriage: Emerging Practices and Identities Among Youth in the Middle East. Middle East Youth Initiative Working Paper No. 6. *SSRN*. Retrieved from https://ssrn.com/abstract=1087433 or https://doi.org/10.2139/ssrn.1087433.

Sreberny, A., & Khiabany, G. (2010). *Blogistan. The Internet and Politics in Iran*. London: I. B. Tauris.

Sreberny-Mohammadi, A., & Mohammadi, A. (1994/2012). *Small Media, Big Revolution. Communication, Culture, and the Iranian Revolution* (pp. 61–63). Minneapolis: University of Minnesota Press.

Stalker, K. (1998). Some Ethical and Methodological Issues in Research with People with Learning Difficulties. *Disability & Society, 13*(1), 5–19. https://doi.org/10.1080/09687599826885.

Statistical Center of Iran. (2016). Retrieved from https://www.amar.org.ir/Portals/1/News/files/Mean%20and%20Median%20Age%20of%20Iranian%20Population.pdf.

Steyaert, C. (2010, December). Queering Space: Heterotopic Life in Derek Jarman's Garden. *Gender, Work & Organization, 17*(1), 45–68. https://doi.org/10.1111/j.1468-0432.2008.00404.x.

Swami, V., & Furnham, A. (2007, December). Unattractive, Promiscuous and Heavy Drinkers: Perceptions of Women with Tattoos. *Body Image, 4*(4), 343–352. https://doi.org/10.1016/j.bodyim.2007.06.005.

Takeyh, R. (2010). The Iran-Iraq War: A Reassessment. *The Middle East Journal, 64*(3), 365–383. https://doi.org/10.3751/64.3.12.

Tavoosi, A., Zaferani, A., Enzevaei, A., Tajik, P., & Ahmadinezhad, Z. (2004, May). Knowledge and Attitude Towards HIV/AIDS Among Iranian Students. *BMC Public Health, 4*(17). https://doi.org/10.1186/1471-2458-4-17.

The Dancing Boys of Afghanistan. (2010). Directed by Najibullah Quraishi. *Clover Films*. Retrieved from https://www.clover-films.com/index.php?option=com_content&view=article&id=8&Itemid=15.

TheGayUK. (2014, March 4). Unconfirmed Reports That Iran Hanged Two Gay Men for 'Perversion'. Retrieved from https://www.thegayuk.com/unconfirmed-reports-that-iran-hanged-two-gay-men-for-perversion/.

Tobias, S. (2005). Foucault on Freedom and Capabilities. *Theory, Culture and Society, 22*(4), 65–85. https://doi.org/10.1177/0263276405053721.

Trew, B. (2016, August 4). Tehran Hangs Teenage Boy for Being Gay. *The Sunday Times*. Retrieved from https://www.thetimes.co.uk/article/tehran-hangs-teenage-boy-for-being-gay-7t2pv97mq.

UN Women. (2018, July). Facts and Figures: HIV and AIDS. Prevalence and New Infections. Retrieved from http://www.unwomen.org/en/what-we-do/hiv-and-aids/facts-and-figures.

Unaids. (2017a). UN AIDS DATA 2017. Retrieved from http://www.unaids.org/sites/default/files/media_asset/20170720_Data_book_2017_en.pdf.

Unaids. (2017b, May 12). Germany—ending AIDS by 2020. Retrieved from http://www.unaids.org/en/resources/presscentre/featurestories/2017/may/20170512_germany.

Undocumented Afghan Refugees Get a Chance at School in Iran. (2017, October 26). *Euronews*. Retrieved from http://www.euronews.com/2017/10/26/thousands-of-afghan-refugees-get-a-chance-at-school-in-iran.

Urban Dictionary. (2001, December 5). Gaydar. Retrieved from https://www.urbandictionary.com/define.php?term=gaydar.

Vahdat, A., & Fattahi, M. (2017, November 29). Iran Challenges Taboos as HIV from Sex Rise. *The Seattle Times*. Retrieved from https://www.seattletimes.com/nation-world/iran-challenges-taboos-on-discussing-sex-as-hiv-rate-rises/.

Varzi, R. (2006). *Warring Souls: Youth, Media, and Martyrdom in Post-Revolution Iran*. Durham and London: Duke University Press.

Verkaik, R. (2008, March 6). A Life or Death Decision. *Independent*. Retrieved from https://www.independent.co.uk/news/uk/home-news/a-life-or-death-decision-792058.html.

Watney, S. (1988). AIDS "Moral Panic" Theory and Homophobia. In P. Aggleton & H. Homans (Eds.), *Social Aspects of AIDS*. London: Falmer Press.

Weinthal, B. (2014, March 14). Experts Predict: Iran Will Remain Deadly. Two Reports Indicate That Despite a New President's Overtures to the Contrary, Iran Will Remain a Deadly Place for LGBTs. *Advocate*. Retrieved from https://www.advocate.com/world/2014/03/14/experts-predict-iran-will-remain-deadly

Whitaker, B. (2006). *Unspeakable Love: Gay and Lesbian Life in the Middle East*. London: Saqi Books.

Whitaker, B. (2007, September 25). No Homosexuality Here. *The Guardian*. Retrieved from https://www.theguardian.com/commentisfree/2007/sep/25/nohomosexualityhere.

Whitaker, B. (2010, December 15). From Discrimination to Death—Being Gay in Iran. *The Guardian*. Retrieved from: https://www.theguardian.com/commentisfree/2010/dec/15/gay-iran-mahmoud-ahmadinejad.

WHO. (2006). WHO Report Iran Who-Aims Report on Mental Health System in The Islamic Republic of Iran. Retrieved from http://www.who.int/mental_health/evidence/who_aims_report_iran.pdf.

WHO. (2016, May 31). 17 Million People with Access to Antiretroviral Therapy. Retrieved from http://www.who.int/hiv/mediacentre/news/global-aids-update-2016-news/en/.

Winch, S. (2005, March). Ethics, Government and Sexual Health: Insights from Foucault. *Nursing Ethics, 12*(2), 176–186. https://doi.org/10.1191/096973 3005ne774oa.

Working Underground: The Life of an Iranian Tattoo Artist. (2013, July 15). *The Observers*. Retrieved from http://observers.france24.com/en/20130715-needles-hijabs-iranian-tattoo-artist.

World Economic Forum. (2015, July 8). These Are the 10 Most Gay-friendly Countries. Retrieved from https://www.weforum.org/agenda/2015/07/what-are-the-10-most-gay-friendly-countries/.

Zanghellini, A. (2012, June 6). Are Gay Rights Islamophobic? A Critique of Some Uses of the Concept of Homonationalism in Activism and Academia. *Social and Legal Studies, 21*(3), 357–374. https://doi.org/10.1177/0964663911435282.

Zeidan, S. (2013). Navigating International Rights and Local Politics: Sexuality Governance in Postcolonial Settings. In M. L. Weiss & M. Boisa (Eds.), *Global Homophobia* (pp. 196–217). Chicago: University of Illinois Press.

Zengin, A. (2016, July). Violent Intimacies. Tactile State Power, Sex / Gender Transgression, and the Politics of Touch in Contemporary Turkey. *Journal of Middle East Women's Studies, 12*(2), 225–245. https://doi.org/10.1215/15525864-3507650.

Zonis, M. (1991). *Majestic Failure. The Fall of the Shah*. Chicago: University of Chicago Press.

Index[1]

[1]Note: Page numbers followed by 'n' refer to notes.

© The Author(s) 2019

J. I. Kjaran, *Gay Life Stories*,

https://doi.org/10.1007/978-3-030-12831-9